D1530876

THE
TONIGHT
SHOW

THE TONIGHT SHOW

ROBERT METZ

ꟼ⋏P
A Playboy Press Book

791.45
M568t

Library of Congress Cataloging in Publication Data

Metz, Robert.
    The Tonight show.

    Bibliography: p.
    Includes index.
    1. Tonight show (Television program) I. Tonight show
(Television program)
PN1992.77.T63M4   79.45'72   79–90920
ISBN: 0–87223–598-X

To my father, whose anecdote-filled sermons influenced my writing; to my recently deceased mother whose marvelous touch on the piano enriched my life; and to my beloved wife, Liz, who makes my nonwriting hours joyful.

Special dedication: To Edward Kuhn, Jr., who also died late in 1979.

Contents

viii CONTENTS

Acknowledgments

Introductory note: It is shocking to report that an invaluable source of *Tonight* information—the old films and tapes of the show—has been erased almost without exception, thereby destroying a significant part of the social history of this nation.

There is always a risk in writing a book about living persons that the outcome will distort the facts despite efforts to give an honest portrayal.

If I should err with regard to portraits of anyone in this book, I do not do it intentionally. It is true that the Carson camp was not cooperative, but I did speak at length to many people friendly to Carson. His ex-manager, Al Bruno, and his ex-producer, Art Stark, both helped put many disparate facts in the proper context.

Most of those important to the show over the years— those with stories to tell and insights to convey—were interviewed in depth. A partial list includes Don Knotts, Louis Nye, Tom Poston, Gene Rayburn, Pat Harrington, Jr., Bill Dana, Walter Kempley, Phyllis Diller, Paul Keyes, Hy Averbach, Tom O'Malley, Bob Shanks, Bob Cuniff, Mitzi Moulds, and writer Sidney Carroll. Jack and Miriam Paar were especially helpful and allowed the author two days at their home in New England. I also had lengthy sessions with Ed Weinberger, Dick Cavett, and Marshall Brickman among other writers for Carson. This list is by no means exhaustive. I spoke with scores of others including some who chose anonymity.

I am obliged to still others for many of the book's vignettes. Mention the fact that you are writing a book about *The Tonight Show* and stories come forth from the most improbable sources.

In addition to the many people interviewed for this book, I referred to many books and hundreds of articles. Among the more important books were Steve Allen's autobiography, *Mark It and Strike It* (New York: Holt, Rinehart & Winston, 1960); Jack Paar's *I Kid You Not*, with John Reddy (Boston: Little, Brown, 1960); *Tonight* by Terry Galanoy (Garden City: Doubleday, 1972); *Here's Ed, The Autobiography of Ed McMahon,* as told to Carroll Carroll (New York: Putnam, 1976); *The Cool Fire* by Bob Shanks (New York: Norton, 1976); and my own books: *CBS: Reflections in a Bloodshot Eye* (1975) and *The Today Show* (1977), both by Playboy Press.

Steve Allen was profiled in *The New York Times Sunday Magazine*—"Portrait of a Master of Ad Lib," by Gilbert Millstein on January 9, 1955. There was a lengthy series by Janet Kern in the New York *Journal American* called "The Steve Allen Nobody Knows," August 1956; and another extended profile in *The American Weekly* in February 1957 called "I'm a Lucky Guy" by Steve Allen and Curtis Mitchell; also, a June 1959 series called "The Steve Allen Story" in the *New York Post* by A. G. Aronowitz.

Jack Paar was good copy, as journalists say, and scores of articles were written and many critical assessments were made. They began with Sidney Carroll's March 1946 piece in *Esquire*—the one that gave Jack broadcast momentum as he returned from the Pacific theater following World War

II. After he began hosting *Tonight* there was "Off-Beat, On-Beam Paar" in *Cue* magazine, Nov. 27, 1954. Jim Bishop wrote a Paar series in 1957 for King Features called "Jack Paar: Portrait of a 'Nice Guy' "; and Gilbert Millstein wrote a profile, "Paar Conquers the Midnight Hour," published in *The New York Times Sunday Magazine* November 10, 1957. *Life* magazine carried "Late Night's Light of TV" on March 9, 1958, by Tom Prideaux; there was a *Saturday Evening Post* piece by Jack Iams called "Jack of All Tirades"; and *Time* magazine's cover story, "Late-Night Affair," published on August 18, 1958, to garner what Paar says was the biggest circulation for the magazine to that date. The *New York Post* published a Jack Paar profile by Dave Gelman and others in September and October of 1958. There was a *Newsweek* profile, "Good Guy? Bad Guy?" in the June 15, 1959, issue.

Major Carson era articles include: "A Write Guy," an early Carson profile by Jack Leahy in the Sunday *Daily News,* August 14, 1960; the *Saturday Evening Post*'s "The Soft-Sell, Soft-Shell World of Johnny Carson," December 22, 1962, by Edward Linn; "The Great Carsoni," *Time,* May 28, 1965. Gael Greene wrote "Johnny's Like Folks" in the January 16, 1966, New York *Herald Tribune Magazine*; Nora Ephron had a *New York Post* series on Carson in January of 1967. There is PLAYBOY's Alex Haley interview with Carson in the December 1967 issue; the Kenneth Tynan interview published in the February 20, 1978, issue of the *New Yorker,* and *The Rolling Stone* interview of Johnny Carson by Timothy White, published March 22, 1979.

Of lesser scope, but nevertheless important, Joan Barthel's "Here's Johnny Out There" from *Life* magazine, 1970; *Los Angeles* magazine's article on Fred de Cordova, "Confessions of a *Tonight* Show Producer," published in December 1975; the *San Fernando Valley* magazine issue of February 1979, "Johnny Carson: America's Favorite Bedtime Storyteller." There was Kay Gardella's three-part series in the New York *Daily News,* April 2, 3, and 4, 1979.

xii *Acknowledgments*

Also, *Look* magazine's May 14, 1979, article "Johnny Carson's Mid-Life Crisis." *The Chicago Tribune* on September 8, 1979, had "What Johnny Means to the Stars of Today and Tonight." *Parade*, September 9, 1979, "Who Needs Talent?" by Steve Allen.

There are the many articles published by *The New York Times* during the Carson years, including Jack Gould's reviews of *The Tonight Show* before and during Carson's tenure along with *The New York Times* Information Bank, which filled gaps in *The Times* morgue. Also, the articles published in *Newsweek* magazine during the same period and *TV Guide* pieces on the show including "And Me—I'm Ed McMahon" by Val Adams in the December 16, 1967, issue.

There was a December 19, 1977, *New West* magazine piece adapted from *Fame*, a book by Susan Margolis (San Francisco Book Company, 1977). The *Washington Post* carried "The Cloning of Carson" on April 26, 1979. *People* magazine profiled Carson on May 21, 1979, after the *Friars Roast* at which he was declared Entertainer of the Year.

In *People* magazine, February 4, 1980, there was an article, "David Letterman: Will He Replace Johnny Carson?" *Los Angeles* magazine's Dick Adler wrote "The Man Who Would be Carson?" in its January 1980 issue.

Foreword

The Tonight Show—which harks back to the very genesis of television thirty years ago—offers democracy's version of the court jester. Each weekday, *Tonight* offers the nation comic relief, putting the day's events into sardonic perspective.

In the feudal tradition the court jester serves at the convenience and pleasure of the king. In our democracy, the entire nation is surrogate for the king, and the jester serves at the pleasure of the populace. Neither survives bad notices for long.

For 15.2 million regular midnight viewers, *Tonight* offers America's very own court jester in Johnny Carson. The show and its star, after so long a success, have become an eternal verity. Not so good as it should be, or perhaps as it once was, but a pleasant anchorage in a storm-tossed world, America's night-light and nightcap rolled into one. As superstar Johnny Carson himself puts it, the show is NBC's "answer to foreplay."

As the remark implies, *Tonight* is at present the frankest show on television short of the raunchy *Saturday Night Live.* Yet one of the talents for which Carson is so highly paid is his ability to rein in nightclub comedians and keep blue remarks at a minimum. And while blue *The Tonight Show* may sometimes be, in the black it most emphatically is.

Tonight, which struggled for an audience for years while pouring red ink onto NBC's accounts, took fire with "Leaky Jack" Paar. Carson compounded the viewing audience so that the show is now NBC's most profitable vehicle by far.

But at its profitable best, *Tonight* was frequently torn by controversy as its Prince of Play threatened to withdraw and perhaps to join the competition—hard-driving ABC, from which NBC captured Carson in the first place over eighteen years ago.

Fully aware of his importance to the company, the hard-nosed Carson negotiated a new contract in spring 1980. There was give-and-take involved: NBC let Carson give up the last half hour of the show, reducing it to one hour; and Carson agreed to do the show four nights a week. Previously he had 25 three-day weeks, 12 four-day weeks, and 15 weeks' vacation. Carson's vacation schedule under the new contract was not disclosed.

What manner of man is this—this Nebraska boy who holds more power than anyone else on the airwaves, a man who, it has been alleged, brought down a president by jesting at his clumsiness? Is he a superman with uncommon intelligence and wit, or a minor talent whose writers pen bons mots Carson merely mouths during monologues and interviews? There is perhaps a little of both in this enigmatic man. But either way, his tastes mirror Middle America. In music his ex-director, Skitch Henderson, classes him as an appreciator of Lawrence Welk and a man who could ask "Who are Simon and Garfunkel?" after the release of their stunning *Sound of Silence* album. After using the duo, Carson then withered Skitch with a memo about the two, who appeared scruffy on the show before scruffy was in.

No ordinary Midwesterner, Carson has a darker nature. He professes to be shy. When under pressure, "terrified" might be a better word. Even when chosen for the show he avoided the press and let Big Ed McMahon field interviewers' questions.

But that was years ago. Does the confident and happily

married Carson measure up to the boy-next-door image he so effectively portrays on television? Can a man who accepts his brother Dick's ambivalently proffered resignation with the impassive question "Can we get Bob Quinn to replace you?" experience emotion at all? His third wife says yes—he cried for hours when Jack Benny died. Can it be that there is an emotional outpost in Carson for those he regards as equals and none for the gray people of the world?

Johnny Carson is undoubtedly America's most powerful clown. Not since Art Stark, the tough-guy producer who kept Carson from going down the tube when his tenure was about a year old, has Carson had a critic within his inner show-business circle. Almost no one in show business will criticize Carson, and then only when the speaker is strictly off the record. For if a court jester becomes king—with more power than a potentate, more wealth than a Woolworth—who will dare to warn the jester that he's become a fool?

Mort Sahl, who once freely criticized Carson for doing "safe" comedy, now has his own NBC show in Washington, D.C. He would not answer the telephone to talk about Carson with the author. Caught in unguarded moments, some performers have lashed out at Carson and said the opposite of what they tell the press. Does Carson "love it when you score?"—when a comic tops him with an ad-libbed line? Perhaps. But one comedian who is on record as saying Carson will help you out if you are going down with a bad shot has confided privately that, in fact, Carson will watch impassively "while you die out there."

There were three major hosts on *Tonight*—two of them superstars. Jack Paar, whose emotions are as close to the surface as Carson's are buried beneath it, frequently feuded with his critics. He gave better than he got, and, as columnist Jack O'Brian has said, read the Old Testament formula for vengeance as "a head for an eye." But on a personal level, Jack and his wife, Miriam, are emphatically generous and forgiving. Jack used to alarm his assistants by the size and frequency of checks sent forth to friends in need. Those who work for stars hope for neat gifts at Christmas. And they are often disappointed. Paar, by contrast, was famous for lavish presents to those around him and once threatened to boycott his own show until raises he put through for staffers were confirmed.

While the public debated what Jack Paar was really like, intimates knew that what you saw was what you got. Though he hated his emotionalism, he couldn't master it —yet that added to his appeal. Viewers stayed with the show long past bedtime because at 12:55 A.M. they just might be witness to a nervous breakdown. Paar is retired now, and he came down from stardom more easily than most. For Jack was the healthiest of the three major hosts —not a sufferer of mental disease, only a carrier, as his sidekick Hugh Downs has said.

Steve Allen, the first host, was quirkily funny in his own right, and the best straight man in the business—more than anxious to help his comedy team, Louis Nye, Tom Poston, and Don Knotts, get their full laughs. But he, too, was an enigma, calling only a handful of associates by their names.

It is astounding but true that Steve disdainfully regarded *Tonight* as a mildly agreeable steppingstone, and was happiest at the final party. Ironically, though, this never-to-be-satisfied man hasn't approached the heights the show took him to. He strives even harder to make his mark—with acting, songwriting, piano playing, and books.

Yet it is Carson who has held the top post longest—more than three times as long as Paar—and is most interesting. Producer Art Stark, who saved Carson on *Tonight* and became his "best friend," was impassively fired. So was Al Bruno, Carson's agent and "friend"—the other man essential to Carson's ascension to success on *Tonight*. Two wives remain behind. There are no sad farewells at the end of the trail with Carson—and no joyful reunions, either. He travels fastest who travels alone.

In contrast to the court jester of prior ages—an often lazy clown who lived by his wits, flirting with death by twitting the mighty king—America's premier *Tonight Show* clown is beholden only to the people. It is they who have the power of life or death over his career. By turning to other channels —which they never have except on guest-host nights—they could end his career within months. Remarkably, though, Johnny Carson has lasted "forever," as time is measured by the talent-pulverizing world of network television.

This, then, is the fascinating and surprisingly brutal inside world of *Tonight*—show-business pinnacle, builder of superstars, controversial critic to the nation. Its people are larger than life, and because of the pressures of the job are even more vulnerable to life's pitfalls—as are the stars' associates.

The show itself has social significance. It is companion to the sick and the lonely, a breath of fresh air for the jaded who have tired of the formula sit-coms. It is, in short, a durable and important American institution, a mirror of our mores and of our times.

Tonight: *Vital Statistics*

May 29, 1950, to August 24, 1951: *Broadway Open House.*

August 27, 1951, to September 24, 1954: *The Steve Allen Show* on the New York City NBC-owned and -operated station.

September 27, 1954, to January 25, 1957: *Tonight!* starring Steve Allen.

January 28, 1957, to July 26, 1957: *Tonight! America After Dark* with various journalist-hosts.

July 29, 1957, to March 30, 1962: *The Tonight Show* starring Jack Paar.

April 2, 1962, to Sept. 28, 1962: *The Tonight Show* with various substitute hosts waiting for Carson.

Oct. 1, 1962, to present: *The Tonight Show* starring Johnny Carson.

THE TONIGHT SHOW

Tonight *in California:*
Will Carson Appear Today?

It is a curiosity that *The Tonight Show,* which a generation ago was born "live" in the electric atmosphere of Manhattan at midnight, has long since been transplanted to languid California to be taped while the sun is still high in the sky.

The studio is in the town archly referred to by Rowan and Martin as "beautiful downtown Burbank," a drab metropolis of busy multilane streets, one-story businesses, and nondescript ranch homes.

The NBC complex itself is cavernous and yet so inadequate that house trailers are used to shelter the executive overflow. But the tourists who came to sit in on the show one fall day didn't seem to notice that.

It was 4:00 P.M., and soon the lucky ticket holders would inch ahead, sated with tacos, Coca-Cola, and soft ice cream from the fast-food shop across the road. Months earlier, they had written for their freebies from hometowns across the nation, and undoubtedly they had planned their visits long before that.

Some are blasé, but most are tingling with anticipation, chatting about Carson exploits, famous putdowns, Art Fern and Aunt Blabby. One visitor seems totally out of place: "This fellow Carson—what is he . . . a comedian?" A visitor

from New Zealand, perhaps, or outer space—certainly not
an American who has ever stayed up until midnight.

Once inside, the guests exhibit a shyness typical of the
superfan, speaking in hushed voices as they await a late
matinee performance by the deity—fifty-four-year-old
Johnny Carson, veteran of eighteen years on *Tonight* and
unquestionably America's biggest comedy star. Yet each
day's visitors are prepared for a disappointment. Unless
they are fortunate they'll be regaled by a substitute host
who, laboring to overcome their dismay, strains for laughs.
Even twenty-four hours or a weekend later, Johnny Carson
is a hard act to follow.

The network is well aware that Johnny is the draw, and
thus the timing of his no-shows—apart from Monday, his
regular night off—is a closely kept secret. Carson is of
primary importance to NBC:

A spokesman for RCA, NBC's parent company, acknowl-
edges that at a time of falling network profits the Carson
Tonight contribution is rising on a percentage basis. (NBC
earned a pre-tax $105.6 million in 1979, down from $121.3
million in 1978. The 1979 profit squeeze reflects NBC's
alarming slide in television ratings generally and its unusually heavy spending on program development to reverse
that trend.)

The network won't specify what *Tonight*'s role is in its
profit picture but some time ago trade sources estimated
that Carson's *Tonight* accounted for 17 percent of the total
in 1978. That estimate brought an RCA protest; but assuming that percentage rate was about right in 1979, the pre-
tax profit on *Tonight* was over $18 million for 1979.
(Corporations generally do not publish after-tax profits by
division.)

Whatever *Tonight* earns, it's a lot of advertising dollars.
The rates are astronomical today relative to the $4,000 a
minute advertisers cautiously shelled out when Steve Allen
first started doing the show for a relatively small national
audience. As always, charges vary according to season.

Thirty-second rates are $14,500 between December 31 and January 28, $18,000 between February 4 and March 10, and $25,000 for the peak viewing season between March 17 and June 9. Full-minute rates are $29,000, $36,000, and $50,000 for those same periods. For those prices per half minute and per minute, the advertiser can buy the right to put his ad in each of the three half hours of the show, a "rotation" system adopted by *Tonight* after it proved popular with *Today* advertisers.

While the price may seem high in the absolute, the advertiser knows that he is reaching an audience of 15.2 million people in the peak season, hence he is still eager. By mid-November of 1979, *Tonight* was sold out for the rest of the year and few spots were available through the first quarter of 1980.

Carson appreciates the significance of those numbers as well as anyone and has been dictating tough terms at contract-renewal time for years. Under the current three-year pact which expires December 31, 1980, the Nebraska boy who parlayed a Rotary Club magic act into the hottest stand-up comedy career in the history of television appears at most four and, usually, just three times a week—in twelve and twenty-five weeks respectively. During the remaining fifteen weeks Johnny takes vacations, sometimes spending a week or so with feature billing at the Sahara in Las Vegas, where he also owns a television station—no gamble *that* investment.

If Carson does get $5 million a year for all this, it is enough to pay 200 junior executives $25,000 a year each. Mike Wallace argued with a noncommittal Carson on *Sixty Minutes* that, everything considered, Carson's annual haul under the *old* contract, would be closer to $6 million, and Carson didn't exactly deny it. Apart from Marxist considerations foreign to our system, whatever sum is correct, it is worth it to NBC, considering something like $18 million, pretax profits.

Summing it up, one public-television executive remarked

some time ago that Carson was so powerful at NBC that if he wanted to work one week a year and do reruns the rest of the time, "The little men in black suits would run down the hall and say, 'Okay, let's let him do one week a year and the rest reruns.' "

That may have been true until Freddy Silverman, who became NBC's president in 1978, demanded shortly after he got the job that Carson appear more often. Silverman was eager to deflect CBS's midnight cannons, which were bombarding NBC in the late-night contest for viewers.

Tonight's waning popularity was a matter of major concern when Freddy came to NBC to put the network in stiffer competition with the ratings leader, ABC. In his prior incarnation, Freddy had helped ABC solidify its lead, and a lifetime before that he was engineering ratings victories for CBS. He was and is the Compleat Network Programer.

In the early weeks of the 1979 fall season, anyway, Fast Freddy shocked the industry by pulling NBC out of the dust of third place and thrusting the network into the lead. He did it with jiggle programing—also called T&A for those scintillating female body parts, tits and ass—but the important thing was that it made NBC affiliates happy for the first time in years. It was short-lived: NBC wound up the 1979–80 season in third place. Nevertheless, Freddy appears to have stanched the outflow of NBC affiliate blood to ABC.

NBC's generally weak programing in recent years lost the network many affiliates to ABC—thirteen at recent count, which dropped NBC to 200 affiliated television stations, or about the same as the other two networks. Prior to this, NBC always had had substantially more stations than ABC and a few more than CBS.

Freddy took up the "Carson Come Home" cause as outspoken late-night advertisers became more and more restive about his frequent absences. In hounding Carson to "no-show" less, Freddy was barking up the wrong money tree. Unaccustomed to criticism, and outraged by it, Johnny announced on April 19, 1979, that he would leave the show the following September 30, the seventeenth anniversary of his debut. For the already reeling NBC, that was something like getting advance notice of an attack on Pearl Harbor while attempting to stamp out the fuse of an atom bomb back at Malibu Beach. The NBC broadcast network executive cadre spent the day in stunned, pulse-racing silence. NBC then announced it would expect Carson to honor his contract and continue to do the show until April of 1981. Under his new contract, signed in May 1980, he agreed to stay on for three years.

But wait. Perhaps it is time for a change—assuming some superstar can be found to duplicate Johnny's success, as unlikely as this may seem. The consensus in the world of broadcasting is that there is simply no human alternative offering anything like Johnny's drawing power. (A source in TV land seriously reported that NBC was impressed with Kermit the Frog, who had pulled well in guest appearances. But few believe Jim Henson's Muppets can sustain the show on a daily basis. Maybe the show isn't all that blue, but it isn't all that green either.) Even on a three-a-week basis Carson is believed to be preferable to anything the network has thought of to date.

The fact that guest hosts preside part of the time draws snide comment from rivals from time to time. Mike Douglas is no comic but a singing host, and thus hardly a competitor. And the idiot cards reportedly lock guests into all but the most edgewise ad-libs. Also, Douglas's syndicated show generally appears at a much earlier hour. Still, in Douglas's own mind he is a Carson rival, and he is critical of Carson's absences. Commenting obliquely, in a reference to his own perfect attendance record, he says that if they come to see Mike Douglas they ought to see Mike Douglas.

Indisputable logic, perhaps, but meaningless in terms of Johnny Carson's contract dispute. Carson had implied that he was looking forward to doing TV specials and feature films for the movie companies. While he has said over the years that he might be just as happy back in Omaha where he had his first radio job and that he doesn't need to perform, one part of his personality wants to be an international star. Judging by the new contract, however, one could speculate that all Carson really wanted was a better deal.

When Carson finally leaves the show it will be crisis time at NBC. *Tonight*, like the equally innovative NBC crown jewel *The Today Show*, is a rare profitable vehicle for the network. (Credit Silverman with a neat fix on lagging *Today* recently through a Phil Donahue implant. Segments of the Donahue syndicated show have brought *Today* back into the lead over the aggressively cheerful *Good Morning America* on rival ABC.)

Obviously, nobody at NBC knows why Carson succeeds so spectacularly, and executives, including Freddy, shrink from the responsibility of picking a successor. A mistake could translate into a monumental boner with disastrous financial consequences for the network and could easily terminate the unfortunate decision-maker's career. Whether Freddy Silverman, who must make that decision, dwells on that is not known. But one guesses that he might —say, at 3:00 A.M. when the rest of quaking adulthood wakes up to worry about life crises.

Meanwhile, Carson continues to enjoy his ample leisure and spends lots of time on his private tennis court, and on the links with such cronies as actor George Segal and Steve Lawrence, the Steve Allen–era discovery.

That tennis court is in the stubby Elysian Mountains of Bel-Air, the exclusive section of exclusive Beverly Hills. Johnny owns a two-acre compound there enclosed by a chain-link fence and guarded twenty-four hours a day by three shifts of NBC security guards. Much smaller Bel-Air estates cost a million dollars or more, which suggests that Carson plunked down a bundle for his super-sized plot.

The community itself features a private security service with guards posted at each of two entrances on Sunset Boulevard. Carson moved into his contemporary ranch-style house about six years ago, purchasing it from comedy-film maker Mervyn LeRoy. LeRoy, whose children were grown, moved to a less spacious home.

Johnny's third wife, Joanna, who, some carpers say, bears a resemblance to Carson's second wife, Joanne, and even looks a bit like his first wife, Jody, has brought considerable serenity into his life.

He'd calmed down a lot since separating from Joanne, and on a night when he was having dinner with the late Jack Benny, Mary Livingstone, and fashion designer Mollie Parnis at "21," Joanna Holland sat in Johnny's line of vision with Jim Farley, Jr. Mollie explains—not literally, of course —"I looked at Johnny and he was having an orgasm. Johnny asked, 'Do you know her?' I said, 'Yes. Would you like to meet her?' "

Carson said yes, with emphasis. Mollie went over and arranged a meeting with the beautiful model. Jack O'Brian, the television columnist, was there too and at a table almost on a line with Joanna's. He comments, "I thought Johnny was looking at me, but actually he was staring at Joanna. He was like a stud with that laser-beam stare." Finally, Farley went to the bathroom, and Mollie went over to suggest that Joanna meet Carson.

The title to Joanna wasn't exactly free and clear when Carson came along. Max Kettner, an exporter and importer based in Geneva, thereafter sued Joanna for $160,000 he said he had lent her to buy a cooperative apartment at 920 Fifth Avenue. In defense, Mrs. Carson contended that the money was an "absolute gift."

There was still another string. Stephen Mallory Associates, a Manhattan interior-decorating firm, later sued Joanna for $43,058—allegedly unpaid decorator bills for a different apartment at 201 East 67th Street, where Joanna's mother resides. Decorators can be dear; the total bill had been $124,000. The suit was unresolved as this was written.

Joanna moved with Johnny to the Coast when *The Tonight Show* went there in May 1972. They were married on October 2 of the same year—Carson's tenth anniversary on the show—but not, of course, before Carson got a final divorce decree one month earlier from wife number two, Joanne. Joanne got a cash settlement of $200,000 and art and miscellaneous items reportedly worth another $200,000, and she receives annual alimony of $100,000 until she remarries.

Everyone, it seems, envies that Carson pot of gold. After the marriage to Joanna, Jack O'Brian wrote that Mollie deserved a finder's fee, and when Mollie saw O'Brian thereafter, she agreed. They say the Carsons have lived happily ever after, given the strains of stardom and its obvious fringe benefits.

Joanna, a steadying influence, urged Johnny to age gracefully—allow his famous boyish face to be crowned with the gray hair that only Clairol knew was there.

To provide for his leisure and convenience she arranged to have the tennis court built on the premises and also put in an office, a separate building behind the house where Johnny works on his monologues in the morning.

Avoidance of crowds is a major preoccupation with the Carsons. Anytime Carson is seen on the street he draws stares and hordes of autograph seekers. He complains that a man even asked him to pen his signature while the two were using adjoining stalls in a men's room. (At his former home in New York City's United Nations Plaza he sometimes wore disguises to avoid recognition, fooling about half the people half the time.)

Carson's Beverly Hills chain-link fence is designed to deflect impertinent tourists, oddballs, and occasional cranks who are drawn by celebrities of Carson's caliber. Yet even in such a sanctum the world intrudes. Carson recently settled out of court the suit he instituted to force Sonny Bono and other less famous neighbors to silence barking dogs in their own retreats. And if the dogs get bothersome again, Carson will be able to jump into his $25,000 Mercedes SLC sport coupe and head for the beach near Malibu, where he is building a second refuge.

While Carson's limited *Tonight Show* appearances do suggest to some he'd like to bow out completely, there is evidence to the contrary. Carson surely must worry about a future without *Tonight*. Years ago, while Al Bruno was representing Carson, Johnny negotiated seriously for a weekly television *Friars Roast* and had all but committed himself before Bruno convinced him that leaving *Tonight* would be a terrible mistake.

Leaving *Tonight* certainly unsettled his predecessors. Steve Allen did it, and, though he won't admit regretting it, he never regained that pinnacle of stardom. Jack Paar may have regretted his leaving too. He certainly attempted a comeback.

As for the visitors to the Burbank studio on that fall evening in 1979, they entered and accustomed themselves to the half-light of the theater while the musicians did an explosively energetic run-through of a number to be played during the evening. During the show itself, Carson would be seen tapping pencils to the music, holding the "sticks" correctly as any dedicated drum hobbyist would. (Not just incidentally, those "sticks" have erasers on both ends so that when Carson throws them at producer de Cordova and de Cordova throws them back at Carson the high-priced talent won't be blinded.)

Doubtless these musicians are among the best dance-band sidemen in the world, and it is one of the curiosities of *The Tonight Show* that the folks at home rarely hear more than a few bars from that orchestra. Its primary function is to serve as a musical claque for Johnny Carson—to hype the show's 500-member studio audience, keep them excited and spontaneous so that the folks back home will feel they are experiencing a live-entertainment event. (The band does tour the West, though, so some fans of the show who never visit Burbank do get to hear it in concert.)

The sensational but largely silent orchestra is only one of several expensive *Tonight Show* props designed to make the show work. Insiders insist that the studio auditorium was ripped apart and redone to resemble the one Carson did so well with back in New York City. Carson reportedly saw the Burbank setup and frowned, and the network gave commands, dutifully remodeling to his specs. NBC was willing to spend heavily to preserve whatever gave the show its astounding popularity back East. By meeting such Carson demands—whether necessary from a performance point of view or not—the network labors to make its most valuable property happy. In pursuit of that goal no expense, however unreasonable, is spared.

Not that the customized auditorium in Burbank is by any means so much waste lumber. Remember, there are 15.2 million people out there in TV land hanging on Carson's every quip.

Here's what the favored 500 see when they visit the show. The stage has three essential parts: the right side (as viewed by the audience), which houses the orchestra in a setting of tiny glittering mirrors; stage center, where a drawn curtain hides imaginative sets for visiting singers; and the primary focus on the left, with its painted canvas backdrop of trees, lake, and mountains behind the Carson throne. To the visitor it all seems drab—and drab it is, for fake scenery photographs better than real. The couch for the evening's guests is equally familiar and has cushioned the backsides of Hollywood's most celebrated stars, who, it seems, would give most anything to cross verbal swords with Carson if they are clever—and most of them are not. Masochistically they come anyway to be skewered by Carson's barbs. Not that they feel comfortable sitting at Carson's right. Many a superstar has candidly told Carson and the world that the idea of facing Carson's one-liners has filled the star with a surpassing fear. More than one has actually dried up, and a few have tarried backstage never to appear after a debilitating case of the "Oh-God-suppose-I-bomb-and-everybody-realizes-I'm-a-fool-without-a-script?" heebie-jeebies. Considering some of the vacuous things many actors say, small wonder their knees quake and their throats constrict.

On the fall day in question, a sign reads: "THE TONIGHT SHOW, THURSDAY, OCTOBER 12."

The band continues its warm-up until the double clock reads 10:30—the countdown on 11:30, when the show will be taped—and 4:30, the local California afternoon time. Producer Fred de Cordova's tactic is to think late-night and get the audience to also—for spontaneity. (In TV, the producer's role is roughly equivalent to that of the director of a play.)

The excitement ebbs a bit as the band under Tommy Newsom, subbing for Doc Severinsen, takes a break. A solitary musician, drummer Ed Shaughnessy, wearing a blazing red tie, bends over his snare and tom-toms, tapping here and turning a key there to fine-tune these bluntest of all musical instruments.

At 5:15 the band is back and another episode in the thirty-year history of Sylvester L. "Pat" Weaver's most dazzling television achievement is about to begin. The orchestra cranks up, and Big Ed McMahon, Johnny's sidekick, slips through the curtain, stage center, and walks to the mike. An old carnival pitchman, Ed is completely at ease as he warms up the audience with old jokes. They laugh at a small joke and he comments, "I can see you're a drinking crowd"—and they laugh again, harder this time. Everyone, it seems, likes to be thought of as a genial party-going drunk—at least in the *Tonight Show* theater and in the collective.

There are other jokes. Ed says a rhythm player's wife has just given birth to twins. "I don't want to embarrass anybody, but I'd like the proud father to stand up and take a bow." In an obvious punch line, the entire band rises in unison and each man points a finger at someone else. It's a surefire laugh-getter; it makes members of the studio audience feel like insiders, for it is clearly implied that the joke is too blue for all those folks out there in TV land.

Still prior to taping, McMahon next teases the audience about a possible no-show by Carson: "Who is our guest host tonight?" There is a groan, though it is Wednesday and Johnny usually takes Monday and sometimes Tuesday off. McMahon adds, "I'm happy to say, it is Johnny Carson." (A recent gimmick to build enthusiasm: announce in anxious tones that Johnny has been in an accident, then bring on an unscathed star to wild cheers.) Finally, McMahon says what everyone wants to hear: "And now . . . heeeeeeeerrrre's Johnny!" The band blows the roof off with the *Tonight Show* theme and the sounds of brass and saxophones blend with that of tremendous applause. (A flashing sign calling for applause seems superfluous.) Carson, dressed in a sport jacket from his own successful line of Hart Schaffner & Marx clothing, steps through the curtain, still youthful after all these years. He makes small talk, comments on the applause and the responsive audience.

When the applause finally dies down, he begins his opening monologue, as fresh and topical—though not always as funny—as the day's newspapers. (An ex-writer explains the kind of difficulty that arises: "How many jokes can you make about Halloween the third year you write for the show?") Johnny sneaks glances at the monologue, which is printed on yard-high poster boards, a crude intrusion just out of view of the camera. Carson's glances down at the printed material have become instant laugh-getters for Carson impersonators—even the bad mimics.

The monologue on that fall day was under par, and even Ed McMahon's booming laughter—he is an important part of the reaction and has boffed at Carson's jokes from the time he emceed *Who Do You Trust?*—doesn't convulse the audience. The so-so reaction does allow Carson his tour-de-force "saves," the "Wasn't-that-a-clinker?" glances at the studio crowd and outspoken comments on the quality of the material. He usually manages to get even bigger laughs in his reaction to his writers' bad jokes than better material might have gotten. Some of those glances are directed at the camera that since the beginning has been the *Tonight* host's reactor device to share "a confidence" with the viewer.

This snatching of victory from the jaws of defeat inspires awe in the business. Carson's very good at it, to be sure, and it's a technique reflecting years of experience.

He finishes the monologue, and with a sweep of his hands, as though he were pushing a load of manure off the stage, he segues to commercials. The television audience hears a few bars of the next swinging number from the orchestra as sponsor products are displayed on the home screen. But in beautiful downtown Burbank, the band plays on.

The Comedian:
A Historical Perspective

Fools and funnymen have fascinated the world since the
beginning of recorded history. Some were witless imbeciles, others grotesque human beings—particularly dwarfs
but also misshapen mounds of fat. And still others, the
most formidable of the lot, were shrewd and calculating
men like the stand-up comedians of today.

The obvious function of the fool throughout history has
been to make us laugh at life, to not take ourselves or our
world too seriously. Thus, the scapegoat-fool slips on a
banana peel, and we laugh because it might have been us,
not he. There is a macabre, often psychopathic overtone to
much that strikes us funny—and the ultimate joke is sometimes said to be death.

The most renowned clowns of history have made others
the butt of the joke. Some clowns were given to playing
cruel tricks on their fellow townsmen. They reported their
sportive exploits with glee, and no little elaboration, to
patrons or prospective sponsors. If the buffoon was clever
and gained notoriety, some man of power, often a religious
leader or a conqueror, would hear about him and perhaps
make the joker a member of his court. The buffoon could
then devote himself to his trade and live high on the hog.
In contrast to the usual patron, a man of urbane sophistica-

tion, most clowns centuries ago were earthy, indolent characters with the wit to avoid hard work and the bold effrontery to express things cleverly and in telling perspective.

Yet, the clown was not a revolutionary dedicated to destroying the system. Rather, he was a safety valve—a corrective to the pretentiousness of the social order—even when that meant mocking the king. The shrewdest rulers kept clowns in part because they needed blunt talk to offset a cacophony of sycophantic trumpeting. The fool told his master what was what, using the leavening of humor to soften the blow. Like Johnny Carson, the clown twitted the powers of government without seeking to bring them down.

The jester of the fierce fourteenth-century Muslim conqueror Tamerlane was a master of the art of baiting with humor. On one celebrated occasion, his patron became alarmed at what the years were doing to his appearance. After glimpsing his face in a mirror, the conqueror wept for two hours in the palace court, and his aides cried with him. The jester's sobs were even louder than the rest, and he cried long after Tamerlane and the others had dried their tears. Finally Tamerlane asked the jester why he was inconsolable. Replied the jester, "If you saw yourself in the glass for a short moment and wept for two hours, is it surprising that I weep longer since I see you the whole day?" Typically for a buffoon, Tamerlane's jester flirted with death by ridiculing the murderous warrior before his closest followers. Yet Tamerlane rocked with laughter, and the buffoon— then as now—triumphed by speaking the unspeakable.

It was characteristic of the most successful ancient clowns to flirt with disaster and death by insulting their powerful patrons. And similarly, Johnny Carson's cutting monologues about officials and presidents are part of his stock-in-trade. In a democracy Johnny Carson does not risk the firing squad by making President Jerry Ford look like a klutz, even though Carson's barbs may have influenced enough votes in that close election to throw the presidency to Jimmy Carter. Carson, since the pull-out in Vietnam, has gotten tougher on politicians in general and the Carters in particular.

While Carson is immune to political retribution, he does court death in the characteristic manner of the king's jester by doing fool things that the average citizen would not— parachuting from an airplane, allowing potentially danger- ous snakes and tarantulas and wild cats to nuzzle him, tak- ing a variety of hazardous pratfalls.

Like the ancient buffoons, Carson does all this to gain the approval of both common man and king, because that ap- proval brings rich rewards—money and power. It is fasci- nating that Carson, like the court jesters, has been able to limit his services to little more than is necessary to satisfy his wants though his limited appearances are far from enough to satisfy the wants of his employer. Nevertheless, Carson is so powerful that three appearances a week have secured him the perks of the job, the astronomical salary, and superstardom. History's greatest fools also showed great ingenuity in limiting their appearances while netting the greatest rewards.

Tamerlane's jester, for example, was obliged to say pray- ers as well as amusing things. Like any self-respecting clown, the court jester resented the extra duty. One day he stood in the pulpit and asked the assembled Muslims, "Do you know what I am going to say to you today?"

"No," they replied.

"And no more do I," said the jester, hastily leaving the mosque.

A week later he asked the same question, but the congre- gation, not to be fooled a second time, answered, "Yes."

"If you know, then I needn't tell you," said the jester, and again he left the rostrum.

The next week the congregation was all smiles, ready to spring a trap. To the usual question, the response was, "Some of us do, but some of us don't."

"Then let those who know tell those who don't," said the jester, making his escape once again.

Tamerlane's jester got away with it because he was on intimate terms with his master, as so many court jesters were. They enjoyed the company and the largess of princes —including those of the church—while orators, poets, and philosophers of considerable learning sometimes languished in poverty. The comedians of today also enjoy the company of kings—we place great value on the individual who can respond to life's ironies with a joke. *Tonight Show* host Jack Paar socialized with the Kennedys, and Carson with Mayor Lindsay of New York. Bob Hope prides himself on having hobnobbed with every president since FDR.

Everyone, it seems, admires the superior shrewdness of a man who by his wits gets away with things mere mortals cannot. For example, today's comedians often use tricks to get forbidden material on the broadcast waves, and Johnny Carson is no exception. It is said that the regular censor was away when Carson did the old burlesque story about the Fugarwe Indians. In the story, the Indians are wandering around in the dark and arrive at a cul-de-sac, where the chief says to a stranger "We're the Fug-are-we?"

Millions of viewers love Carson for his risqué stories and envy his ability to get away with it. The day after the Academy Awards ceremony, which Carson did for ABC, he was back at the old stand with a joke about Superman. He's finally marrying Lois Lane, Carson quipped. He doesn't know it yet, but she's using a Kryptonite coil.

There are grim overtones to comedy, and the best comedians are obviously willing to exploit them. The comedian reminds us that we are one heartbeat away from eternity. He doesn't always do it politely. Characteristically, the clown in action is amoral and will use the most shocking —even brutal—methods to get laughs. The late Lenny Bruce, commenting on the trial of a young mass murderer accused of planting a bomb on an airplane which killed the man's mother and everyone else on board, said, "Anyone who blows up his mother and forty people *can't be all bad.*" Bruce also specialized in erotic and toilet humor. In his famous obscenity trial the late newspaper columnist Dorothy Kilgallen, a fan, was dumbstruck when asked to defend a Bruce routine which she hadn't seen and which was about intercourse with a chicken. Lenny was a dope addict, philanderer, and voyeur, among other unconventionalities. Yet he saw better than anyone in his time the colossal irony of life and the hypocrisy of its institutions and was willing to go to mad lengths to reveal his vision. Lenny was not only a con artist in the slang sense of that word, this man who envious stand-up comedians admit could put any rival in his pocket was actually convicted of playing confidence games for profit.

Bruce didn't invent comic amorality. Actually, it is an old, old tradition in comedy. The fourteenth-century German comic master Till Eulenspiegel was cruel in exercising his wit. In the village of Budenstetten he was engaged by a curé with whom he was constantly in and out of trouble as he practiced his merry pranks—including a gross maneuver which caused the curé to relieve himself during services. As stage manager of the Easter play, he situated an old foe, the curé's venerable chambermaid, at the tomb of Jesus to play the part of the angel of the Lord. Till and two peasants took the parts of the three Marys. When the chambermaid-angel asked, "Whom do you seek?" one of the peasants, on instructions from Eulenspiegel, replied, "We are looking for an old one-eyed concubine belonging to the curé." In the uproar that followed, Till was once again forced to flee.

Thereafter he often took service with tradesmen but always got into trouble by mischievously obeying orders literally, with absurd results. This is a familiar method of modern comedians, including *The Tonight Show*'s Steve Allen, who learned the technique from his mother, vaudevillian Belle Donohue. Belle, playing a featherbrain, wandered on stage to ask the MC, "Is it all right to come out now?" "Yes," said the MC, and, urging her to begin, said, "Get going!" Whereupon Belle turned around to exit again. Just so, Steve, in interviewing a man from his audience, asked, "What is your name, sir?" Answer: "Tom

Francis, Central Tool and Die Works, Pittsburgh, Pennsylvania." Steve: "That's a rather long name, Mr. Pennsylvania." Mild stuff, certainly, but amusing and serviceable—yet a far cry from the tough talk that goes into the humor of some comedians.

Many comics today, like Lenny Bruce and Till Eulenspiegel, are addicted to jokes that are coarse, gross, and even brutal. On *The Tonight Show* we watch the cruelty of the frequent substitute host Don Rickles with a mixture of shock and amusement. Rickles is praised by some who know him offstage as a warm, likable fellow. But in performance the milk of Rickles' kindness curdles. He adopts a slashing style against those who share the stage with him and with the guests he interviews in the studio audience.

A while back, Rickles interviewed a man who had been retired for many years. Rickles adopted a pseudo-indulgent manner as though dealing with someone in second childhood. It wasn't so, but the man's piping voice suggested that it might well be so—and if not now, maybe soon. Rickles smiled and said something nice, then ordered the old gentleman to stop looking down at his crotch or "it's back to the home." The humor is representative of Rickles' amoral stage personality. It is more than a little brutal. Watching the old man squirm, the viewer thinks as he chuckles, "Better he than I." We laugh, perhaps, so that we won't cry over the actual fate of the man—a fate which each of us knows realistically may sometime be our own. Thus by proxy we laugh at the approach of death—the ultimate joke.

The sixteenth-century German buffoon Hans Clawert, an illiterate who had a lucrative quack practice, had no fear of death. As he breathed his last, a victim of the plague in 1566, he bequeathed his soul to the good God, his fowling net to his patron, his anvil to the smith, and cards and dice to the devil, and so departed.

An abbot, we are told, gave extreme unction to a medieval buffoon named Scrogin and told him that if he believed he had received the holy spirit he would have received it. But Scrogin recovered. The abbot then lent Scrogin a horse for his return home. The buffoon never returned the animal, sending instead a message that if the abbot believed he had received the horse he would have received it. When finally at death's door, he asked to be buried at Westminster Abbey "under one of the spouts of the leads for I have ever loved good drink."

Just so, we admire cigar-chomping humorist George Burns, who laughs at death—once-removed—in his mid-eighties. The miracle is that he works at all.

Most clowns have attempted to avoid work in the traditional sense and yet have lived better than the working man. Scrogin's joyous and well-rewarded exploits have a modern equivalent—the near-extortionate fees the *Tonight Show* guest comics later command in Las Vegas. A few weeks of appearances in Vegas and they'll have earned more than most of us in a year. They may do nothing else all year, apart from additional guest shots on *The Tonight Show* to keep interest and the price up. With typical cynicism, the comics call the Las Vegas largess "fuck you" money. They are smart enough to pile it up quickly and then relax and let the world go to hell.

But how did this strange profession evolve? What led some clever individual to think that he could earn a living by doing offbeat, funny things of no worth in the material sense?

The ancient practice of keeping half-wits and grotesque human beings at court was certainly an encouragement to the consciously funny man. In ages past, kings paid fortunes for hideously deformed individuals, particularly dwarfs, and they preferred those who were imbeciles. In fact, one wealthy Roman slaveholder demanded his 20,000 sesterces back when he discovered the wretched creature he had bought still had his wits.

Having wit and to spare, the professional buffoons quickly sensed a market, and assumed a craziness that somehow impressed the patron—particularly if the fool was willing to lambaste his master with insults. While it may seem curious, direct insults aimed at the master, not just oblique witticisms designed to tell a hard truth in acceptable terms, were sometimes an essential for the successful fool.

In the brilliant treatise on the role of comedy in history called *The Fool,* first published in 1935 by British publishers Faber and Faber, Ltd., author Enid Welsford points to the fact that for centuries human beings, particularly the fortunate ones, have sought the ridicule of others as a means of warding off bad luck. The discussion throws more light on the often complex role of the fool. The ancient Greeks, Romans, Estonians, Carpathians, townsfolk of Berlin, and residents of many parts of India all sought to be ridiculed. Welsford wrote:

"The explanation should not be difficult to grasp for those who dread mentioning their good health without touching wood. It is a form of that universal human instinct, the dread of what the Greeks called the sin of 'hubris' or presumption.

"The malign power of the Evil Eye is not only found in concentrated form in some human beings, it exists in a vague undefined way suffused throughout the universe, or such at least is the impression. . . . To praise oneself or be praised by others is a sure way of attracting this queer cosmic jealousy, and conversely, the surest way to evade its unwelcome attention is to deprecate oneself or be mocked by other people. . . ."

Apprehensive citizens in the past have sometimes provoked their immediate neighbor—throwing rocks into his house, for example—with the idea that if the neighbor reacted with greater abuse, bad luck would be transferred from the provocateur onto the revenge seeker. This was common practice in the Indian sectors of Behar and Bengal. But practical citizens have regarded it better to hire a permanent scapegoat whose official duty is to dispense abuse and accordingly bear the community ill luck on his unimportant shoulders.

It was sometimes difficult to find someone prepared in cold blood to abuse important persons in order to rid them of their burden of ill luck. Enid Welsford noted: "For that purpose it will be necessary to employ someone who is either too stupid or too helpless to decline the undertaking."

Johnny Carson is neither stupid nor helpless and need not fear ill luck. The show remains secure after eighteen years and a score of finely tuned writers. The bite of his humor is soft, like that of a playful family puppy. *The Tonight Show* has become a palliative like the neighborhood bar where the restless gather for a little light amusement—to watch a confused drunk, perchance, or to listen to the tragicomic yarns of the unhappily married or the lonely traveling drummer. But the walk to the television set is more convenient on a cold or stormy night. It's an easy out, and, besides, it offers viewers the professional merrymaker at the top of his form. The show itself is carried along by momentum as it exploits all the classic devices of comedy.

Clowns of old often wore motley, garish clothes as a simple but effective way of raising laughter through incongruity. Thus *The Tonight Show* brings us Doc Severinsen and his outrageous costumes—an amusing knockoff, it could be said, of the great nineteenth-century English clown Joseph Grimaldi, whose extravagantly grotesque costumes were a caricature of the dandies of his day. The clowns of old were often gross in size, men of gargantuan appetites, and while Carson remains svelte, attractive, and well spoken, he has his hard-drinking foil Ed McMahon, who resembles Falstaff, the fat, merry, ribald, and boastful knight in Shakespeare's *Henry IV.* As Enid Welsford explains: "This great primal joke of the undignified nature of the human body, repeated for centuries, literally ad nauseam, forms a most important part of the stock-in-trade of the buffoon and reached its highest development in the person of that 'ton of flesh,' that mountain of a man, Jack Falstaff."

As for Carson himself? His style is an amalgam of the best of the modern clowns. Rich Little, the master mimic, has commented on Carson's wisecracky Bob Hope delivery, his Jack Benny stare, his Rickles putdown, his Steve Allen laugh. At times he adopts motley clothes, dressing as Art Fern and Aunt Blabby. And Carson as Carson—witty, at times slashing in his putdowns, and clever enough in repartee with guest comedian and politician alike to best them all. And, in the tradition of the great buffoon (and the rest of us), Carson is in it for the heavy money, the freedom and power it brings. For the clown's ultimate irony is that while jesting at kings and popes, at guests and audience, at danger and even death, when he enjoys his laughs, it is on the way to the bank.

Carson has mastered it all, and he is today America's premier clown, its favorite funny guy from the general store, the corner pub. Carson is the nation's master comedian and court jester in the forum of the comedy kings— *The Tonight Show.*

Pat Weaver:
The Man Who Invented Tonight

NBC executive Sylvester L. "Pat" Weaver, the father of *The Tonight Show,* certainly didn't come to the network from central casting. At six feet four inches, he was a lanky stringbean of a man. Refreshingly good-looking with his shock of red hair and jug ears, he looked more like a retired tennis champ than a jaded broadcast executive. He dressed nattily too, and was in every way the antithesis of the corporate drone in appearance and in mental set and habits. His craving for exercise included daily swims and, in season, skiing. He was physically active even in his NBC offices. There he was given to jumping on a bongo board—a seesaw for the feet—and rocking to and fro to the mystification of visitors from the outside world. Conventional he was not.

He also exhibited one of the most casual attitudes to be found in any executive suite. From the moment he arrived at the network as vice-president in charge of television in the late 1940s, he would refer to the redoubtable David Sarnoff, crusty chairman of NBC's parent, RCA, as "Fang." Not in Sarnoff's earshot, perhaps, but Sarnoff was Fang with abandon to everyone else Weaver encountered—including even Sarnoff's sycophants. He was that sure of himself.

When Weaver wasn't giving flip monikers to enemies and friends—super-rich Nelson Rockefeller was "Rags" to Pat —Weaver composed monumental memos about the brand-new medium, television. He had a massive background in show business, and particularly radio, but nevertheless he saw little of radio in television's future. Meanwhile, most other broadcast executives were electing the obvious route: TV should be radio with pictures, they said. But Weaver thought that approach would straitjacket a medium he had perceived would become the greatest device for communication and entertainment in history. It would make a mutant of Everyman, make the entire world as familiar through pictures as the corner drugstore.

No, Pat Weaver wasn't the prototypal executive in a gray flannel suit. Like an errant Boy Scout, he was not only irreverent in the chapel of corporate cant, he was also disobedient in the temple of tradition. Needless to say, he was feared by those network executives and advertising chiefs who were satisfied with and committed to the status quo.

And that's part of the reason he was called to NBC. The onetime premier network faced a major crisis, and Weaver, who had been a wunderkind in radio programing, was ordered to resolve it in a way that would put NBC back on top. He was given a free hand and told to grab NBC television, mired in conventionality as it was, by the ratings bootstraps and wrench it upward and into the lead. General Sarnoff sensed that innovative measures were called for to beat the competition, which in those days meant CBS.

CBS's solid lead in television was a bitter irony at NBC. Until the late 1940s, CBS had been regarded as broadcasting's upstart network. Now the junior network was flying high, following its most impressive coup: Chairman Bill Paley had captured virtually the entire roster of NBC's top radio talents—Jack Benny, Burns and Allen, Amos and Andy, and other top stars—as the result of a stunning 1948 raid which appealed to the performers' bank accounts through tax loopholes CBS helped them exploit. CBS was now using this old talent and some new faces to dominate most of television's prime evening hours while piling up profits that were the envy of NBC and of the business world in general. It was up to Weaver, then, to bring the CBS juggernaut to a halt and make NBC the number-one television broadcaster.

If anyone could do it, Weaver could—or so his friends and followers believed. From his early years in Los Angeles, where Pat's father was a wealthy roofing-materials manufacturer, Weaver had been impressive. At thirteen he read Edward Gibbon's forbidding *Decline and Fall of the Roman Empire,* along with dozens of other scholarly tomes that other boys his age stacked to reach the cookie jar. No sissy, Weaver was active in sports and developed many other interests. His success with each new endeavor bred a lifelong breezy confidence, which was appealing to many who believed it stopped short of arrogance.

As might be expected of so bookish a lad, Weaver earned high marks in high school. His father, an ambitious man who once waged an unsuccessful campaign for mayor of Los Angeles, looked at Pat's report card and presented his son with a new Ford. Weaver proved to have a flair for mechanics, too; he promptly customized the car. He used it to squire pretty girls, including starlets from the nearby Hollywood community. A talented amateur dancer, he earned trophies in Charleston contests with such unknowns as Loretta Young, Carole Lombard, and Joan Crawford.

After graduation, Pat took an entirely different automobile to Princeton—a Marmon roadster, which helped establish him locally as a bon vivant. Peripatetic as always, he baffled everyone with his high marks and his election to Phi Beta Kappa in his junior year. He capped his scholastic attainments by graduating magna cum laude. Eager to see the places he had studied as a philosophy major and bent on becoming a writer, he went first to Paris and then on an extended visit to the ancient ruins in Greece and Italy.

When his money ran out he returned to the States, arriving in mid-Depression. A stint as a salesman in New York City was unrewarding, and he soon returned to the West Coast, where he was taken with that noisy infant, radio. Like many another man in the young, traditionless industry, Weaver was able to do most everything he liked in the early days—writing and broadcasting the news, for instance. He also composed, cast, and acted in radio dramas. Broadcast conditions were primitive at the time, and Weaver sometimes competed with backfiring autos from a nearby garage which lent a disconcerting counterpoint to his more serious efforts.

In those days, the sponsors' advertising agencies produced most of the radio shows, and it was perhaps predictable that Pat Weaver—a so-so actor and scriptwriter—would enter the agency business. Pat found employment with Young & Rubicam, a leading radio agency, and was soon tapped as representative to one of the agency's most difficult stars—Fred Allen, a top radio performer who wrote most of his own material. Fred Allen's literary output was awesome, and if there was one thing he wouldn't tolerate it was sponsor interference. Every time an Allen barb found its mark in a sensitive target, the sponsor got letters and Allen got reprimands. Worse than that from Allen's point of view, the network and sponsors attempted to cull the scripts in advance and avoid those embarrassing letters. One of Weaver's first official acts was to boot two men out of the broadcast booth when they attempted to rein in the irascibly funny Allen as he rehearsed his show. Perhaps it was just as well Weaver didn't know it, but the kickees were Lee Bristol, president of Bristol-Myers, Allen's sponsor, and Merlin Hall "Deac" Aylesworth, president of NBC. Weaver's rash act in running interference on that momentous occasion won Fred Allen's undying loyalty.

Young & Rubicam was suitably impressed with the way

Pat handled a star who could be as cantankerous as he was funny. Two years later, in 1937, Pat was named supervisor of all Young & Rubicam radio programs. Thereafter, his confident air was instrumental in selling many shows to sponsors—even bad ones. He was, in short, something of a miracle man in the eyes of his radio cohorts, a judgment Pat Weaver shared in all immodesty.

Judging from his later service to one of the monumental presences of business, he must have been. Young & Rubicam handled a minor American Tobacco Company product, and, as a result, Pat came to the attention of its president, George Washington Hill, a man of such force and personality that he became an American folk hero. Sidney Greenstreet portrayed a character modeled on Hill in the movie called *The Hucksters,* which was the talk of the nation for months.

When Hill asked Weaver to rescue American Tobacco's Lucky Strikes from third place in the cigarette derby—after Chesterfields and Camels—Weaver realized something new and different clearly was needed. For his part, Hill sensed that Weaver's flair would do the trick, but probably didn't anticipate the dramatic switch from Hill's hard-sell approach that Weaver would call for.

In Weaver, Hill had not found a yes-man. Like the bird that flits in and out picking the teeth of the crocodile, Weaver knew just how to handle himself to avoid Hill's sharp bite. Each morning the tobacco ace would stride into the conference room, his many aides already at their stations, standing in rapt attention like docile lapdogs awaiting the command to sit. Hill would eyeball each fiercely in turn as he drew two packages of Luckies from a pocket and began chain-puffing his way through the meeting. Lighting his first butt and slapping the package on the table, he would bark, "Tobacco is what it's all about, gentlemen!" While his aides cringed, Hill would fire questions at them and illustrate the generally unsound replies dramatically. One idea caused him to balance a large potted plant on the edge of a wastebasket. It crashed to the floor, of course, because, as Hill explained cogently, the idea had "no foundation." The aides withheld comment whenever possible for fear of unleashing an unnecessary tornado. Weaver would sit with his feet propped jauntily on the desk, parting his shoes occasionally to aim and fire an idea at Hill, thus exhibiting a nonchalance that unnerved the others all the more.

One day, Hill read in its entirety Weaver's twenty-four-page typed memo which constituted a masterful overview of advertising history. Weaver traced advertising back to the "first social contact that man had with man." The memo's passages sailed through history via the voyages of Minoan merchants, and into the rise of medieval guilds, the beginnings of the machine age, and up through American Tobacco's latest and, in Weaver's view, rather unsatisfactory commercial. The climax: Drop hard for soft sell and adopt a campaign for "The finer, the lighter, the naturally mild Lucky Strike tobacco." Hill bought the idea and was wise to do so. Within three years, Luckies were again leading the cigarette race, with Chesterfields and Camels in the place and show positions.

This and other American Tobacco campaigns rounded out Weaver's training in the uses of radio. He had a full appreciation of the role of the sponsor from the viewpoint of one of the toughest sponsors in the business, and he knew the role of entertainment after working with some of the most demanding and talented people in the medium. Weaver was ready for television.

But first a word about World War II. Shortly after Pearl Harbor, Weaver, a summer yachtsman, applied for a Navy commission and soon found himself plying the Atlantic in a convoy escort vessel, so safe from hostile fire that he wore swim trunks most of the day, sunning himself on deck while a steward freshened his drinks. Bored and feeling guilty, he was delighted to be tapped for the Armed Forces Radio Service, a West Coast dispenser of morale-building programs. There were so many transplants from Young & Rubicam there that Armed Forces Radio was known as the Y&Rmy. Weaver's efforts included the much-admired *Command Performance* dramatic series. It was a harbinger that his works often included classical numbers, reflecting his still-controversial view that broadcasting owed a bit of culture to the listener, something he would continue to press for in television.

When the war was over, Weaver returned to American Tobacco and an ailing George Washington Hill, whose rasping voice reflected a lifetime of tobacco abuse. Hill died soon after, and Weaver mourned the genuine loss of a friend—and the $250,000-a-year vice-presidency Hill hadn't gotten around to bestowing.

Pat returned to the agency business but was quickly bored by the same old stuff. He thus welcomed the NBC programing job in 1949 and set about reshaping broadcast attitudes and practices as only a man of his wide background, ingenuity, and force of personality could.

He was soon faced with heavy opposition from advertisers and the agencies. First, there was television's astronomical cost, and the way Weaver solved it. Radio, which relied on the theater of the mind for "scenery," could be produced for peanuts—especially the endemic fifteen-minute show. Even longer radio productions thrived on budgets that were a fraction of that required for full-dress television productions. In radio, a leading washing-machine product, Oxydol, could have its own *Ma Perkins* soap opera, and did, too.

Weaver and others thought a half hour was the minimum time span for effective network television, and even that period seemed constricting to Weaver, who believed that some shows ought to run an hour and a half—a revolutionary idea at the time. Obviously, few advertisers could afford singlehandedly to bankroll the "spectaculars" Weaver was calling for. And any show running ninety minutes, featuring high-priced talent and expensive sets on a regular basis, could soak up the annual television advertising budgets of half a dozen sponsors.

Weaver's solution was both ingenious and diabolical: relieve the ad agencies of the responsibility for producing television shows and claim the production role for the networks themselves. The networks would thereby control content and at the same time would be in a position to sell participations to as many advertisers as necessary for full sponsorship. Pages in the television magazine, as it were.

This approach would also permit Weaver to override advertiser objections to another pet plan. Hewing to the subtheme of his Y&Rmy days, Pat was determined to upgrade the public taste by sandwiching an occasional classical artist between the light entertainment—a pianist between a comedian's pratfalls, for example.

But it was Weaver's determination to capture the production reins that sent shivers down advertising men's spines. Once the advertising agencies became aware of this Weaver plan, they felt both betrayed by an old associate and, even more to the point, threatened. If Weaver won, the admen would no longer rub elbows and knees with stars of stage, screen, and radio. Instead, they would be relegated to the unexciting business of filming commercials, a function about as appealing as emptying the stars' garbage.

As it turned out, they had little choice. Weaver had read the signals well and early. He was right—it wasn't feasible for single advertisers regularly to sponsor Weaver's "spectaculars," and the viewing public loved the new concept. Weaver pioneered with *Your Show of Shows,* the hour-and-a-half-long comedy presentation with Sid Caesar and Imogene Coca, a show that virtually changed the Saturday-night habits of a nation. Restaurateurs and movie-theater owners groaned as their best night became a stay-at-home evening for much of their clientele. Pat Weaver was definitely on the march.

Meanwhile, he was scribbling feverish memos about two new shows that were to be the jewels in his television crown—*The Today Show* and *The Tonight Show*. The precursor of the latter show was called *Broadway Open House* and appeared for an hour between 11:30 P.M. and 12:30 A.M. Monday through Friday.

In a memo concerning the prospects for the show, Weaver wrote that "to get a good station lineup . . . after 11:30 P.M., we must program.

"Therefore, we must have facilities available and we must have an economical and saleable operation. . . . We must remember that our [affiliated] station lineup will be pretty bad and it may be difficult to get a good program and afford to put it into this period because of the low time scale [advertising charges at such a late hour]. At 11:30 [P.M.] I would like to see us do *Broadway Open House* for an hour. . . .

"The *Broadway Open House Show* would be as originally planned, to wit: a zany, light-hearted show on every night at the same time for people in the mood for staying up. . . .

"Will the Sales Department work with Program[ing] on the *Broadway Open House* bit on the basis of it being sold in quarter hour units, either on a strip [every-night] basis or just in [individual] units?"

Then out of the dictaphone came one of Weaver's brilliant ideas which made up in common sense what its expression lacked in syntax. Vetted a bit, it went like this: "It is my feeling that if we have a *Broadway Open House* and a quarter hour between 12:00 to 12:15 in the morning which is devoted to moving [for example] a relatively unknown brand of spaghetti [for] very little money, a job will be done of such proportions that we will find ourselves locked in with a lot of small advertisers that we can do a great job for and [that] will stay with us and will not attempt to make us change the program and louse it up."

Pat Weaver knew what he was about, all right. And when the NBC sales staff headed by Matthew "Joe" Culligan offered the late-evening hours to potential sponsors, they

started with the little guys—little guys who were, like Alpo
Dog Food, to become big guys as time wore on.

To Earn a Profit: Black Ink on the Bottom Line

As soon as Pat Weaver arrived at NBC, he began turning
out interoffice memos with a disturbing theme regarding
the infant television. Unless broadcast programing in the
new medium progressed beyond radio-adapted quiz shows
and amateur hours, he claimed, people would stick to radio
and TV-set manufacturers would starve.

Whether NBC regarded this prospect as real or a figment
of Weaver's fertile imagination, it must have been regarded
as an alarming idea. NBC's parent, Radio Corporation of
America, now RCA, was the nation's leading manufacturer
of electronic equipment and also held most of the important patents for television-set manufacture. The parent
company expected the television-set market to be a vast
one, wanted to dominate it, and was therefore looking to
a new era of high profits.

If the airwaves could be used to convert listeners to viewers, history might well repeat itself for RCA. A generation
earlier, RCA's canny and irascible boss, David Sarnoff, had
weighed the prospects of infant radio and foreseen an
enormous public appetite for sets, predicting that the market for radios would grow by tens of millions annually.

His competitors were also enthusiastic, but Sarnoff's
forecasts were regarded as visionary. Sarnoff, in their eyes,
was just a telegrapher who had gained fame by being in the
right place at the right time—at the telegraph desk at John
Wanamaker's in downtown Manhattan the night the *Titanic*
went down. Sarnoff covered himself with glory in reporting
those last moments of the ship and the rescue of many of
its passengers.

Thereafter Sarnoff joined RCA, a joint venture of American Telephone, its affiliate Western Electric, General Elec-

tric, and Westinghouse. Proving his merit, he soon rose to the top of the enterprise, which was later to become an independent company.

Despite the skepticism of his rivals, Sarnoff planned his production schedules on the basis of the anticipated market and proceeded to exploit it. What followed was one of the most impressive marketing coups of the twentieth century. Sarnoff's projections were uncannily precise, and shareholders of RCA got rich while those of many of Sarnoff's timid competitors watched in dismay as their companies went out of business or were forced to content themselves with undersized fruit from the radio-manufacturing cornucopia.

Sarnoff's success as a broadcaster was also unequaled. The nation's top talent flocked to radio, and most of the stars worked for one of RCA's NBC networks—either the Red or the Blue. For in the beginning, NBC was pervasive and enjoyed a near-monopoly position in network broadcasting.

When TV came along, the General was still in command at RCA, but then the Columbia Broadcasting System raids decimated the NBC talent roster. Meanwhile, in 1943 the Federal Communications Commission forced NBC to sell its Blue network and it became ABC. In the late 1940s, Sarnoff was nursing his ego and his pocketbook over the loss of Jack Benny, Burns and Allen, and the other onetime NBC stars. No wonder Sarnoff gave Weaver his head. Pat, who was entrepreneurial by nature, argued persuasively that his approach would add to NBC's profits. Broadcasters are among the most profitable of companies and, run well, almost indecently so. When a hit show is fed to affiliates by the network, the local station owner needs merely to step back and let the money roll in. Thus when Pat Weaver was selling the morning *Today* show to reluctant affiliates—they preferred to sleep late and send out test patterns on their respective channels until midmorning—he dangled the carrot of big new profits. The affiliates, a few of the more ambitious among them grousing about the moneymaking local shows they had to give up, took the bait and began sharing in growing network ad revenues from sponsors, some of whom took single spots and others "strips"—a full week of advertising at the same hour each day.

Weaver's night-show problem was different. Most affiliates were already offering late-night programing, mostly old, old movies. Local ad revenues from the sale of gimmicks and gadgets were modest but steady. Pat Weaver envisioned a highly profitable vehicle for the affiliates, involving national advertisers. The affiliates would share in much higher ad revenues, and so would NBC.

Matthew "Joe" Culligan, who was a sales and marketing specialist at *Good Housekeeping* before he joined the broadcast world to sell national advertisers on *The Today Show,* attempted to do the same thing for the new night show. Culligan is an ebullient supersalesman who has never lost his zest. His latest book is called *How to be a Billion Dollar Persuader: How to Sell Anyone Anything.*

Today was a huge success when Steve Allen's *Tonight* came along, and yet the advertising agencies were skeptical. They argued that midnight was sleep time for working America and that it wouldn't be worthwhile to aim for viewers at that hour. But executive producer Richard A. R. Pinkham, who generally went with Culligan on his sales rounds, would stand in front of the admen and read *TV Guide* listings for the evening's late television programing. Mostly there were movies starring Richard Arlen and Mary Beth Hughes, Sabu and Johnny Weissmuller. Hollywood had sold few of its popular recently made pictures to what it regarded as a lusty infant that promised to grow up and become a dangerous competitor.

Building on the success of *Today,* through which Dave Garroway and J. Fred Muggs, the chimp, had been introduced to advertisers, Culligan used Steve Allen to plug the new show.

Culligan commented, "Because the Hudson Theatre was

such a madhouse—they smoked all kinds of things and it was teeming with creative people staging musical numbers, etc.—we decided to do a half-hour kinescope production of selected portions of the show. The show was sold out before it went on the air.

"Tonight was profitable from the beginning, thanks to *Today,* which gave us a base and which had already proved the point about the wisdom of participating advertising from the ad-taker's point of view." Culligan soon had a sales staff out beating the bushes, and, he says, "As before, I recruited the advertising sales staff from the NBC pages."

Ad rates then brought the advertiser a national audience for as little as $4,000 a minute. The first clients were a widely variegated group, some of whom had graduated from the *Today Show*—advertisers like Saran Wrap, Dial Soap, Alpo Dog Food, and Fedders Air Conditioning. But the principal thing was a combination discount rate whereby the advertiser got a substantial discount, 15 to 20 percent, for buying both *Today* and the night show.

Advertisers and their agencies were soon hopping on the midnight bandwagon. The show began to gather steam and proved to be a marvelously profitable new medium for the affiliates and for many of the nation's smaller companies that were first experiencing the heady stimulation of the national marketplace.

Two Nonstarters

Jan Murray: Ready, Willing, and Unavailable

Comedian Jan Murray might have been as famous as Jack Paar, or possibly even Johnny Carson, if his agent hadn't been so opposed to his hosting *Broadway Open House.*

The opportunity came before the show debuted. Jan's agent had called to say that NBC was auditioning a number of performers and that the network wanted Jan to try out too. But the agent was against it because, among other things, he thought five shows a week would prove a killing pace.

Jan explained in a telephone interview that he thought otherwise—that the night show would be a light-entertainment and interview show with occasional easy-to-do impromptu sketches. He was sure he could handle it and, more important, accurately predicted that it would prove to be the biggest, most important variety performers' showcase in television.

The agent had another motive. At the time the *Broadway Open House* feelers came, Jan was about to sign for his first network television show—CBS's *Songs for Sale,* which spotlighted as yet unpublished works of aspiring songwriters. To the agent, *Songs for Sale,* to be broadcast simultaneously on TV and radio, was a surefire success and the best route for his talented client. But as Jan viewed it, the night show was a bigger plum and one he wanted very much to have.

Jan didn't believe the show had to be stand-up comedy —something at which he was not particularly adept. He would have built the show around his strength as a story-teller—"I don't just pound jokes like Rodney Dangerfield and Henny Youngman. I tell true anecdotes." Performers on the West Coast who know Jan love to invite him to parties because he regales them with true stories from his own experience.

Thus when NBC approached Jan's agent to ask him to audition for the show, Jan was buoyant despite his agent's misgivings. Jan auditioned, but heard nothing for some time. A few weeks later, however, NBC indicated that it was inclined toward Jan and wanted to discuss the show. But it was too late: Jan had already signed to do *Songs for Sale.* He comments, "My agent was very happy because he thought *Songs for Sale* would run forever and that the late night show wouldn't last at all. I personally was heartbroken."

Creesh Hornsby: The Man Who Might Have Been King

While Weaver was mulling the debut of *Broadway Open House* in the summer of 1950, he recalled his days as a producer in radio, and, in particular, he thought of Jack Benny and his gang of characters as a promising model for the new television show. Jack played off his outspoken "girlfriend" (in real life his wife), Mary Livingstone; his sassy black valet, gravel-voiced Eddie "Rochester" Anderson; and Dennis Day, who acted as Benny's naive, well-meaning foil.

Don Wilson, the jovial announcer, was the nice guy who would chide Benny gently about his monumental pride and parsimony—running gags that kept Benny's show at the top of the ratings for years. In one classic episode, Benny is walking down a lonely street late one night when he is

accosted by a gun-wielding thug demanding, "Your money
or your life." Seconds pass. Laughter builds as more seconds pass. The bandit finally growls, "Well?" Benny, with
some asperity: "I'm thinking it over."

Benny's humor translated readily to television, and the
TV generation remembers him best for a sight gag the
radio audience never experienced. In it the indignant
"Well!" of radio days was followed on TV by a turn of the
head and a fixed, fey stare. The TV studio audience seemed
willing to laugh at that posture as long as Benny chose to
hold it. Actually, the length of the hold was precisely measured by the comedy actor, and it reflected a sense of timing so perfect that thoughtful comedians, including Johnny
Carson, have since studied Benny as they have no other
performer.

Benny and his gang were not available for the late-night
show, nor was Fred Allen, whose *Allen's Alley* also used a
comical company: Titus Moody, a laconic Vermont farmer
who said little more than "Yep," and said it for several
years not so long ago on the Pepperidge Farm commercials; Mrs. Nussbaum, a Bronx housewife with a heavy Yid-
dish accent who mangled logic as hopelessly as she did the
English language; and Senator Claghorn, an outrageously
pompous and overbearing southern politician who
wouldn't look at a compass because it pointed north.

Weaver believed the ideal and most durable format for
the midnight show would be to have the host play off similar foils in skits and running gags.

Somehow, though, the idea was eventually abandoned
for something quite different—probably because a certain
comedian came to Pat's attention at the time the show was
being readied.

In effect, the NBC executive decided to go the wild route.
He chose for the spot a dark, odd-looking young comedian
who had done well on West Coast television. He chose Don
"Creesh" Hornsby.

Creesh broadcast out of the most overstuffed attic

Weaver had ever seen. It was filled with "weird junk," as Weaver recalled in an interview, and the comedian had "some sort of relation" with things in the attic. There were, for example, a stuffed owl and a grandfather's clock that would talk back to Hornsby. "Hornsby would talk to the broadcast audience while referring back to these inanimate and animate—but not human—stooges." Weaver also thinks there may have been toy trains chugging about the chaos of that attic mess.

When the entertainer wasn't playing the piano or doing anything else of consequence, he ran around the room yelling "Creesh! Creesh!"

Hornsby's material was "good" and held up for hours on West Coast broadcasts and thus seemed promising for *Broadway After Dark*. Weaver explains: "We thought Hornsby might have a chance, though his stuff was really wild. We reasoned, 'What the hell, it'll be late at night and who cares?'

"The main thing was that Hornsby had proven popular with a big audience with a totally unbelievable formula. We thought, 'If it works [on our late telecasts], fine, and, if not, we can go to a more conventional format.' "

Hornsby arrived in New York City with his family and prepared for his debut and that of NBC's new midnight mélange. It was just two weeks before the debut—in May 1950.

Hornsby never reached the studio attic. A few days before he was to go on he contracted infantile paralysis. According to some reports, the comedian was a Christian Scientist and did not consult a doctor. Hornsby died the weekend before the show was to commence.

Stopgap—Vaudeville at Midnight: The Jerry Lester Seasons

Creesh Hornsby's death left the National Broadcasting Company with no fallback plan for *Broadway Open House.* The following Monday night—in the summer of 1950— NBC viewers were offered a chatty husband-and-wife interview team who were known to radio listeners as Tex and Jinx. Tex was also a successful, and flamboyant, public relations man, and Jinx was a former Miss America. They bombed that first night and were off the show pronto.

Wayne Howell, an NBC staff announcer, then as now was luckier. So was Milton DeLugg. They shared the stage with Tex and Jinx and went on to enjoy long and profitable runs in supporting roles. Accordionist DeLugg, who is now musical director on *The Gong Show,* directed the *Broadway Open House* staff orchestra.

Thus, the spectacular premier so eagerly awaited in broadcast circles never came off. However, Pat Weaver had anticipated that Creesh might prove to be too wild even for America at midnight. He had already been mulling alternatives. Recovering quickly, he lined up guest appearances by leading comics, many of whom were old friends from radio.

Weaver's hope was that some comedian would strike sparks—provide the magic needed to make the show work against the competition of old movies and the local sponsors of those turkeys who provided the late-night revenues and profits for NBC's affiliates, which were thus reluctant to clear time for NBC's new show.

The problem is that no one really knows why a loosely structured entertainment like *The Tonight Show* works—though Fred Allen's and Jack Benny's radio and television experience suggests that relying on a gang of colorful characters for comedic purposes can be a good starting point. In any case, as would become clear, seasoned, imaginative performers can impose their own sense of order on a loose and unfamiliar format and turn it into exciting entertainment.

In the beginning, though, it was helter-skelter. The show became an amorphous and continuing experiment—and with the talent in charge.

Wally Cox had his turn. Cox, who was to become famous starring as the bookish, bespectacled professor in the amusing and understated *Mr. Peepers* situation comedy, walked on one night to do the routines which were gaining him notoriety in the coffee shops of Greenwich Village. The skits were sheer whimsy—some purporting to be about kids he knew when he was a boy. Wally, who is remembered as a skinny, nondescript little man, would paint an amusing and mildly cuckoo word portrait of a playmate of yesteryear, then grin and say, "What a crazy guy," rocking slightly and smothering his amusement in spasmodic breaths.

As announcer Wayne Howell explains, "Wally would do his little routines and just walk off the stage. There was nobody there to host."

Martin and Lewis took the show one night in a kind of impromptu manner. On *Broadway Open House,* the youthful Jerry Lewis immediately mounted a determined attack on sponsor Anchor Hocking's "unbreakable" drinking glasses. After considerable effort, Jerry struck a blow for truth-in-advertising, shattering one of Anchor Hocking's invincible goblets. The duo that was to become America's foremost comedy team didn't get the late-night assignment, but that reflected Pat Weaver's initial comedian rotation strategy more than sponsor pique. Pat's policy brought viewers a different comic every night for some weeks.

When NBC called Jerry Lester he was living in a Manhattan apartment and winding up a television show on Dumont—"trying to retire from television," as he explains. Jerry's wife is an earthy woman he takes fishing in the Ozarks. Affectionately, she is "that hillbilly of mine" to Jerry and a woman whose goodwill Jerry is determined to have. She had told Jerry not to do TV because it was "too much [work]." So Jerry told NBC's representative to forget it and added, "Please don't call me again—I'll get in trouble with my wife."

But Jerry's agent pleaded with the ex–burlesque hoofer and banana to do at least one gig. As an enticement, he told Jerry that Martin and Lewis had received an automobile as payment for their appearance. That just about did the trick. Jerry answered NBC's third or fourth call with the question: "How much do you pay?"

"What do you want?"

Jerry turned to his wife and asked, "How much does that stole you want cost?" She told him.

She told him and that was the price he said he wanted. NBC, in effect, agreed to buy Mrs. Lester her stole.

As Jerry tells it, his brand of humor was just what the audience was looking for, and he adds that NBC realized this almost from the outset. "I went on with no makeup and no jokes," he said, and the studio audience, the viewers, and the executives of NBC were all impressed.

"After the show, there was a line of NBC executives outside my dressing room. They asked, 'What are your commitments?' And I said, 'First I have to take my wife to dinner.' "

The executives brushed this aside and explained that

what they wanted was for Jerry to finish the thirteen-week initial span of the show, which then had about eight weeks to run.

Elated by the reaction of the audience, and the freedom to create his own show, Jerry agreed to finish the run, doing the Monday, Wednesday, and Friday stints. Comic cellist Morey Amsterdam, later to become a stalwart on *The Dick Van Dyke Show*, did the Tuesday and Thursday shows, also with Wayne Howell, Milton DeLugg, and the orchestra. Amsterdam was good, but basically, Morey's output was a letdown after Jerry, and he became a kind of bookmark holding the television page until Lester returned the following night.

By contrast, Jerry's popularity was enormous. By the end of five weeks, Jerry was famous and the show was on its way to becoming a national habit—at least as far as Omaha, then the western terminus of the so-called coaxial cable which piped network shows to affiliates outside New York City.

NBC executives, alarmed because they had no options on Lester, dropped by to negotiate with an emerging TV phenomenon. Jerry explains, "This is the spot every artist should find himself in. I really dealt. I told them I'd do the five additional weeks and that was it." He sounded as though he meant it, but he didn't. Later he was to form a production company and sign a lucrative long-term contract.

The show was wacky, spontaneous, vaudeville-based, and, at times, vague. And there were lulls, too. Jerry used gimmicks to cover them. Gimmicks like Dagmar—real name, Jenny Lewis. For the first two or three months, Dagmar sat on a stool right in front of the band with an off-the-shoulder dress and an enormous overhang that may have influenced the wit who dubbed television the boob tube. Dagmar seemed to fit that phrase on both counts. She was a prototypal dumb blonde. A large sign under the stool read, "Girl Singer," but she never opened her mouth and never sang. Letters rolled in from mystified viewers asking, "Who is that big-busted girl?" Dagmar affected a disdainful silence through it all. Finally, one night after Jerry did a particularly bad skit, she said, "Drop the net, Mac!" and became a speaking member of the company. Most of what she said defied Webster's. For example, she defined "isolate" as an apology for tardiness.

Just how Jerry himself worked was a little obscure—possibly even to Jerry. The opening spot would determine the entire show. Jerry gives an example.

Wayne Howell would say to Milton DeLugg, "Let's be nice to Jerry—he has a terrible toothache."

Dagmar would come in and say, "What's the matter?"

"Jerry's got a toothache." And, with luck, they were off and running.

Jerry explains, "We worked from a script about two pages long, double-spaced, with two lines to explain each sketch. . . . We created a door gag to open each segment."

In one such skit, La Guardia Airport was the topic. There was a flight attendant at the boarding counter who said, "Four minutes to Flight 807." People would move through the door.

Jerry says, "Finally, I would come in and start moving through the door. The flight attendant would say, 'Hold it! You're too late.' I'd say, 'But I have to get in there.' With that you hear the roar of a takeoff. I'd say, 'Gee, I can't understand that—I'm the pilot.' "

Often there was a "Jerry Tale" at the end of the show—a takeoff on Jack the Giant Killer, for example. The Jerry Tale writer, now dead, had been an upstate college professor. He wandered into Jerry's office one day and said that while he had never been a comedy writer before, he was sure he could do it. Jerry hired the man on the spot, and not just because he came to the interview barefoot. "He was a weirdy, all right, but he was marvelous."

In time, Jerry was reviewed in *The New York Times*. Broadcast critic Jack Gould said that it "remains a mystery" exactly what Jerry did on television. "Mr. Lester presents a concoction of music, talk, dance and noise which has a peculiar fascination for a viewer whose resistance is low after a night of watching television."

Not that it was all good stuff. Commented Gould, "Mr. Lester prides himself on working without a script, a fact which has given rise to the old Broadway quip that there must be somebody who writes the lulls on his show."

Gould found qualities of a "big private joke" and warned that it was practically mandatory for viewers to watch several times to make sense out of the program. "As a matter of fact, *Broadway Open House* frequently is so beyond credulity that it exercises an almost hypnotic effect on the viewer. It is a sort of theatrical counterpart of a wrestling match. In the morning you may wonder why you lost sleep over it, but chances are you will watch it again."

In Lester's lexicon, everything that was okay was "George," and when a commercial came on, the studio audience cooperated happily to sing "Stop, Look and Listen." The year 1950 was clearly an unsophisticated one.

There were shades of Creesh Hornsby and of other comics as well. Thus on occasion when nothing else was happening Jerry would lead an energetic community sing of "The Bean Bag Song." The song was the theme of Jerry's Bean Bag Club, which evolved after someone called Jerry a bean bag and he promptly decided to institutionalize the concept.

There were echoes of other comics too. Gould said some of Lester's jokes were Milton Berle rejects, a particularly harsh judgment in that Berle was known among comics as "the Thief of Badgags." (When Lester was in bloom, Berle was such an explosive TV success he was nicknamed "Mr. Television" by the media.)

Continuing his review of Lester, Gould said Jerry loved to climax a reading of a line with a "high, dry, disdainful monotone which sends chills down the spines of admirers of the one and only W. C. Fields."

Lester "mugs" and "if that doesn't work, mugs some more. . . . It is the kind of performance that once was known as parlor comedy; now it is called television."

Maybe Jack Gould wasn't overwhelmed, but everyone else seemed to be—particularly the folks out in television land, who flocked to personal appearances of the *Broadway After Dark* company. Jerry loved to take the show on the road, partly because it was highly profitable for his production company. In all, 45,000 Clevelanders bought $2.50 tickets to see a Lester confection at the local armory. In Cincinnati, the music hall was sold out five times in one day and Jerry says he had to return 100,000 requests for tickets. His adoring fans in Baltimore broke down the dressing-room wall, seeking a glimpse of the clown prince. Wayne Howell, who like Milton DeLugg had become a personality in his own right, says, "We each had to have a cordon of police, and there were twelve people on the show. All of us were known individually—even the orchestra members.

"One time we flew to Detroit immediately after the show ended in New York. Our private plane arrived at 4:30 A.M. in the morning." Howell, more blasé than the fans, was astonished that "5,000 people were waiting for us at that ungodly hour." He adds, "We enjoyed these personal appearances. We always took our girlfriends, and it was always a real swinging party. One time I went up to the cockpit and there was Dagmar flying the plane with one hand and fending off the pilot with the other."

Inevitably, perhaps, frictions developed. Dagmar, who had a real talent for comedy—an unusual sense of timing —became a bone of contention. To offset Dagmar's impact, another girl was brought on, actress Barbara Nichols—who had enough oomph to challenge Dagmar as the show's blond sex symbol. Jerry called Barbara "Agathon," and when he did magic tricks—the gimmick was that they never worked—would say, in his W. C. Fields voice, "Agathon, bring me my wand."

The show wasn't entirely spontaneous, despite the fact that one or two lines of copy typified an entire script. (For example, "Wayne walks on stage and Jerry leapfrogs over him.") A young man named Simon and called Doc was one of the writers, but Jerry and his gang were not impressed. The writer, now famous as Neil Simon, has become the hottest Broadway playwright and movie scripter in the business. Wayne Howell says that some of the material in Neil Simon's first two plays had a familiar ring—"He used a lot of stuff in them that he had written for the show."

The supporting cast impressed Jack Gould, and he called Dagmar's comedy role "a treat." But for Jack, the standout was a young man named Ray Malone, "the most graceful, imaginative and personable dancer to come along since Gene Kelly," Gould wrote. "His routine on a person crossing Fifth Avenue, for one example, is a remarkable demonstration of the art of tap."

Gould had sensed Jerry's concern about the possibility of being outdone on his own show. "Night after night, when Mr. Lester lets him on the air, Mr. Malone is one of those rare dancing artists who thinks not only with his feet but with his mind."

Ray was certainly unusual. He was turning on with pot a generation before it was accepted by the nation's youth and thus made popular. Wayne Howell says, "Our whole floor smelled like a reefer paradise." Pot wasn't Ray's only habit. Some years ago, he died tragically of alcoholism in the Bronx.

As for Wayne Howell, he is still at NBC.

When Wayne started doing *Broadway After Dark* he got "absolutely nothing" for the chore. Like any staff announcer for NBC, it merely fell to his lot to announce on that particular show. But the midnight vehicle carried commercials, and each participant was free to negotiate any deal he could. Jerry, as the packager, was the boss. Howell explains, "I asked Jerry for a raise and got $25 a night—same as Dagmar got in the beginning. Toward the end she was getting $2,000 a week and I was paid $900. We also got paid extra for the side trips. I got $500 for going to Cleveland, for example." Big money in 1950, when the dollar was worth several times what it is today.

And, of course, Wayne got the visibility and other side benefits that go to a "personality" on television—a Doc Severinsen, for example. Whether Wayne enjoyed being mobbed in Baltimore or not, it was certainly an interesting, even exhilarating, experience.

More to the point, perhaps, Wayne was hot and was soon earning substantial sums of money from three syndicated disc-jockey shows. One called *Musical Merry-Go-Round,* on NBC radio, was featured between 9:00 and 9:30 P.M.

When it was finally over, Wayne remained as a staff announcer at NBC radio. He no longer has the stardom and instant recognizability. But Wayne still has his fans: "My mother keeps asking me when I am going to replace Johnny Carson."

Jerry Lester lives in Florida, touring from time to time with former stripper Ann Corio in *This Was Burlesque.* It's old-fashioned burlesque and thus not too different from what Jerry did for many months on *Broadway Open House.* It is also quite successful. Jerry has all the kinescopes of his shows and thinks they may be quite valuable. But his efforts to sell and/or syndicate them have failed so far. His type of humor may work in the burlesque theater for an audience seeking nostalgia, but the *Tonight Show* viewers evidently are seeking something a bit more sophisticated. They were to get it in Stephen Valentine Patrick William Allen—but not before a long hiatus on the NBC network.

After Jerry Lester left *Broadway Open House,* Morey Amsterdam's off-night Tuesday and Thursday appearances were terminated. Other comics did *Broadway Open House* for a while, but none enjoyed notable success. The attraction went off the air on August 23, 1951, after a year and three months. NBC did not offer another midnight show to affiliated stations for over three years, despite the fact that a late-night variety show continued as a major element in Pat Weaver's grand scheme for the NBC network.

The Tonight! *Star-to-Be:*
Steve Allen

The Unhappy Childhood Years

Steve Allen was the quintessential child of vaudeville, and, true to the cliché, sometimes slept in a steamer trunk. On-stage, his mother and father, billed as Montrose and Allen, did their comedy act. Vaudeville luminaries like Mae West spoiled the child backstage, and, as they used to say in Hollywood, Mae was joined in this pursuit by "a cast of thousands."

Nevertheless Steve's early childhood was lonely. He seldom had companions his own age; seldom enjoyed give-and-take with his peer group. Deprived of the kind of home life most children take for granted, Steve craved attention to an unusual degree. He appeared to need love and acceptance more than most, as stories of his early childhood clearly indicate. It is understandable perhaps that he chose show business for a career.

Obviously, with vaudevillians as parents his penchant for the spotlight is understandable, particularly on his mother's side. But Belle's early struggle to be noticed was for quite different reasons. Unlike her son, the lonely backstage child, Belle competed for attention with fifteen lively siblings. Steve has described his grandmother,

Bridget Scanlon, as a "meek, patient country girl." With all
those children, most of whom survived, the household was
so raucous that Belle's father, a "fierce, bearded Irishman"
from County Cork, ultimately fled back to the Emerald Isle
alone.

Thereafter Belle's family settled in Chicago. Curiously,
Belle was allowed to leave home at the unusually early age
of nine with two women down the block. She became part
of their aerialist act with Barnum and Bailey Circus. (As the
patriarch of the aerialist family, the Flying Wallendas, has
said, the only time he was alive was when he was on that
wire. The rest of the time he was "just waiting." He craved
the risk, the thrill of a standing ovation, of having an audience in the palm of his hand—something that every extro-
vert and star can understand; something that all three hosts
of *The Tonight Show* know well.)

Belle was still knocking about show business at twenty-
seven when she married Steve's father, a carefree vaudeville singer named Billy Allen, the son of a Pennsylvania
Dutch couple, Emma Mae Brademeyer and William Allen.

Billy and Belle developed a comedy act, with Billy playing straight to Belle's Dumb Dora humor—she got laughs
by the centuries-old tradition of giving Billy's words a lit-
eral interpretation for foolish results. It's a variation on the
old Abbott and Costello routine "Who's on first?" Costello
asks that question and Abbott answers with a resounding
"Yes!"—since the man on first is named Who. Costello
keeps trying. "At the end of the month, who gets the
money?" Abbott: "Every dollar of it. Why not? The man's
earned it."

Then along came Belle's only child. He was born on the
day after Christmas in 1921—arriving, as Steve has put it,
more pathetically than he intended, perhaps, "like a forgotten Christmas present."

A few months later in San Francisco he *was* forgotten.
While the family was on the circuit, baby Steve became so
sick that he was left in a San Francisco hospital while his

mother and father performed in other cities. One of his mother's sisters, Steve's aunt Rose, was informed and went to San Francisco to look after the baby. It was she who months later delivered the infant to his parents in Chicago. Steve has said of the occasion, "I marked the reunion by slapping my mother's face with all the strength that I, a little more than a year old, could muster." He does not remember the incident himself, but his mother told him about it and added that she was so startled by the blow that she reacted in sudden anger and returned it. At that point, Aunt Rose took the baby out of Belle's arms and considered keeping Steve herself. The crisis passed, though, and soon Steve was traveling with his parents again.

Life was certainly hectic on the vaudeville circuit for the young family. "Mother used to wash my diapers in hotel sinks, after which Dad would hang them on lines he'd string across the nearest vacant lot or fire escape. He was a practical man, Mother tells. Once she suggested they quit show business. 'I'd like to live like a wife,' she said. 'Impossible, dear. I couldn't support you.' "

The question became academic when Steve was eighteen months old. His father died. Oddly it seems for a woman with such a young child, Belle continued her show-business career, with the company MC taking up the straight-man role. Steve was dragged along.

He was pushed into the background, as might be expected, but he was obviously determined to be noticed and almost began a stage career of his own while still a toddler. Occasionally unattended backstage, he would step into view of the audience and stare solemnly at a melancholy diva as she warbled her songs. It was a comic sight. The child's impromptu appearances were soon written into the act, but baby Steve inexplicably stopped his walk-ons almost immediately and could not be persuaded to resume them.

Thereafter he wandered about offstage looking for excitement, finding an audience of sorts. He was sometimes discovered in the dizzy reaches of the theater flies, where upraised curtains and sets are stored. As might be expected, this alarmed and exasperated his preoccupied mother.

When possible, Belle hired bellhops to look after Steve back at the hotel, but even there he caused concern. Steve would slip away and man a hotel elevator, for instance, stopping between floors until his mother was called back to the hotel to beseech him to come down. Enjoying the attention, Steve would call out, "Look at me, Mama Belle."

The early years were frightening, and unsettling. Steve recalls, "I can dimly remember waking up alone in the middle of the night in various hotel rooms, wondering where I was and where my mother was. Sometimes I would get up, get dressed, and go out into the night looking for her. After a few experiences of this kind she would have to send me home, and I can recall then wanting to run away from wherever I was living to look for her."

There can be little doubt that these early experiences made a profound impression and led him to seek inner solace. Even today, he often seeks privacy. Let Steve have an audience and he is away and laughing. But off camera, he can be and often is remote even with people who know him well.

For instance, Steve's *Tonight!* producer, Billy Harbach, puts Steve up in the Harbach Park Avenue apartment when he is in New York City so that Steve won't have to endure the loneliness of a hotel. But though Harbach and Steve are friends of a quarter century, Steve will sit alone in the Harbach drawing room, playing the piano for hours, even when Harbach is there and free to talk with him. Harbach doesn't resent this or find it odd in his friend. Rather he recognizes this as just the way Steve is. Nevertheless, most would regard this conduct as rude even in a friend.

Steve's life as a vaudeville baby ended when he reached school age. Belle then settled him by turns with members of her large family. They were the Donohues, whom Allen remembers fondly as "flighty Irish."

"Mother and all the members of her family were, I think, born in the wrong century. None of them had any luck driving automobiles, using telephones, or even opening packages according to printed instructions. Cans of food were as often as not opened upside down, and cereal boxes, the type that had phrases like 'Cut along the dotted line' or 'Open here' printed on them, were instead opened as if by the paw of a grizzly bear—and an angry one at that."

He has further characterized them in a manner that may ring a familiar note with observers of certain Irish families: "As if there weren't enough things wrong in the Donohues' life, they could be thrown into a panic by a knock on the door or the ring of a telephone. Sensible people'd just open the door or answer the phone, but with the Donohues there was a great deal of scurrying around, grabbing for slippers or bumping into each other. It's a wonder someone wasn't knocked cold in the rush.

"Also, the family was a peculiarly isolated unit which loved itself and mistrusted the world, and a bell ringing represented an intrusion by the world."

He remembers that he was frequently unwell and that various aunts were overprotective. "When we rode on streetcars my aunts would try to force me to take the only vacant seat while they stood up. I was quite tall for my age and was greatly embarrassed. . . . When I was twelve I unconsciously began trying to break away. The corner drugstore became my favorite hangout. My aunts demanded that I get to bed early to protect my health, and if I stayed out, they fought furiously over who was to blame."

Nevertheless, he loved his relatives and found them to be "fascinating—warm-hearted and generous, but wild, unpredictable and terrible-tempered." After a number of unhappy experiences in which Steve at an early age interrupted illogical Donohue arguments—they called him "Philadelphia Lawyer" at the time—he realized how impos-

sible it was "to communicate with the adults around me."
So he clammed up, causing the Donohues to call him "the
Sphinx" thereafter.

Steve said that it wasn't easy to remain calm in those wild
Donohue households. "In times of stress, when the crock-
ery began to explode, Mother, or whatever aunt was my
current guardian, and I would flee to some new neighborhood and open a new camp." Yet, the Donohues were a
major influence, and "such talent as I may have was undoubtedly inherited from this covey of nervous wrecks."

He remembers his aunt Maggie as "the steadiest of the
lot," and the only woman Railway Express bill collector in
Chicago. When she invited Steve and his mother to live
with her, it was the beginning of a better life. "We had a
real dining room and I could now return dinner invitations
from the other kids. . . ."

But inner peace eluded the young man, and he was still
inclined to roam when troubled. Soon he was planning to
run away with his best friend, Richard Kiley, later to gain
fame as a male lead in Broadway musicals. It was Steve's
second year of high school, his marks were poor, and a girl
he thought special snubbed him. He urged Kiley to flee
with him, figuring that the $7 he had saved would do for
the both of them. When Dick held back, Steve hopped on
his bicycle and, at sixteen, rode into the sunrise without a
care in the world.

But after he crossed the Illinois border into nearby Indiana, he grew tired and eventually left his bike with a
garage owner. He thinks it may still be there. Steve then
stuck out his thumb and was soon speeding south, learning
to appreciate the unusual qualities—and the essential
goodness—of strangers and ordinary folk. The experience
undoubtedly contributed to his knack for interviewing total
strangers in later days on the air.

Some time later when hitchhiking palled, Steve switched
to the rails. It was during the Great Depression, a time
when thousands of unemployed men were cadging rides on

the nation's freight trains and ducking railroad detectives, some of whom were not above throwing men off moving trains to their deaths. On one ride on a flatcar he met the "dirtiest, meanest-looking tramp" he'd ever seen and was so unnerved he retreated to a gondola car loaded with pipe. As the train came into a station he suddenly saw the face of the old tramp above him, blazing with fury. The man shouted that he was to get out of the space between the front of the gondola and the load of pipe pronto or become "mincemeat." Steve scrambled out as the train jerked to a halt and the pipes plunged through the space he had huddled in moments earlier, battering the front of the car with impressive force. Thus Steve was saved by a man he took to be a threat.

The young man begged and bummed his way, learning to swallow his pride and accept handouts when hungry. First he went to Texas and then to California. Meanwhile, Steve's mother had alerted her sister Nora that Steve might turn up at her California home. He did. The aunt welcomed him and persuaded Steve to finish a year of high school in sunny California. Steve then returned to Aunt Maggie's in Chicago, and a new piano which had been purchased for him, and to greater contentment than he experienced at any other time in his young life.

At Hyde Park High in his junior year he met an inspiring teacher named Marguerite Byrne who was organizing a school magazine as faculty adviser. Steve asked to contribute, the teacher encouraged him to write, and soon he was submitting verse outside the school—to the Chicago *Tribune.* This brought a note from Charles Collins of the newspaper asking, "Who's writing the stuff a kid named Allen is sending us?"

Marguerite Byrne told Collins it was Steve's own stuff, and they began publishing it. After Steve entered and won a local Civitan Club contest for the best essay on Americanism—it paid $100—he began to feel contented with his burgeoning career.

Meantime, he learned to play his piano. "Life looked pretty rosy, I recall, with my stuff breaking in the Chicago papers, living with Mother and Aunt Maggie, having my own piano, making a few dollars each week by playing high school dance jobs, and my shyness drying up a little. What more could a guy want?"

Allen's Early Radio Broadcasts: *From the Ground Up*

Not an attack of asthma, certainly. But during his junior year, an old problem with asthma returned with a vengeance and Steve was forced to move to a warmer climate. Typical of the Donohues, the step was taken without preamble. "There was no planning to it; my mother and I simply got on a train, got off at Phoenix, and began walking around town in the heat of late summer, looking for a place to live."

They found two rooms in an ancient rooming house directly across from Phoenix Union High School, and while his mother unpacked, Steve enrolled for his senior year. He found his classmates as warm as the sun, and was soon settled in, writing the humor column for the high school paper. At the end of the school year, the faculty adviser asked four boys if they had plans for college. All but Steve did. The adviser said that he was entitled to grant one journalism scholarship to Drake University.

"Where is Drake?" asked Steve.

"Des Moines, Iowa. They have a good journalism school. What do you say?"

"I'll take it."

Steve returned to Chicago for the summer and then took the train to Des Moines. Luckily, there was no other student qualified to write a humor column for the college paper, and Steve got the job—the first freshman ever allowed to write a regular feature.

He was quite happy. He took a course in radio, played

with a school dance band, and even fell in love—though he neglected to tell the girl about it. There were the usual happy college times, the football games, laughs in the dorms, and the serenades in front of sorority houses.

But the scholarship was for one year only, and, unable to afford the tuition and room and board, he returned to Chicago for the summer. His asthma returned, and soon his mother and he were back on the train to Phoenix— again without any planning whatsoever.

This time, Steve enrolled in Arizona State Teachers College, just outside Phoenix, but within months quit school to take a part-time job at radio station KOY. Steve reasoned that if he didn't take the job, he'd spend three years in college only to ask for the same job again.

He had the usual man-of-all-trades announcing assignment and obtained a wealth of experience in his three-year stint at the station. He was allowed to turn his hand to anything he pleased as long as he didn't ask for additional money. So he wrote commercial copy, newscasts, a few chapters of a popular Arizona soap opera called *Love Story Time,* and an occasional dramatic show. He also did some acting, spun records, played the piano, and sang.

It is perhaps understandable that someone destined to host one of America's foremost comedy shows would kid around on the air—just as Jack Paar and Johnny Carson did.

Steve had noticed that commercial copy prepared by the station was read in parrotlike fashion by the average announcer, who did not look forward to reading the same dreary copy day after day and thus paid little attention to what he was reading. Steve decided to forge a commercial message that had been on the air for some time. In his version, the first couple of lines made sense and the rest made fun. But the problem was that the authentic copy was dog-eared and dirty. Fresh copy would be suspect. So Steve adopted the practice of some wary bill collectors who are expected to face the wrath of deadbeats again and again.

They forget those unpleasant calls and simply wipe up the office with the uncollected bill to suggest that it has been handled daily. Just so, Steve kicked his retyped commercial around the studio, after forging the initials of each announcer several times to suggest that his version of the commercial had indeed been read on the air frequently.

Steve says, "You might think that you could not get very far into such a commercial without realizing that a trick had been played on you, but that is because you are not a radio announcer." He set his alarm for the particular time this morning message was to be read on the air. Then he lay in bed laughing long and loud as one announcer read the following message in a singsong voice:

"Say, men, if you're in the market for a new suit, why not see the fine new worsteds and tweeds at Thew's Clothing Store on Central Avenue? Yes, Thew has a fresh delivery of good-looking new models priced to please your pocketbook. Believe me, when you try on one of these fine suits you'll find a number of small green cabbages in the pockets because Thew insists that a man working on his income tax is a man who will refuse to step on a crack for fear he'll break his mother's back home again in Indiana. And among men who know good clothing you'll find a great many chain-smokers, tobacco-chewers, and cotton-pickers. So remember, one if by land and two if by sea. There isn't a better car on the road and I'll be glad when you're dead, you rascal you."

During the war years, Steve Allen left the station, briefly, to join the army and get married, but as he ran up the hills of Camp Roberts near Paso Robles, California, armed with a machine gun, his asthma returned, and he was discharged and returned to station KOY with his bride.

Steve Allen's comedy training then began in earnest. It was 1943, and Steve and Wendell Noble, who were both doing "voices" on KOY programs, got together to form an act, Noble and Allen. Wendell produced a couple of joke books, they put some old comedy routines together, and Wendell sang a few songs played by Allen. They got a few bookings and some worthwhile experience, but little came of it. He needed help and was to find it in Jules Green.

The Man Who Put Steve on the Road to Riches

If clothes really make the man, Jules Green, a short, wiry man with blond hair, should have become a top producer in Hollywood early in life. Jules represented the best in masculine haute couture, because he was a man of taste. But he also had the good fortune to find "one of the world's great tailors" in his native Pittsburgh and was thus able to dress as he wished to from an early age.

Jules's friends were to become accustomed to his well-intentioned but pointed critiques of their attire. They also learned to expect his periodic flights to be meticulously fitted and suited in his steeltown tailorshop. The shop was a sartorial oasis in a city of roughly clothed workingmen, some of whom fed coal from the neighboring Appalachians into open-hearth infernos that in turn showered all of Pittsburgh's citizens—worker, homemaker, executive—with "black snow." (Pittsburgh has since undertaken a massive civic cleanup effort that has laundered the air and the city's reputation to boot.)

Fired with career hopes even before he reached maturity, Jules made his first trip to Hollywood when he was in his early twenties. But that trip and a later one to what Rona Barrett calls "Tinseltown" were unavailing.

Yet Jules was no fool. He was not one of the many thousands of pathetic creatures who have assaulted Hollywood with more ambition than talent, an overweening ego, a surfeit of naiveté, and a cheerful smile. Jules had grown up in show business, though his boyhood place in the business was once removed and a giant step away from the stars themselves.

Jules's father was the working showman in the Green family. All during Jules's youth, Mr. Green ran several silent-film houses. The old man never lived to hear the talking screen. He died the year before Al Jolson set America agog in 1927 with the scratchy sound track of *The Jazz Singer*. But as Jules grew up, he bathed in the glow of the flickering screen and was developing by osmosis or sheer talent a shrewd sense of the business. Thus his early forays to the West Coast entertainment capital were as natural for him as slipping into a hand-tailored suit.

Since Hollywood was not ready for Jules on either of his first two tries, he returned crestfallen but undiscouraged to Pittsburgh and a twelve-year career with Warner Brothers' Tri-State Theatres, which had movie houses in Pennsylvania and neighboring West Virginia and Ohio.

In 1948 it was back to the West Coast, and that time Jules clicked at the age of thirty-four. He landed a job with a curmudgeon who was a highly successful agent and packager of radio shows—James L. Saphier. Saphier had an impressive seven radio shows on the air at one time, and his most important client—later for television as for radio—was that show-business legend Bob Hope.

Some time after Jules reached California for the third time, Green listened to Steve Allen's whacky 11:00 P.M. comedy show on the local CBS outlet, KNX. The show was largely impromptu, relying heavily on Steve's glib witticisms.

Steve had earlier been told that "funny" wasn't what the KNX management wanted. In due course, Steve got a memo saying, "We hired you to play records, not to do a comedy program." Fearful that the sport—and his growing following—might fade into the night, Steve followed instinct and read the executive memo on the air. This brought a barrel of fan mail, all on Steve's side, which he collected and dumped on the memo writer's desk a day or so later. Broadcasters never argue with good ratings. Quoth the chastened executive, "Well, you win. Go ahead and talk, but play a little music, okay?"

Steve bent slightly, playing a few records and audibly breaking the rest of the wax discs, to the delight of his many listeners. Steve was right about the incidental role of records to his success. Nobody complained. For he was turning a dead hour in early-to-bed Hollywood into stay-up time for the biggest audience in town, collecting laughs and rave notices along the way—particularly for ad-lib interviews conducted with members of the studio audience.

This feature began one evening in the confusion of a last-minute no-show by scheduled guest actress Doris Day. Left in the lurch, the undaunted comedian simply dragged mike and extension cord down the aisle and into paydirt with lines like these:

S.A.: And what is the name of the gentleman on your left?
Woman: I have no idea.
S.A.: Keep your eye on your purse!
Second woman: Mr. Allen, is your family here at the studio tonight?
S.A.: Why do you ask—is your husband a burglar?
S.A., to another guest: What do you do for a living, sir?
Man: I'm retired.
S.A.: I noticed that you were sitting here in your pajamas, but I didn't know the reason.

That last gag and lots of others worked better for the listening than the studio audience, but on-the-scene visitors as co-conspirators laughed with abandon. Steve seemed never at a loss; he quipped amusingly in response to hundreds of straight lines that might have stopped lesser comedians. In Jules's studied judgment, Steve was unique. He believed Allen could become a major star on late-night television, which was then a highly promising media infant.

Like others, Jules believed television would soon be the dominant broadcast medium. Prepared to act on this judgment, he took the initiative and called Steve, telling him that if he ever became a free agent, he'd like to hear from him. At the time Allen was with the powerful William Morris Agency, and the account executive handling Steve was someone known to Green: "I was close to that man and I wasn't about to pirate Steve," Jules says.

But talent and agents often disagree—or simply don't click together, don't see eye to eye on progress. A new association is especially likely when an extremely ambitious man like Steve Allen has reached a pinnacle of sorts—tops on local radio—and wants to push on to a higher peak. Agents can be highly skeptical of their own talent and unwilling to spend money or push for things that don't come without effort. The budding talent gets the old "Don't call us, we'll call you" treatment from agent as well as auditioner. Thus when Steve's William Morris contract ran out months later, Steve telephoned a man he thought would be more eager to sell Steve Allen. Jules duly brought him into the Saphier office.

Jules's immediate goals for Steve were modest enough—but important. Steve was getting about $175 a week; his program previously had been lengthened to a full hour by KNX without a salary increase. Jules sealed the bond with his new client by getting Steve a raise to $250 a week. The raise more than absorbed Jules's 10 percent agent's fee.

Jules felt that a more serious problem was the KNX studio where the show was broadcast. While that studio was a big step up from the original broadcast booth, which could accommodate a dozen ectomorphs, the newer quarters were still too small to house Steve's fans. Besides, it was designed for radio drama, and as such it had no stage. The actors simply stood before the microphone and did their lines while an audience of a hundred or so on the same level sat in folding chairs.

Jules campaigned at KNX and soon Steve was in the much-larger Jack Benny Theatre, a specially designed radio-comedy studio that had an elevated stage where Steve could talk to his studio audience in comfort—even while

playing his piano. Soon Steve was filling the 500-seat theater nightly and developing style and features that would
serve him throughout his late-night broadcast career. One
such feature, his audience interviews, wasn't new. Both Art
Linkletter and the late and lamented Tom Breneman had
used them in somewhat different fashion. But Steve's special brand of literalized humor made the interviews seem
fresh and original. "Do they hear this show in northern
California, Mr. Allen?" "They hear it—but they don't get
it."

Technically, Steve belonged to CBS, and Jules regarded
this as a potential obstacle. Jules wanted Steve in New York,
where network television seemed bound to spend its lusty
infancy. But CBS's California talent chief, Harry Ackerman,
was no fan. Jules mulled this over, then called Ackerman to
say, "Look, Hare, you don't think Steve is talented, but
everybody else disagrees. I want Hubbell Robinson [CBS
talent chief in the East] to see him."

It was true: Ackerman didn't dig Steve. But he was willing
to be overruled for the good of the network. Jules says,
"Hare set up a three-way phone call with Hubbell, and the
result was that I took Steve to New York."

Jules had hard days ahead of him. For some time he lived
in a single room in the Barbizon-Plaza Hotel while touting
Steve for a late-evening TV show. To this day, Jules is
convinced midnight is Steve's natural broadcast habitat. In
his quest for a midnight TV show, Jules tried all three
networks and even asked NBC's Bud Barry to make a kinescope pilot of Steve that Jules could offer to the affiliated
stations individually.

Meanwhile, Steve was doing television game shows, including *What's My Line?* where he coined a question that
was to become a cliché on the show: "Is it bigger than a
bread box?" He developed as a songwriter, doing a number of songs of his own, and in time he became host of that
unknown-composers' showcase *Songs for Sale.*

Jules had settled in as James L. Saphier's New York partner, with whom he argued long and loud on the telephone and by mail over any number of things. Finally, Jules became so disgusted with his stormy relationship with Saphier—"a difficult, cold-ass man who is dead now"—that he thought of giving up and returning to Pittsburgh. But Steve, with whom Jules never had a written agreement, liked Jules's analytical approach, and his sometimes critical but generally helpful efforts in his behalf. Steve asked Jules, "If you leave [Saphier], can I come with you?"

That was a major factor in Jules's decision to break up the East Coast–West Coast partnership. The two agents split, arranging to share East Coast client commissions "up to a point." Inevitably, a fight broke out over the agreement that ultimately led to three separate lawsuits. Says Jules, "I won all three of them. It cost me $65,000."

Under Steve's and Jules's oral agreement, they set up RoseMeadow Corporation (Steve had married his second and present wife, Jayne Meadows, by this time). The company was owned 80 percent by Steve and 20 percent by Jules.

The primary problem remained, though: to get Steve off "daytime junk" and onto late-night television. Failing that, Jules figured he'd return to Pittsburgh anyway.

Finally, Ted Cott of NBC-TV's local television called Jules to say, "I want to talk with you." He offered Steve the job as host of the local Knickerbocker beer late-night television show that Cott had pirated from ABC. The offer to Steve came with this condition: "I'm not going to pay Steve one penny over $1,500 a week."

Jules jumped at the offer, and so did Steve, who was temporarily at liberty, having just quit an unsatisfying midday CBS radio network show in disgust. Of Ted Cott's salary offer to Steve, Jules comments, "I was prepared to take $1,000."

Steve Allen was on his way to becoming the first regular host of what would be *The Tonight Show,* and Jules flew to Pittsburgh to see his tailor.

Up the Ladder: Steve Allen Goes Network on **Tonight!**

When the Steve Allen midnight variety hour began to click on NBC's local station, Pat Weaver's night-show concept was dusted off and offered to Steve for the network. It was a proposition bound to appeal to Steve & Co.—or so NBC thought. Apart from Steve, the man in the troupe who had the most to say about the proposal was Steve's manager, Jules Green.

The way the deal was structured, $11,000 to $12,000 a week would be divided up by the show's small company of performers, and Jules, as agent for the package, would receive 10 percent of that sum as his compensation—$1,100 to $1,200. He would, of course, lose his 10 percent override on Steve's earnings, but so what? The net result of a network contract was a quantum jump in income for Jules and everyone else.

Since Jules had endured more than two years in a single room in the Barbizon-Plaza Hotel, and had recently married Nancy, his sweetheart, then and now, he was eager for more money. NBC's lawyer, Gus Margraf, sized things up and naturally assumed acceptance was a formality.

He was clearly taken aback when Jules told him no: "Either we own the show or no deal." Jules continued to take that position while NBC insisted that it must own the show. Steve and Jules had solid evidence that without artistic control, which they felt could only be obtained through actual ownership, the show could be tinkered to death by NBC.

NBC could chose the talent both in front of and behind the camera and veto appearances of anyone the network didn't like, and also do other things to the detriment of the show. For example, NBC could do too many "house ads" for the good of the show, scheduling appearances of performers in forthcoming network attractions—even over the production company's protest.

Margraf, who felt that Jules was being unreasonable, attempted to vaporize resistance by invoking the witch doctor: "Jules, if you have a problem," he said, "you can call Pat"—Pat Weaver. Recognizing this offer as an illusion in the day-to-day rough-and-tumble of television, Jules invoked the magic word signifying total disbelief: "Bullshit!"

Steve Allen's determination to control the show was based on a number of considerations. First, Steve and Jules knew—or at least perceived—that NBC wanted to make *Tonight!* a lighter version of *Today.* Rightly or wrongly, they believed *Tonight!* would become a news show, basically, with entertainment features—not the successful impromptu comedy-variety show they were doing. They were amazed that NBC felt it could improve on success and appalled at the perceived consequences if the network had the power to attempt it.

Whether or not NBC wanted drastically to alter the content of the show, the network clearly planned to make important changes. For example, NBC executives felt that Dwight Hemion, Steve's director, was first-rate and of network caliber, and they were right, as his efforts on *Tonight!* and his distinguished career thereafter amply prove. But producer Billy Harbach was first-rate too, Steve & Co. felt, yet NBC would not concede that Billy was strong enough to make the switch from local to network show.

NBC may have been influenced by widely quoted stories of Harbach's reaction under pressure, which Steve & Co. found more amusing than distressing. Billy operated at a high level of energy and, when in high dudgeon, was capable of bizarre comments that suggested he was a distant relation to the Reverend William A. Spooner. Spooner was an English clergyman—he died in 1930—who convulsed worshipers for years with "spoonerisms," unintentional transpositions of sounds in spoken language such as "Let me sew you to your sheet" instead of "Let me show you to your seat."

There was the time Billy Harbach jumped into a cab with

Louis Nye in a rush to get to NBC, ordering the driver to take them to "CI 7-8300, and hurry!" CIrcle 7-8300 was NBC's telephone number.

On another occasion, Harbach walked into Steve's office to discuss the program, and Steve asked if Billy was chilly.

"No, why?"

"Well, you're walking around indoors with your overcoat on."

"Oh," he said, with a look of surprise. "I forgot to take it off . . . no! Wait a minute . . . I forgot to go home." At that he ran for the elevator.

Billy had a terrible memory for names—even big names. Once he ordered his secretary to call Charlton Heston for a rehearsal, shouting, "Get me—uh—Charleston Huston; er, uh—Carleton Hudson. You know, Chester Moses." He referred to Fric and Frac, the comedy skating team, as Trick or Treat, and called Shai K. Ophir, the superb mime, Ootie Shankar.

Billy had a way of adapting descriptive words and phrases to his own uses. When the show was returning from a visit to Havana, Cuba, Jules Green asked when various members of the group were dispersing. Said Billy, "I'm dispersing Wednesday." On another occasion, during which the producer was arguing hotly with Jules, Billy exploded, "There you go, Jules, for the first time you're wrong again." Once, while attempting to estimate the dimensions of a set, Billy asked vaguely, "How many feet in a foot?"

Who could blame NBC, wrong though the company was, for having doubts about a man who recited the Holy Trinity as "The Holy Father, Your Son, and the Ghost" and who excused himself from a production meeting with the words "Let me be right back"?

If NBC had the control it demanded, the picture on the small screen would be different too. Steve, Jules, and the others were proud of the fact that they had discovered a teenage singer, a highly appealing entertainer, named Steve Lawrence, and the gang took equal pride in the discovery of Eydie Gorme, who wowed viewers with her unusually wide vocal range and who became the young baritone's wife. Despite their obvious popularity and importance to the show, NBC was insisting that when *Tonight!* went on the network it would do so without their services.

Jules recalls that while NBC obviously believed that the show was good, the network "wanted to strip it." When NBC said no to Steve and Eydie, it offered any vocalists Steve might want for substitutes, and Steve said, "Okay, give us Frank Sinatra and Dinah Shore."

That made the point. The two were major stars even then and well out of reach. Steve was making it clear that he had no intention of sacking his vocal duo, though he did add one of a team of brothers who were traveling with Kay Thompson's act—Andy Williams. Steve was able to do this and keep his first team because he won the argument for artistic control. NBC finally accepted Jules's terms and signed an agreement whereby Steve and Jules's corporation, RoseMeadow, owned the show.

There were to be more disagreements, including one Jules won hands down that had such an important effect on television that Jules feels he ought to be getting a perpetual royalty.

The question was how much to pay guests on the show once it hit the network. Mort Werner, who was in charge of THT—Pat Weaver's holy trinity, *Today, The Home Show,* and *Tonight!*—contacted Jules to say that NBC planned to pay up to $750 for talent.

Jules asked what Mort had in mind, and Mort said NBC would pay some guests $500, some $600, and so forth, to a limit of $750.

Jules thought Mort's mind was wandering when he suggested a sliding pay scale for talent on *Tonight!* Jules reasoned that once word got around that top talent got $750, no self-respecting performer would agree to work for less.

Says Jules, "We expected to have as many as four or five guests a night, and someone would have to spend full time in negotiation if we had a sliding scale."

Jules told Mort he'd pay all guests scale—nothing more. At the time, scale was $265.50 per appearance—and that's what everybody got. Everybody, that is, except the music and variety acts. Those groups were paid on a different, somewhat lower scale. Thus four members of an act might get, say $600, and not reach the minimum for an individual. RoseMeadow books would reflect the payments and the contributions to union welfare plans and all the taxes, including withholding, so that there would be no charges of kickbacks, etc.

Jules is justly proud of the compensation scheme, which has, of course, led to problems from time to time. Sometimes performers would refuse to come on the show for fear that Ed Sullivan, who paid much better for appearances on his Sunday-night variety show, would not book them again. Jules expected that, but could deal with it.

But he could not deal with what he saw on the television screen years later. Jules and his wife, Nancy, were watching Jack Paar on *Tonight!* at a time when Paar was unhappy with a lot of things, including the fact that he was limited to scale in his efforts to persuade people to appear on the show. Muttering about the problem audibly to his nationwide audience, he said, "Who started that, anyway?"

Jules was mortified that his master stroke was being demeaned, and he startled Nancy by shouting at Paar's cherubic face on the TV screen, "I started it, shmuck!"

Stardom: The Style of Tonight! with Steve Allen

Writer Stan Burns found her. She was one of those typical Greenwich, Connecticut, matrons—proper, a trifle brittle, well educated, sporting the tailored look of Peck & Peck, the fashion house. She was an expert on house pets and had brought a magnificent model home: the exterior was an exact replica of a Victorian house. Several of her pets were inside, some playing and some sleeping.

The camera focused on the building, and Steve Allen asked the woman, "What is this thing?"

"Oh, that," she said amiably, "that's a cathouse." The remark was punctuated by Steve Allen's familiar raucous laughter, and the studio audience joined him. *Tonight!* was off and running. As Skitch Henderson says, "Steve Allen could do an hour and a half on a gag like that."

And so it was in the beginning. Steve Allen was fresh and uninhibited and a master of ad-lib. The show was a free-form vehicle with bits in which Steve played straight to the regular company of comedians, music from pianist Steve and the singers and from Skitch Henderson and the band, short interviews with strange New Yorkers and members of the audience.

The original writers were Stan Burns—a husky ex-marine whose off-camera humor was as sick as his personality was sweet ("This is the airline of the stars, folks . . .

Carole Lombard, Grace Moore, Will Rogers . . .")—and Herb Sergeant, tall, dark, and tweedy. The two writers recognized Steve Allen for the zany character he was and found all kinds of silly things for him to do. Some of it was physical. Steve would dive into a vat of Jell-O, and on another occasion was dunked in hot water with thousands of tea bags tied to his clothes.

Frequently the crew would open the back door of the Hudson Theatre and aim a camera outside. People would walk by, look at that camera, do a take, then drift back to look inside, right into the camera, as Steve Allen did an amusing ad-libbed voice-over—until the drunks came by to hog the camera.

On other occasions Steve would walk into the night in a policeman's uniform and stop cars—a risky thing to do in New York City. The bright lights from the theater kept the drivers from realizing that they were on national television. To the first motorist, Steve said, "Sorry, sir, but this is the border patrol and we're making a spot check for contraband."

"What band?"

"I just wanted to know if you're smuggling any fruits or nuts."

"No. Absolutely not."

Roaring laughter from inside the theater. The next car nearly ran Steve down. Finally a taxi came by and Steve flagged it down.

"Where to, chief?" asked the driver.

"Just take this to Grand Central, and hurry," said Steve, opening the door and throwing a giant salami into the back seat. The driver yanked the flag down and roared off, never to be heard from again.

Steve's conversations with visitors, regular and otherwise, offered amusing counterpoint to the rehearsed parts of the show.

An elderly regular, Mrs. Sterling, had little money, and would ask for gifts.

Steve: "Good evening, Mrs. Sterling. How are you this evening?"

Mrs. Sterling: "Mr. Allen, you're wonderful. . . . Say, you're not working too hard, are you?"

"Up until now I wasn't, no."

"That's fine. Say, I'd like to have one of those Pomeroy cameras."

Mrs. Sterling even asked for Polaroid seconds for "my daughter." Viewers didn't know it, but gifts were a two-way street with Mrs. Sterling. Steve says that from time to time she would rush up to him outside the theater and hand him a small paper bag or package containing candy or handkerchiefs.

Another regular who came two or three nights a week was tall and thin and named John Shafer. Mr. Shafer spoke extremely rapidly.

"And what's your name, sir?"

"Well, my name is Shafer, John Shafer. I work as a farmer upstate. That is, it's not my farm, you understand, but my uncle's farm; but I figure eventually it'll be my farm, I mean if everything turns out all right. We raise quite a few nice things on the farm. It's about a hundred acres and we've been up in that section for the last two, three generations. I just come down to town once in a while to see the sights and have a little fun. Watch your show once in a while and thought I'd drop in and see it. What was it you wanted to ask me?"

One night Steve Allen asked what Mr. Shafer had done the night before.

"Well, I seen this movie, *Mogambo,* with Clark Gable and this Ava Gardner woman and it was a pretty good picture, but to tell you the truth I couldn't figure out what old Clark was so interested in this Gardner woman for when I figgered he would've been better off with this blond girl, what'sername, this Kelly girl. Her father's from Philadelphia. 'Course it sure was something when all those old gorillas came running around and old Clark had to step lively to keep things on an even keel."

If Steve's regulars sounded a little wacko, okay, it was part of the charm of the show. It was mostly ad-libbed and filled with random characters from the cracker-barrel school of Americana. There was a short, stocky man with a strange accent who came to the show when it originated in Hollywood one summer. He said he would like to sing. What song?

"Allagazanda's Ragatima Band."

What key?

"A."

Skitch Henderson struck up his own band and the man sang the song—all on one note. He visited the show to sing again and again, never wavering from his A note.

Then there was Professor Voss, a robust man in his late sixties with a slightly German accent. He took long walks bare-chested on the coldest days, which tied in with his unusual ideas on diet and exercise.

Once Steve said, "Tell me, professor," as the man sat half naked in a large tub filled with ice and freezing water, "to what do you attribute your remarkable physical condition?"

"Well, it's water that does it. You've got to start off each day by drinking plenty of water."

"Do you do that?"

"Oh, yes, indeed. The first thing you must do when you get up in the morning is drink four quarts of water!"

"Wow, four quarts. That's a lot of water. And what do you do then?"

"Well," he said matter-of-factly, "you stand about three feet from the toilet—"

At that point, Steve Allen cut the professor off as the audience roared.

Steve would also read letters to the editor from the *Daily News,* punching out the angry sentences from Brooklyn and the Bronx as the boys in the band yelled mock support of the writer—"Yahhh, Yahhh!"

There was a marvelous tentative quality to the show in the beginning—and not always enough material to fill the gaps. Steve would play the piano if nothing else worked, and his associate from Los Angeles days, Skitch Henderson, and a small group within the band would ad-lib original numbers.

From Skitch's vantage point, *Tonight!* was almost as tacky in the early days as *The Noble and Allen Show.* Though Skitch was NBC's musical director, the company refused to let Skitch use staff musicians because that would have involved heavy overtime as the late hour *Tonight!* was done live in New York City. NBC told him to hire musicians elsewhere and to pay them scale—$240 a week. Skitch also got minimum pay for leaders, $480 a week.

Theoretically, it should have been easy to find competent musicians. When members of the big bands of the 1940s tired of one-night stands and foul-smelling buses, they mostly settled in the Big Apple and looked for work. These refugees from the big bands were among the most skilled and creative musicians anywhere.

The network studio bands generally had their pick of the crop because they offered something the best jazz musicians rarely find—steady employment at good pay. The NBC staff band read like a *Who's Who* of jazz, and the pay generally reflected lavish increments for sponsored shows. But under the network edict Skitch was forced to look around for competent men who would play for minimum scale.

Fortunately, he got Eddie Safranski, a top bass player who had been with the highly innovative bandleader Stan Kenton. Skitch also snared Bobby Rosengarten, a highly regarded percussionist.

Meanwhile, the network had just disbanded its famous NBC Symphony, and Skitch got three refugees from that august organization—the bass trombone and two French-horn players. They were, says Skitch, "fantastic" musicians, but, unfortunately, not the jazz musicians the assignment called for. He also found a fine trumpet player known as Doc Severinsen, and a first-rate saxophone player who unfortunately drank too much and is now dead.

That was it: piano, drums, bass, one trumpet, one bass trombonist, two French horns, and a sax. Put them all together, they spelled "Mother, help us." The ensemble would have been a reasonable facsimile of a balanced band had there been at least three saxes—assuming the French-horn players doubled on trumpet.

Somehow, they got by. In time the musicians began to work well together. Skitch and a group within the ensemble were able to offer musical interludes to bridge the chaotic nonprograming that characterized the show in the beginning months.

There were vocals from Steve Lawrence and Eydie Gorme. Steve Allen announced, "I discovered Steve and Eydie . . . in the back seat of a car." Steve Lawrence developed into a fine light comedian as well as a vocalist and eventually appeared on Broadway. To broaden the vocal appeal of the show, there were young Andy Williams and Pat Kirby, who soon quit to return to New Jersey and have a family. She was replaced by Pat Marshall, who later—much later—married Larry Gelbart, creator of the television series *Mash.*

But it was the comedy regulars who gave the show its unique quality. Steve Allen was a roving journalist questioning Don Knotts as the nervous man on the street, Louis Nye as the campy Madison Avenue–type Gordon Hathaway, and Tom Poston, who couldn't remember his name. In a very real sense the three represented the insecurity of the man on the street in a mighty and frightening city, the nameless millions who never get a chance to talk to the camera, or, getting it, blow it.

Even the announcer, Gene Rayburn, had his chance to fly. Gene, who had been the clown of the 1940s radio disc-jockey comedy team Rayburn and Finch, found announcing confining. In the beginning he was a bit unnerved—afraid to intrude and push back into comedy. But he asked for and got a news show—part of Pat Weaver's original concept was that the show would offer news and weather along with the light entertainment—that he delivered from a sound-proof studio constructed by NBC carpenters in the basement of the theater.

The news featured a funny "tailpiece" taken directly from the news when one was available. Otherwise, he and a clever writer who worked on the segment would write a phony. But then NBC executive Davidson Taylor, a humorless man with an overpowering tendency to intrude, vetoed the spoof, and Pat Weaver, who evidently had his hands full with more demanding problems, let him get away with it.

Nothing daunted, Gene began doing the weather in a humorous fashion—he had had a hundred hours of Air Force meteorology. But then Gene was staggered by hepatitis and couldn't leave his home in Westchester County. Broke and about to go off the payroll—he was on an appearance-by-appearance basis—he appealed to producer Mort Werner for help. Werner, never one to desert a talent in trouble, promptly ran a broadcast-quality telephone line from the Hudson to Gene's house. Thereafter, a leggy model in an abbreviated nurse's uniform would stand before the weather map and Gene's mellifluous voice would say, "There's rain over Appalachia—put some measle marks over the mountains, nursey. No, no, not over Canada, over Pennsylvania, that's it—just a little to the left now. And there's snow in Ironwood, Michigan"—a running gag; there was always snow in Ironwood.

It was that kind of show—zany, improvisational, and fun. Everyone had a good time and there was rarely a feeling of being left out. It was not a competition. Steve wanted his fellow comedians to get the best out of the material, and he didn't try to top them. *Tonight!* was *The Tonight Show* at its early best—a show that might have survived forever. But in Steve Allen's view, he had merely planted his foot on the first steppingstone and would hop, skip, and jump to superstardom. It is often a problem in show business. Those who get the farthest sometimes say goodbye and pursue a new destination, unaware that they have already arrived at the top.

Lost Perspective: Steve Allen Jumps the Tonight! Ship

When Steve Allen became host of *Tonight!* he was by most accounts a shy and self-effacing young man. But, says Skitch Henderson, "He took on the aura of a star within a few months."

For the new host quickly sensed his importance to an enterprise that was rapidly becoming a premier television institution. Steve's ego expanded accordingly. He did continue to be supportive to his fellow performers. (Louis Nye says that when he or another performer inadvertently delivered a punch line in the midst of sound-muffling laughter, Steve, a superb straight man, would say, "I didn't quite get that," or some such words, and the line could be said again —"You'd lay it out real good the second time.") But former associates say Steve became assertive, even disparaging at times of nonperformers working the show; that he demanded perfection of close aides and spoke condescendingly of those with run-of-the-mill functions. Once, when a prop was placed badly, he said to an associate producer, "Send whoever does that for a living to me." This kind of putdown galvanized some, but it didn't necessarily cut tensions or lead to flawless work.

When Greyhound became a sponsor, a live greyhound was used in the commercial. Steve had the dog handler informed repeatedly that the dog was to be kept at bay, for Steve despised dogs and hated to be touched by them. Somehow, though, the greyhound sensed Steve's rejection and attempted to overcome it. Despite the handler's best efforts, the greyhound would infuriate the star by thrusting his muzzle into Steve's hand moments before each live commercial ended.

Even key associates experienced Steve Allen's wrath. Arthur Cantor, the Broadway producer, once served Steve as a publicity man and at one time felt he and Steve were friends, though Arthur recalls that Steve exercised a restraint one would not expect from someone really close.

Once, in the course of their professional relationship, Arthur broke an ironclad rule in inadvertently sending out pictures of Steve and his wife, Jayne Meadows, without clearing them in advance. It may have been that Jayne, who tends to photograph heavy, revealed a sagging tummy, or perhaps Steve, who was vain about his looks too, thought the photos of himself unflattering. In any case, Steve learned of the mistake and demanded that Cantor recall the pictures. Arthur knew that journalistically this would be a mistake. Press agents simply didn't recall photos, and he told Steve so. Arthur argued that to ask would cause some editors to use the photos out of spite. When Allen insisted, Arthur simply refused to carry out the order. Characteristically, Steve took matters into his own typewriter, batting out a lengthy form letter to editors all over the nation asking for the return of the pictures. Surprisingly, most returned them—some with friendly notes. Not so surprisingly, Arthur and Steve parted company shortly thereafter.

The more popular *Tonight!* got to be, the more assertive Steve Allen is said to have become. Early in Steve's tenure, Jules Green served as Allen's mentor with laconic and sometimes blunt critiques of sketches and comedy ideas. Steve accepted the criticism at first. But as can happen with men who say funny things, Steve Allen soon began taking himself too seriously. He became convinced that his knowledge of comedy and its techniques was so comprehensive that he didn't require assistance.

He may have been unaware that others in the company thought he miscast himself in sketches, attempting to do "characters" he couldn't manage and demeaning himself professionally with lampshade-on-head humor more acceptable at private parties. As he became more and more sensitive to criticism, Jules Green, his most effective critic, found it impossible to rein Steve in. In fact, Jules discovered that Steve could not even accept the fact that others were making substantial contributions to Steve's enormous success.

For instance, Skitch Henderson often corrected the scoring on songs that Steve Allen wrote, thus saving Allen embarrassment. Steve never said a word about the changes; never thanked Skitch for his trouble, Henderson says.

In view of Allen's distorted sense of his importance, it is perhaps understandable that he was to perceive himself to have outgrown *Tonight!* He was ready for prime time—in his view, the late-night show had been a preamble. He therefore challenged Ed Sullivan's phenomenally successful 8:00 P.M. Sunday-night television variety show, doing this, it should be noted, with the approval of NBC. Meantime, he continued to do *Tonight!* part of the time, but ultimately dropped entirely the weeknight broadcasts that had brought him superstardom.

Steve Allen had failed to grasp the importance of the daily network television show and was in fact pleased to give it up. Skitch Henderson recalls that he never saw Steve so happy as at the party commemorating his final departure from *Tonight!* in 1956.

In retrospect—now that it is clear that *Tonight* is the most important comedy showcase in television—it is easy to fault

Allen for his lack of perspicacity. In his defense, Steve Allen did reasonably well against Ed Sullivan. *The Steve Allen Show* even won a Peabody Award as best comedy show in 1960. Still, the potential of a weekly comedy show was far less than that of a nightly one, as Johnny Carson has so amply demonstrated since. Anyway, Steve Allen gave up the Sunday-night show and left NBC in 1960 after seven years with the network.

In the two television seasons following his years on NBC, Allen appeared in a weekly comedy hour on ABC-TV. But in 1963 he returned to late-night television with a show for Westinghouse broadcasting that he refers to in his press kit as his old *Tonight!* show. He stayed with that show for three years and experienced indifferent success. Thereafter he emceed three seasons of *I've Got a Secret.*

There were other projects. Eventually, Steve did a syndicated show called *Laugh Back* with old *Tonight!* clips interlaced with fresh sketches from veterans of the NBC years. The show was not well received. One *Tonight!* comedy regular, a reluctant guest on the limp and uneven *Laugh Back,* turned to a fellow guest in irritation to ask, "Do we need this? Do we owe this man something?" Maybe they didn't need it, but Steve Allen seemed to. To his friends and critics, *Tonight!* was Steve Allen's pinnacle—and though he does not say so, his efforts to resurrect the show both directly and through clips suggest he thinks so too.

Clearly, Steve Allen has found it difficult to adjust to a world that remembers him most fondly as host of the original *Tonight!*—live from New York on NBC.

The Making of a Millionaire

Wealthy television stars don't always keep their money, though some of them try hard. They tend to be "careful." Without doubt, TV stars have good reason to be careful. Their careers dangle over the precipice from the twine of the thirteen-week contracts standard to their business. The few who become important enough to wrest long-term agreements from broadcasters generally manage this only after many years of thirteen-week purgatories. For a study in muscle-twitching anxiety, observe a TV personality in the twelfth week of his travail as he looks at the charts and discovers his rating is sinking.

No wonder some TV stars become paranoid about money, treating their staffers at Christmas with dime-store key chains or, in the case of one celebrity, cheap umbrellas wrapped in butcher paper.

But the TV star proposes and God—who evidently is unimpressed with marquee value—disposes. TV personalities become profligate without meaning to as they fall prey to scorned wives and, in a surprising number of cases, to managers who are incompetent, perfidious, or both.

Steve Allen was as careful as any, and luckier than most, particularly in Jules Green, who was lucky in turn to get acquainted with Jack Dreyfus, a living Wall Street legend. Dreyfus was uncommonly good at making money and a superb organizer. Many years ago, he founded Dreyfus Corporation, which quickly became one of the biggest names in Wall Street and the manager of investment companies or mutual funds—the firm invests in the securities of various companies and sells participations or shares in the fund portfolio to individuals—with billions of dollars in assets. Jack, who would rather fade than trade, retired many years ago while still in the prime of life to the relative obscurity of his estate near New York City, a superachiever dropout.

But at the time Steve Allen's show was getting under way, Jack was deeply involved in Wall Street and had picked out an obscure company called Polaroid as a future giant. In retrospect that may sound like a mean accomplishment. Polaroid was the first advertiser on the show.

Folks were indeed amazed back then as Steve demonstrated the new picture-in-a-minute camera, but the shares were known only to guys like Jack Dreyfus who were willing to risk the vagaries of the volatile over-the-counter market for new and untried companies. Nevertheless, the cognoscenti thought the concept exciting and were impressed with the ingenuity of its inventor, Dr. Edwin Land, who, just incidentally, was also endowed with movie-star looks and physique.

The stock was already selling for many, many times its per-share annual earnings when Polaroid began advertising on Allen's show. That is, as they say in Wall Street, Polaroid sold at a high price-earnings multiple, and the shares were therefore thought to be too dear by men like Jules Green who had been in the market and had had bad experiences with volatile high-price-earnings stocks.

Nevertheless, Jules kept hearing about the presumed brilliance of Polaroid's future from a fan of the show, the very Jack Dreyfus who was then establishing so grand a reputation in Wall Street.

Jack's brother-in-law was head of Polaroid research, and when the company began advertising on the show, Jack began dropping into the Hudson Theatre on 43rd Street just off Broadway several times a week to watch the show. Jules and Jack became friendly, and Jack would say to Jules, "You've got to buy Polaroid—it's like shooting fish in a barrel."

Says Jules, "At the time, I was not interested in the stock market. But one day I received a stock certificate for a hundred shares of Polaroid from Jack with the message, 'I insist you own these shares. Pay me when you can.'"

At the time, they were $40 a share in the over-the-counter market, and, despite his misgivings, Jules sent Jack Dreyfus a check. The stock continued its climb, and Jules eventually bought a lot of Polaroid stock for Steve Allen, for Steve's wife, Jayne, and for RoseMeadow Corporation.

The shares continued to move onward and upward. Jules became a big fan of Polaroid and began touting the shares to friends and acquaintances. People later came up to Jules to say they didn't know how to thank him and added, "You told me to buy Polaroid way back when and said that you would guarantee me against loss." Jules says he has no recollection of being that bullish. Anyway, the stock progressed so well and so rapidly that the musicians, convinced Polaroid was about to fall out of bed, would boo Jules upon his arrival at the Hudson every time the stock rose 10 to 15 points on a single day. It happened many times.

But Jules and others were certain that when the shares were listed on the New York Stock Exchange, the play would be over—at least for a time. Thus, Jules began selling his Polaroid at prices ranging from 260 to 285 a share. (They never traded above 200 again, because the shares were split—stockholders getting several shares for each one they had held originally—so that the price would be in a more popular range on the Big Board. Most companies whose shares were rising rapidly in value tried to keep the price of their shares in the 20s during that era and would use one or more stock splits to accomplish this.)

Polaroid was far and away Jules's most successful investment for Steve, though he says that most if not all the stock market investments he made for the star—all without fee, he states—were profitable. In any case, when Steve took the show to the West Coast and Jules decided to remain in New York, the corporation was dissolved.

Under the tax laws, Steve and Jules had both benefited from the corporate umbrella. Federal individual income-tax rates were still at the World War II level and ran up to a maximum 91 percent. Thus, the corporation was set up as a legitimate means of minimizing the tax on Steve's large salary. He was paid a modest sum relative to his earnings—at one time he drew about $1,000 a week. The remainder, less deductible expenses, was left in the corporate treasury to be taxed at the top corporate rate of just over 50 percent. Some of those deductible expenses were items most people pay on their own—wardrobe and some automobile costs and business-cum-pleasure expenses, for example.

Thus the bulk of Steve's (and Jules's) earnings was taxed at the corporate rate, and so when the corporation was dissolved in about 1960 half the earnings—the untaxed part—were left. The capital-gains tax on the remainder was 25 percent. Since tax had already been paid at a 50-percent rate on the corpus of the company, only half of the balance constituted capital gains. Thus effective tax on the company when it was collapsed was just 12.5 percent.

The result: Jules handed Steve $1 million in cash in 1960, a sum that, adjusted for inflation, would be worth a good deal more today. Says Jules, "I did it out of friendship. I handled his investments without a fee, and I don't think I ever lost money for him in a stock."

Steve is not a big spender—"careful" would describe him accurately. He has given his staffers baskets of sponsor Hebrew National's salami and other cold cuts for Christmas. When he moved the show to California in the late 1950s, he bought a lovely but by no means palatial home in Encino, California, in the San Fernando Valley; he and Jayne live there to this day.

Steve Allen does broadcasts on public television, does radio commercials, and contracts to write books in such rampant fashion that some have thought he might be broke. But Jules says, "I'd be very surprised if Steve hasn't managed to hold on to his money. He could have moved to Beverly Hills but didn't. They don't drive a Rolls-Royce, either." In fact, said Nancy Green when I interviewed Jules and Nancy at the Dorset Hotel in Manhattan, "Jayne takes buses."

Years of Nostalgia, After **Tonight!**

Steve Allen seems in recent years to have found that which he has fought so hard to avoid—diminishing stature. By failing to focus on one of his several talents, he appears in large part to have dissipated them all—as his own press kit ironically suggests.

The kit asserts that Steve has been known to work on more than fifty projects all at the same time. To assist him in this effort he is never without his pocket dictating machine. Jack O'Brian, the columnist, recalls watching in pained disbelief as Steve Allen sat prominently placed in a popular Manhattan restaurant talking into his recorder for well over an hour. While Allen was alone at the time, he will sometimes interrupt his conversations with friends and associates to pop that mike to his mouth and rattle off a memo or two.

According to the kit, Steve is involving himself in the fight to ban atmospheric nuclear bomb testing, speaking in behalf of the United Nations, and fighting in the continuing civil rights battle. He is quoted as saying, "I'm not worried about my TV rating. I'm worried about Mankind's rating."

Some might add that, by involving himself in global issues such as these, Steve jeopardized his career as a popular television entertainer as viewers yawned and grew bored awaiting the next humorous segment of the show. In that connection, a former NBC executive who earlier had worked for a prominent governor remembers a letter from Steve to the governor in the early 1950s telling the governor to be alert to a particular issue. Said the executive, "I thought to myself, who cares what Steve Allen thinks?"

Obviously, Steve does. The kit mentions "the many battles yet to be fought and the many things yet to be done."

Steve Allen's touting of his accomplishments and talents in the press kit and elsewhere are in stark contrast to the picture he paints in feature articles where characteristically he states that he has been "lucky" and that it takes no talent to be a talk-show host. This divergence of approaches has prompted one acquaintance to comment, "His is the humble approach to megalomania."

There are solid Steve Allen accomplishments, and *Who's Who* mentions them along with some not so solid ones. (*Who's Who* subjects supply their own fact sheets.) Under "Allen, Stephen Valentine Patrick William" is a rundown of his radio and television career including "creator, host Tonight Show NBC, 1954–56." The bio says he wrote the narration for and appeared in the movie *Down Memory Lane,* and notes that he was in *The Benny Goodman Story.* The fact that it does not say he played the title role suggests editing. That fact is prominently displayed in the press kit. The *Who's Who* bio states that Allen wrote more than 3,000 songs—the press kit says well over 4,000. Some of the difference may be in songs Allen registered with ASCAP that Skitch Henderson claims to have ad-libbed with the *Tonight!* band. Skitch is still annoyed about this and says that Steve was registering the orchestra's ad-libbed tunes on the show for a year before Skitch discovered it. Whether Allen or anybody else collected royalties on these numbers —assuming they were played again—is unclear. Presumably both the 3,000 and 4,000 numbers include the 350 songs Steve says he wrote in one week to win a bet with Frankie Laine.

In *Who's Who* Steve lists his best-known songs—"South Rampart Street Parade," "This Could Be the Start of Something" (his *Tonight* theme), "Picnic," "Impossible," "Houseboat," and "Mary Hartman, Mary Hartman." He lists a number of books, including *Fourteen for Tonight,* 1955; *Bop Fables,* 1955; *The Funnymen,* 1956; a novel, *Not All of Your Laughter, Not All of Your Tears,* 1962; and *The Ground Is Our Table,* about migratory labor.

Meanwhile, in his press kit he claims to have a dozen books "in the works," which would suggest that he personally is writing all those tomes. However, a book on crime in America is actually being researched and written by a free lance for a fee. In Allen's defense it might be noted that he may feel that it is important to America that the subject of crime be discussed in a knowledgeable manner in a book and that he's willing to share his advance—$6,000 of it—to see that such a book is written.

At the moment, the most significant thing Steve Allen is doing is the public-television show *Meeting of the Minds,* which had its genesis on *Tonight!* and which Jules Green argued was too talky and undramatic to be spun off. Under the concept, Cleopatra, for example, meets Theodore Roosevelt, Thomas Paine, and St. Thomas Aquinas. To quote the intemperate language of the press kit, the series met "unanimous acclaim" from both critics and viewers. That is, in a world in which most viewers watch the three networks and let PBS languish in fourth, fifth, or sixth place depending on the number of available independent commercial television outlets.

The press kit includes a sheet titled "Steve Allen from A to Z." "Zany," the sole entry under the last letter of the alphabet, Steve Allen surely was during the *Tonight!* years, and it was in that vein that he was most effective. For all his so-called accomplishments, his reign on the show was certainly his most important and the one for which he will be remembered.

Indeed, he came back to the format again and again like some dog returning fitfully to sniff the clothes of a long-departed but not especially cherished friend. The last time Allen returned to the old *Tonight!* format was for Westinghouse in 1963. It was the same old format, with Steve being submerged in a tank of Jell-O and the silly laugh and audience interviews.

To use a show-biz catchphrase, it was over, already. Why? Gene Rayburn has a theory that anyone who leaves the *Tonight* format can never succeed with it again—once the habit is broken with viewers. Rayburn didn't say it, but presumably his theory would apply to Carson too.

As for Steve Allen, he probably never achieved super-stardom as he claims in the press kit, or, if he did, he has not kept it. He is in many ways like John Gilpin, who jumped on his horse and rode off in all directions. He makes one want to echo the Broadway director who told a scattered performer, "Don't just do something, stand there."

Or as one former aide puts it, "He had that wonderful brilliant career that reached its zenith with *Tonight!* and he can't realize that the world is different and that he would have to be a different person to make it today."

Ernie Kovacs: Interim Host

In the fall of 1956, when Steve Allen decided to give up the Monday and Tuesday segments of *Tonight!*, NBC chose an innovative comic named Ernie Kovacs to do the first two days of the week.

Kovacs was already familiar to *Tonight!* viewers because he had subbed for Allen while Steve starred in the feature film *The Benny Goodman Story* and had filled in on Mondays and Tuesdays in the summer of 1956, along with another candidate some felt should have gotten the Monday-Tuesday assignment permanently—one Jack Paar.

Steve, meantime, continued his appearances on Wednesdays, Thursdays, and Fridays and appeared again on Sunday in a more structured version of his show, to challenge CBS's long-dominant variety vehicle at 8:00 P.M.—Ed Sullivan's *Toast of the Town*.

It may come as a surprise, but NBC was not happy with *Tonight!* While critics thought Pat Weaver's live late-night entertainment a flower in the television wasteland, NBC shook its corporate head every time it looked at the bottom line. True, some segments of the show were fully sponsored, but others were not. Hard to believe as it may be at a time when the show is NBC's most lucrative, it was not then producing much profit for NBC.

NBC thus decided to reduce the length of the show to sixty minutes. And so it came to pass, starting October 29, 1956, that *Tonight!,* Pat Weaver's nighttime pastiche, signed off at 12:30 P.M. and was in danger of going off the air entirely—Steve Allen and Ernie Kovacs notwithstanding.

The network show already had been shrunk. It was airing on the network beginning at 11:30 P.M.—as it does today. A fifteen-minute segment at 11:15 P.M., which Steve had done for the local audience, had been dropped sometime earlier.

The shorter format would be a break for any performer; it is universally agreed among performers that ninety minutes of live TV five nights a week is a grind and will sap any entertainer's stamina in time.

Ernie Kovacs was no warmed-over radio performer. Lots of his early stuff would never have worked on radio at all —including a much-talked-about half-hour telecast of sight gags in which not a single word was spoken. Indeed, Kovacs was so uninhibited and so inventive in his use of the television medium that critics didn't know what to make of him. They called him inspired and zany at his best and ragged and even tedious when below par.

But in a television age marked by timidity in exploiting the new medium, his better sketches were startlingly refreshing. One featured performers with the upper halves of their bodies missing. There was an inspired variation on that inspired routine of a mummy unwrapping its bandages. The viewer saw more and more emptiness. Finally there was nothing where the wrap had been—no body, nothing.

His technique might be called borderline schizophrenia at the very least—like the time Ernie stood behind a guest on the show and peered through her head, his eye showing through a spot in the middle of her forehead. Some of these tricks involved the use of two cameras, one on each of two

different sets along with black hoods and clothing shown
against a black backdrop for those invisible bodies. These
were fairly easy to mount, as was the gimmick in which a
ship was launched in a tub of water and the one in which
a parade of characters stepped out of a beautiful woman's
bubble bath.

Other effects were far more complicated and expensive.
Ernie once sat at a special set in which milk poured from
a bottle—the lip of which was held directly over a glass—
splashed way off to one side in apparent defiance of gravity.
In fact, the set was placed on an angle from the horizontal,
along with the camera that caught the action.

On another occasion, an auto salesman patted the fender
of a brand-new car and it fell through the floor. Later a
grossly overweight ballerina pirouetted to the basement in
the same fashion. The car joke might have been a bit too
real—it cost $13,000. It played a role in Kovacs's continu-
ing war with sponsors and television executives who sometimes found that it hurt when they laughed. Mr. Kovacs was
as free-spending personally as professionally and was eventually in hock to the IRS, partly because of the twenty
Havana cigars he smoked each day at a cost of nearly
$7,500 a year. He showed his exasperation with broadcast-
ing's often-limiting budgets in a closing credit on one
program that read, "A Production of an El Cheapo Sub-
sidiary."

Kovacs's unique antics caused nearly everyone to call
him "zany." In a tongue-in-cheek article before he joined
NBC, Kovacs, a Trenton, New Jersey, native whose father
had been a tavernkeeper, professed to be worried about
the label. An undesirable adjective could be attached to
anyone, he pointed out, noting that he had a friend
when he was a kid "whose antipathy toward the chem-
ical formula of two parts hydrogen, one part oxygen, one
part Procter, and one part Gamble resulted in his being
called 'Stinky.'

"I worried about Stinky. I thought he was facing a pretty rugged future. But a jigger of chlorophyll did for Stinky what nothing can do for zany.

"It started when I pretended I was frying the cat in the oven. I ran into the living room where Mother and Dad were entertaining an old friend—an ex-con who was hiding out from the law and had to do all his visiting at night— yelling, 'Cheddar is on fire! He's in the oven!'

"Mother, Dad, and the ex-con (whose alias I can't recall now) raced into the kitchen. Dad opened the oven, and there was a cardboard cutout of a cat, with a little sign around its neck, saying, 'Phew, that was a close one.' Public Enemy, who was standing by Dad, pointed to me and said, 'Your kid sure is zany, Andy.' (It was either that or 'Your kid sure is Andy, zany.') Anyway, that was the first time I heard the word, and I've borne the stigma to this very day. . . .

"The appellation is hardly justified. What, may I ask, is irrational about wanting to saw off a TV camera's tripod while we're on the air? Anyone who has been in this business for more than one guest shot has had that urge. Or what's so eccentric about portraying a Chinese named Walter Puppybreath who sings 'The Seagull's Revenge' while a happy stagehand drops two dozen eggs (one at a time) from a point above the singer's head?"

Commenting that he wrote all his own scripts, Kovacs added that some of them ran to a total of "maybe three or four words." He explained, "I use the fronts of envelopes. Lincoln used the backs. The difference begins there."

In the article, which concerned *Kovacs Unlimited,* a CBS offering, he continued:

"On a hot day, I write the show in Central Park. The entire cast goes with me. They're very fond of me, and besides, I always pick up the check in the delicatessen. We have some pastrami, a few cans of beer, and the usual picnic fare. I never get around to writing anything in the park, but while everyone else is picking up the empty cans, I inscribe the following on a slice of pastrami: 'Be sure to open the show saying that it was written near the bird sanctuary in Central Park.' This makes for a boffo opener, and the rest of the forty-five minutes is no problem at all."

Maybe so, but a young production assistant who worked for NBC didn't think so—though she was amused by the fun-loving Kovacs. Mitzi Matravers had started in television broadcasting's lowest-level job during the summer of 1956 when NBC began alternating Paar and Kovacs on *Tonight!* on Mondays and Tuesdays. She remembers Paar calling her into his dressing room on her first meeting with Jack. He gave her messages from fortune cookies and said, "Tell me, which of these are funny?" Mitzi said, "I told him which ones I liked and he did those." Paar said to her, "If I ever get a show of my own, I hope you'll work for me.

Impressed with Paar's talent and discipline and appalled by Ernie's nonchalance, Mitzi rooted for Paar. "After that summer, it was obvious that Jack should have gotten the show, but they chose Kovacs.

"Ernie just couldn't take that kind of discipline," she says. On the day of the show, "Ernie would be in a smoke-filled room playing poker with a lot of NBC executives and directors and I would knock on the door as production assistant and say, 'Ernie, we don't have any scripts for to-night.' He would go to a file cabinet and pull out an old script—we had new material too, but he was too lazy to work on the scripts. The old scripts would come from other shows he had done.

"Ernie's sketches would run on ad infinitum. There were some brilliant things, but they demanded special effects for which there was no budget and no rehearsal time either. Frequently, a sketch would be leading to one great finish and would be so badly timed that the point would be lost in the middle of the station break—the whole thing would be kaput.

"The skits were hysterically funny when they came off. But he was ill prepared and wasn't putting in the time, and the money was slight, and he must have been aware that NBC was putting enormous effort into a new midnight show tentatively scheduled to debut that January."

Much of Kovacs's stuff did come off. Viewers would long remember his version of Tchaikovsky's *1812 Overture*, punctuated by the snapping and dicing of celery, eggs smashed against a skillet, and file drawers offered as wind instruments.

Kovacs spoofed the American Western in many arcane ways, including a Bavarian Lone Ranger performing in lederhosen with a sidekick who says, *"Guten Tag,* Kemosabe." Fascinated with the humorous possibilities of foreign languages, Kovacs offered Wolfgang van Sauerbraten, the German disc jockey who would plug a deodorant called Pffft "for gesvetzin." "Whom Dunnit?" was Ernie's panel show featuring a studio-audience guest shot by a well-known personality, Dr. Harvey Serene, curator of the Museum of Portugal—"Our time has expired and so has our guest."

And there was Kovacs as Percy Dovetonsils, who would lisp his latest poetic ode, and his Nairobi Trio of three musical gorillas who performed intricate compositions, following a conductor's banana baton. And always those technical gimmicks—like the time Kovacs opened a biography of Thomas Edison and an incandescent lamp shone brightly out of its pages.

Later Ernie's best sketches, including those he did on *Tonight!,* were rediscovered and offered on educational broadcasting to a new generation of fans. It happened in 1977, fifteen years after Kovacs, who had retired from television to act in movies, hit a slick stretch of pavement in Los Angeles early one morning and wrapped his station wagon around a utility pole. The king of surreal comedy died instantly.

Mitzi was right. NBC canceled *Tonight!* in December. Both weekday versions—Steve Allen's and Ernie Kovacs's —went off the air in December 1956 as NBC prepared to launch its new late-night entertainment, *America After Dark.* Pat Weaver still argues that it was NBC's attempt to make the world forget there ever was a Pat Weaver. Broadcasting's most imaginative executive had been shunted aside so that General David Sarnoff's son, Robert, could have the top job at NBC.

If Pat Weaver hadn't stood on the only rung on the executive ladder at NBC above Bobby Sarnoff, he might have survived. But Bobby's father, General David Sarnoff, boss of NBC's parent, RCA, wanted his favorite son to be chairman of NBC. And now that Weaver had rescued NBC from potential oblivion in television, he was expendable.

The Sarnoffs knew there would be a public outcry if NBC fired Weaver. He was popular with the television critics, who had followed his programing with appreciation and who regarded him as the freshest-thinking executive by far in the burgeoning new medium. So they took a different approach. Despite long-standing promises to Weaver that his executive role would never be undercut, NBC fired key Weaver aides while he was away. Weaver was unable to protect or even warn his carefully chosen associates, and, so compromised, Weaver stepped through the NBC revolving door for the last time.

NBC De-Weavers the Network: America in the Dark

America After Dark was so bad viewers went next door to turn it off.
—Walter Kempley

Mitzi Matravers agrees with that former *Tonight!* writer's assessment. When *Tonight!* was dropped, Mitzi remained at NBC and helped usher in *America After Dark,* a turkey so rank that NBC suffered midnight indigestion for the duration.

The new program, which columnist Jack O'Brian promptly dubbed *America in the Dark,* was the only show Mitzi ever worked for that fired its producer the morning after opening night. "I came to work that day and his office had been cleared out," she says. "He was gone."

On paper, *America After Dark* didn't sound too dreadful. But in execution, it resembled the successful Steve Allen format about as much as a telephone directory resembles a lyric poem.

The idea was to capture the flavor of America's nightlife through televised segments from a variety of locations throughout the land. The show boasted some promising apprentices as writers—such well-known people of today as Liz Smith, the widely syndicated New York *Daily News* scoopist; Martha Wineman, who would later write distinguished articles for *The New York Times Sunday Magazine;* and David Rabe, the playwright. The way things turned out, it's a wonder they all didn't sell their typewriters and become tap dancers.

As for the show's substance, nightclubs may have seemed like a good bet, considering the format, but anyone who has sampled America's nightclubs in locations outside of Las Vegas, where the gambling take pays for top stars in lush settings, must have known that NBC was in trouble before it stepped into its first gin mill. Generally speaking, the nation's nightclubs are tawdry, and with few exceptions most of what goes on in them is dull. Even if what's on the customarily tiny club stage is worth hearing, it is not easy to catch over the loud conversations of the drunk and disorderly. Comedians who have worked the circuit call such joints "toilets."

NBC's plan was to tune in on nocturnal happenings with host Jack Lescoulie in the Big Apple. Jack was to call up six well-known newspaper columnists in three major cities for features. Hy Gardner, Bob Considine, and Earl Wilson were in New York; Irv Kupcinet held forth in Chicago; Vernon Scott and Paul Coates were fifth and sixth in Los Angeles. There were no winners.

Newsmen in other cities were to be tuned in from time to time for remote pickups of the kind of offbeat stories Charles Kuralt does so well for CBS's *On the Road.* None of the stringers, it seemed, was remotely up to it.

NBC was making an all too familiar mistake: attempting to make broadcast personalities out of newspapermen, most of whom sound and look about as well on television as businessmen who recite their own commercials. The show was in so much trouble from day one that NBC not only fired the producer, it called its resident script doctors immediately. NBC vice-president memos flew and the pit grew.

NBC gave Lescoulie someone to talk to—a Judy Johnson who also sang. She needed backup, of course, and NBC hired musicians—first the Lou Stein trio. But in a panic effort to keep the rating above (would you believe?) a 1, NBC knocked Stein out of the box and threw in the Mort Lindsay quartet. Then NBC substituted the Johnny Guarnieri quartet, later retiring it too—all in the space of a few months. The musicians were good scapegoats but were not responsible. They didn't mold the format.

But NBC News had a hand in it. That department was to offer newsbreaks as they developed—say, a fierce storm along the coast, and in a sad but worthwhile early remote, a fatal plane crash at Rikers Island. NBC News also offered such staples as weather reports and sports results. Anyone who awoke during these segments after a long nap might have thought he was catching *The Evening News*.

For the kind of overall picture viewers were rapidly tuning out, consider an evening early in the run when Earl Wilson roamed the aisles of Beauty City in New York talking to folks like Dagmar, Gretchen Wyler (the musical-comedy dancer), and Miss Sweden—busy personalities too wrapped up in careers to visit the beauty parlor during the day. They were, in some benighted booker's sense of the NBC master plan, a part of the scintillating night scene. Each was as interesting as any woman should be while soaking her head at midnight. That same night the show looked in on a "Hollywood" party. The best you could say was that the Brentwood, California, house where the drinks were served was architecturally unusual. Unlike their soul sisters in New York, Jolie Gabor, Ann Miller, and Linda Darnell were carefully coiffed, but what they said was duller than dogfood. They may have convinced themselves that the real, live Hollywood party was fun—but they didn't convince viewing America.

There were other more successful segments—but they smacked of the old *Tonight!* Eli Wallach came by the New York studios after his Broadway curtain in George Bernard Shaw's *Major Barbara* to do a Sacha Guitry reading from *Debureau* in which a clown tells his son what it means to be an actor. J. J. Johnson, "boss" trombonist, as they say in *Downbeat* magazine, rose to the occasion and blew the roof off the studio with the help of Lou Stein's trio.

Leonard Feather, jazz editor of PLAYBOY, was tickled to tell about his *Encyclopedia Yearbook of Jazz* and brought things back to ho-hum reality.

The poverty of the evening's entertainment—and of the format itself—was apparent when Earl Wilson went back to Beauty City to watch the girls emerge from the driers. NBC topped that by crashing the California bash two more times. The chitchat became less intelligent at each stop—if that's possible.

Clearly it was not a vintage evening for the show. But then there was no good wine to be quaffed by viewers on *America After Dark* during the half year the show was allowed to languish before NBC administered the *coup de grace.*

Says Mitzi, one of the few survivors, "The show fizzled out in July 1957." But the fizzle was all too long for viewers who had been switching channels fruitlessly in a search for the likes of Steve Allen, Ernie Kovacs, or even Jerry Lester.

NBC chairman Sylvester "Pat" Weaver had departed in 1956 more appalled than anyone else by the decision to substitute *America After Dark* for *Tonight!* There had been muttering that Weaver was a spendthrift, and he had, in fact, offered some shows that lost money and bordered on the visionary during his regime. But he also gave life to a plethora of distinguished and, at the same time, solidly profitable ideas in the commercial world of American broadcasting.

He brought NBC ninety-minute and two-hour "spectaculars," the television shows that decisively broke the half-hour prime-time television straitjacket, and, not just incidentally, allowed NBC (and, in turn, the other networks) to wrest control over programs and their content from individual advertisers. After Weaver left, NBC renamed his "spectaculars," calling them "specials."

And to cite just one more success, there was Weaver's Saturday-night comedy smorgasbord, with a ninety-minute live centerpiece, *Your Show of Shows,* starring those extraordinary clowns Sid Caesar and Imogene Coca. (The entertainment died a natural death in 1954 after an amazing six-year run.)

Weaver was particularly appalled at NBC's assault on what his aides called "THT," his *Today, Home, Tonight!* format. Over time, they were to become profit generators of enormous importance. As early as 1954, while Weaver was still NBC's chief, *The Today Show* had become the biggest one-show grosser in the history of show business. NBC wisely stayed execution, but, says Pat, the Weaver-eradication campaign resulted in a change of name to *The Garroway Show.*

While the substitution of *America After Dark* for *Tonight!* was perhaps NBC's most visible boner in its efforts to eliminate the smell of Weaver, what it did to *The Home Show* was the most ridiculous, in Pat's view.

The Home Show, the network's midday television magazine for women, was already a big success, with Arlene Francis as hostess, and probably hadn't even reached its full potential. Weaver maintains that the show was grossing $5 million to $6 million a year and "throwing off" another $2.5 million or so in profits. But RCA accounted it differently, and canceled.

Pat Weaver had once asked the accountants how much the NBC Symphony cost the network, only to receive an answer reflecting the fact that costs could be assigned or not assigned to a particular show depending upon how one chose to keep the books. The accountants answered Weaver with a question of their own: "How much do you want the NBC Symphony to cost?"

Goodbye *Home.* Says Weaver, "NBC sent the entire $5.5

million back to the women's magazines. We were getting people who didn't like soaps and quiz shows."

One of the last things Earl Wilson did before he said goodbye on *America After Dark* was to call Jack Paar and tell him that NBC wanted him to star on a resurrected *Tonight!* One story has it that the forewarned Jack Paar shrewdly did everything he could think of to get the show, while flatly stating in response to NBC's inquiry that he wasn't interested.

Paar is probably lucky one Pat Weaver idea didn't work out. Pat had followed the career of a local TV host in California for years, and sometime before Weaver left NBC he told his aides to sign the young entertainer—so that he could be put on hold for an opening sometime in the NBC schedule. There was no special plan: "We had lots of people who we didn't have much use for and would put them in comedy development to try to get a formula for their success."

But his aides didn't follow through, and Johnny Carson stayed put.

Following the *America After Dark* disaster, Sarnoff and Co. had nothing to lose in giving *Tonight!* one more shot. But they weren't too optimistic about recapturing the old crowd of late-night viewers. Some affiliates had switched to a fairly successful formula—old movies. The advertisers had abandoned *America After Dark* at or shortly after its inception. NBC apparently decided not to get locked into a set format until it could assess things in both viewer and commercial land. At least that was Paar's belief.

He noticed that when he agreed to host the resurrected show, now called *The Tonight Show,* he was given a contract that ran a mystifying twenty-four weeks. In broadcasting, one either got a thirteen-week contract, or, in a vote of high confidence, a twenty-six-week contract. Nobody ever got the twenty-four weeks Paar was signed for. Jack checked the calendar. Twenty-four weeks would take the show right to the end of the year—to December 31, 1957. Says Jack, "Obviously, they were going to drop it at the end of the year."

Another Star Is Born: Jack Paar

Early Life and Times of a Broadcast Maverick

If Jack Paar were in grade school today, he might well be classed as a hyperkinetic child and, no doubt, would have his share of problems—just as he did back home in Jackson, Michigan, half a century ago. He was smarter than the rest of the kids and bored by the routine of grade school. But without the high-priced psychiatry so common today, his mother and his teachers managed to help Jack survive a hostile environment.

His mother—who like his father was of Dutch descent—realized that if Jack spent a few days at home playing hooky it probably wouldn't hurt him and might even do him and the school some good. Thus, while Mrs. Paar was a good Protestant—Presbyterian, Episcopalian, or Dutch Reformed as the opportunity presented itself—she was quite willing to tell lies for her beloved Jack when he didn't want to go to classes. Some of her notes to teachers bordered on the bizarre—like the time there was a heavy snowstorm and Jack didn't feel like wasting the happy occasion behind a desk. Jack stayed out and Mrs. Paar wrote his teacher that her boy had missed school that day because he was suffering from snowblindness.

The teacher, like anyone who has had to deal with a disruptive individual in an otherwise manageable group, probably accepted Jack's many absences with only mild concern and, quite possibly, with positive relief.

Fortunately for Jack and the millions who watched *The Tonight Show* years later, one of his teachers found a particularly appropriate means of dealing with Jack's frequent intrusive remarks. This clever teacher finally told Jack that if he would shut up and stop amusing the rest of the kids during lessons, he could have a few minutes with the class at the end of the session to use as he saw fit. And so it came to pass that each afternoon just before final bell, the teacher would allow those children who had been good to stay on. It was their privilege to be entertained by Jack Paar, boy comedian.

Paar let little stand in the way of his urge for verbal expression—even the stuttering that dogged his speech for years. After Jack read how the Greek orator Demosthenes dealt with the same problem by shouting at the sea with a mouth filled with pebbles, Jack retired to his room, his cheeks stuffed with more-sanitary buttons, as he shrieked at the walls articles from old newspapers and magazines. Little by little his speech patterns improved.

Jack's father, a railroad division superintendent, was a rough-spoken man who fished a lot when not on the trains. Sometimes he fished with Jack, though the boy found it as difficult to sit still out of doors as in. When at home, the elder Paar used his dry wit to counterbalance a seemingly placid but somehow dominant wife. (As Jack has put it, "My mother was the stronger force.") The family moved periodically, and they had several homes in the Midwest. When Jack was born on May 1, 1917, the family was living in Canton, Ohio, but he was raised primarily in Jackson, Michigan. His memories of childhood are surprisingly somber —"I was born an old man." This attitude may reflect two vivid experiences involving death.

When Jack was five, his older brother was killed by an

automobile. And when Jack was ten, his best friend died. Jack was baffled: "My heart was breaking, and all I could think of was to break balloons through the [funeral] service. Then I went home and bawled."

Jack's room carried a crayoned sign reading, "Keep Out, This Means You." This reflected Jack's penchant for solitude and his passion for neatness. "My room was the most attractive in the house, and I didn't want it cluttered up. . . . I used to make my own bed and clean up the room myself. I couldn't stand things like ashtrays with stuff in them—I had a compulsion to empty them."

At age fourteen he spent eight straight months in that bedroom, sipping eggnogs as he recovered from mild tuberculosis. (Jack remembers experiencing periods of melancholy as he lay on his back staring at the ceiling, and the melancholia persisted, as most fans of *The Tonight Show* in the Paar years surely must have imagined.) But Jack's father sensed Jack's loneliness and so installed a workbench at the boy's bedside, teaching Jack everything he knew about carpentry and electronics. Jack was soon building his own radio receivers.

After Jack recovered from TB, his father sent him away to work with a railroad gang in freezing weather to toughen him up. Jack did grow stronger and proved it in high school to the satisfaction of nearly everyone but "The Black Panther." As "Roughhouse Paar," Jack won the school wrestling championship by defeating his young Negro rival, but promptly lost the title in a rematch. "Always quit while you're ahead" was the lesson Jack learned from this one, and, again, he put that theory to work throughout life.

It was at about this point that Jack was stopped on the streets of Jackson by a radio announcer doing a man-in-the-street broadcast. Paar expounded on the Michigan prison system at considerable length—the announcer had to wrest the mike from Jack's hand—and thereafter Jack was hired by the station, to sweep up and empty wastebaskets for $3 a week, working from 9:00 P.M. to midnight.

Lowly though the assignment was, it is doubtful that he would have landed it had not Jack and his mother written at least a dozen letters commending the young man's dissertation, though Jack's mother had missed the broadcast.

Newly employed, he played hooky more than ever, hanging around the radio station during the day, buying cigars for the news editor to ingratiate himself. The principal would call Jack's home, and Mrs. Paar, ever his ally in such endeavors, would impersonate a colored maid and say, "Ah'm sorry, Mrs. Paw is out."

Jack spent a great deal of time practicing to be an announcer. He quickly acquired a microphone, placed it in the attic, and read into it from plays, books, and magazines in an effort to develop a radio style. Apart from the family, no one heard or was aware of these sessions—the mike was dead. But while he was still sixteen, he got his hands on a live mike when the station offered him a full-time job at $12 a week.

Jack figured he had had enough of books and went to his faculty adviser to say, "I'm wasting my time and you're wasting yours." On that manifesto he resigned. But on his way out the door he remembered his athletic locker key and, with commendable thrift, returned it to collect the dollar deposit.

He continued his cleanup chores and was trusted to tell the listeners only, "This is station WIBM, Jackson." The problem was that he hadn't quite licked his stutter.

Jack remembers the thrill of being in the ground-floor glass-enclosed studio (the quarters had been an auto dealership) and stating that phrase as his awed high school friends pressed their noses against the window. Cautious though he was, his friends occasionally caught him furtively emptying the trash.

Restless, he quit to take a job at station WIRE in Indianapolis. Homesick, he returned to Jackson in six months and at age seventeen became WIBM's regular newscaster. One evening before his regular spot, he became miffed after the local *Town Crier* used up virtually all his time. Into the live mike, Jack muttered, *"The Town Crier* has taken so much time with his items about Mrs. Howell spraining her ankle, the Reillys' missing fox terrier, and next Tuesday's strawberry social at the Methodist Church that I won't have time for the news of Mussolini's attack on Ethiopia. Goodnight."

The station manager grabbed Jack as he came out of the studio and fired him. In retrospect this episode might be regarded as clear-cut evidence that Jack Paar was some talker—but no patsy.

Jack Paar Learns the Trade

Jack left Jackson in search of fame, taking a series of announcing jobs in the Midwest and East. From the beginning he was irrepressible and, in his own odd Midwest Republican and Protestant way, anti-establishment.

One night when Jack was a staff announcer at Pittsburgh's WCAE, the engineer put on the wrong record, and this caused Jack to burst out laughing. The engineer rushed in and punched Paar. The station sided with the engineer, and fired Jack.

Next stop, Cleveland's WGAR. Jack became well known in radio land with station breaks like "This is WGAR in Cleveland, broadcasting out to a certain someone in Lexington, Kentucky," or " 'All the Things You Are,' for a certain someone who cares." They were love notes to a traveling actress Jack was smitten with. WGAR was a CBS affiliate, and when the network heard about the billets-doux, WGAR got an abrupt Teletype that read, "Tell Paar to stop making love on our network."

The mishap was minor compared with Jack's war with the Cleveland library. Jack ignored many overdue notices and a registered letter on the misplaced book. Thus, late one night he was squired to the local slammer by two policemen. Irrepressible in court next day, he chided the judge for "putting the Magna before the Carta." The judge didn't smile but made Jack buy the book and pay a fine as well.

While still in Ohio, Jack met a beautiful girl who auditioned on the piano at the radio station. He doesn't remember her well—except that he married her twice. Her name was Irene, and though they were in love, their first marriage ended in divorce two years later. Three or four months after that they married again. This time, the union only lasted a few months and again off to family court. As Phyllis Diller later commented about the replay of the Liz Taylor and Richard Burton nuptials, remarriage to the same person is like "having your appendix put back in."

By the time World War II rolled around, Jack was already a combat veteran—if you count marital and career encounters. His Cleveland period ended abruptly when he chose to comment sarcastically at the station picnic about the intrigues of executive wives. Pink slip in hand, Jack headed for Buffalo's WBEN to avait developments in Europe.

Shortly after Pearl Harbor, Jack volunteered for the Army.

A Young Comedian Makes His Mark: Hello, South Pacific

Jack Paar has summed up his years in the service as follows: "I never understood the Army and the Army seemed to make no effort to understand me." But actually Jack was one of World War II's most successful court jesters precisely because he had an excellent grasp of the Army's methods and its hierarchy. And while the Army didn't try to understand him, it certainly was concerned about him— once he hit his stride.

Jack was sent immediately to a staging area in Indiantown Gap, Pennsylvania, and went through the Army's rigorous

physical training while becoming a member of the 28th
Special Service Company, a troupe of entertainers. At
camp, there was little time for play—with one notable exception. Jack's company commander, Sam Booker Carter,
had been a sales executive with the Hershey Chocolate
Company, in nearby Hershey, Pennsylvania. Captain
Carter arranged for Hershey to give a dinner dance in
honor of Jack's company, a motley collection of jugglers,
magicians, burlesque comedians, and even a string quartet.

Jack has described what followed:

"At the dance I met a slim, pretty, ash-blond girl. She had
a freckled nose and looked very sexy in a Republican sort
of way. Her name was Miriam Wagner and she was related
to the Hersheys."

Jack told Miss Wagner that he did not dance, adding,
"But I'm interesting to talk to."

"She eyed me doubtfully, but we sat down to talk. I never
talked faster in my life."

They met on July 3. Romance exploded like a firecracker;
they were engaged on the Fourth. It was love—not money
—that caused Jack Paar to act so impetuously. Miriam was
the great-grandniece of chocolate magnate Milton Hershey, and her maternal great-grandmother was Milton's
sister. Yet she was no Hershey heiress. Nor was anyone
else. When Milton died he left his $84 million to an orphan-
age.

Later, the legend would persist that Miriam was an heiress. Not that she was poor. Mr. Wagner was a dairy farmer,
and his biggest contract was with the Hershey plant. He
also owned some land which he sold to Hershey.

The Wagners were of Dutch descent, thrifty and conservative. They were not impressed with the boyish young
private who so abruptly asked for Miriam's hand. When Mr.
Wagner asked if Jack had been to college, Paar remembered a couple of classes in astronomy he had attended in
Cleveland on a lark and reported honestly but misleadingly
that he had "attended Western Reserve University." Some-

how Jack passed muster and the two were married in Hershey's Dutch Reformed Church on October 9, 1943. An Army buddy, one Jose Melis, sounded the wedding march on the church organ. Unlike his two slippery alliances with first and second wife Irene, his union with Miriam was to be binding.

After a short interval, Jack was sent to the West Coast and was soon sailing for Guadalcanal on an Army troop transport. On that long and arduous voyage Jack got a flash of inspiration he was to build on for the rest of the war and, it might be said, during his entire career.

The enlisted men were on such short rations they were constantly hungry. The entire food setup seemed designed to show them how subordinate they were. They stood in line for hours to get each of their two meals a day. In stark contrast, the Army officers aboard were fed three times a day and their food was several cuts above that of the men, featuring pies and cakes from the ship's bakery.

One day there was a submarine alert and Paar seized the opportunity. He jumped into a lifeboat and stated, "I've been asked to make an announcement that there was a Japanese submarine in the vicinity, but unfortunately the Navy gun crews have driven it off. I say unfortunately because the enemy submarine was trying to bring us food."

Jack may have decided right then that the essence of the Army dilemma was the class system. Certainly nothing enraged the GIs more than forced exposure to an undemocratic class system that reflected European social stratification and not the free United States society. When Paar began making the South Pacific circuit—on a one-a-day, island-hopping schedule—he quickly pieced together a series of anti-brass routines and became one of the best-loved comedians in the entire South Pacific. The only problem was that insulting an officer was one of the most serious offenses an enlisted man could be charged with.

Characteristically, Jack Paar had chosen to enter forbidden territory.

Jack's competition in his war theater included such superstars as Jack Benny and Bob Hope, and yet he topped them all. It was all the more remarkable in that back home Jack Paar had no following or even a foothold in the entertainment world.

What's more, the showcase for Jack's talents was lowercase vaudeville—the Special Services shows were mass-produced and unpretentious. They consisted of an MC and a few specialty acts—acrobats and jugglers. On occasion, three GIs with balloons in their shirts lip-synched the Andrews Sisters. Sometimes there was a small musical group or, more likely, just a piano. Jack played devastated Guadalcanal shortly after it was captured from the Japanese and went on to such battlegrounds and hospital depots as Fiji, Suva, and Munda.

Playing himself—and sometimes calmly smoking a pipe as he spoke into the mike—Jack often began, "Gentlemen . . . and any officers who might be present . . ."

He might go on, "The captain himself is censoring the mail again this week—so let's cut down on the big words. . . . Also, I don't care what you think of the colonel—stop using your thumbs when you salute. . . . The commander is sorry about the foul-up on our Christmas packages from home. We'll get them as soon as they finish breaking them. . . . Why is it that on every invasion the officers are so far behind the line they get bombed by the Nazis? . . . About this blitz you're going to go on. The colonel has given orders you are to bring back more prisoners. He needs a new kimono. And try to bring back some girl prisoners. Last Saturday in the officer's club they were dancing with each other again.

"Don't forget the general's birthday. The officers and nurses will have candlelight and wine. The enlisted men— warm beer and an old flashlight."

The officers would squirm a lot, and then begin to laugh

with the GIs—although a little less heartily perhaps. In the classic tradition of clowns, Jack was abusing the more fortunate members of his audience and was pointing out that the bad luck went elsewhere—to the enlisted men.

It was perhaps inevitable that the irrepressible comedian would go too far. At a Navy hospital in New Caledonia his troupe was putting on a show for several thousand men, many of them wounded and in wheelchairs. But the show was delayed until the commodore arrived an hour late.

He appeared with a pretty USO girl on his arm. As they made their way to their seats, Jack said, "You wouldn't think one man and a broad would hold up five thousand men." The men howled, and Jack ad-libbed the clincher: "The USO girls were supposed to do the Dance of the Virgins for you, but they went to the Officers' Club last night and broke their contract."

The men screamed with laughter—but the commodore did not. After the show, Jack was placed under arrest for insulting the officer and was threatened with a court-martial. Fortunately, Jack's old company commander and ally, Sam Booker Carter, was standing by. Outside the lockup Jack heard Captain Carter order his release, saying that Paar was an Army man and couldn't be held in a Navy area. In the confusion over Captain Carter's rendering of the rules of war, Jack was released and the captain rushed him away.

It was perhaps providential in view of Jack's collision course with disaster that the war was nearly over by then. Jack was to be among the first to go home. Consequently, he agreed to cut ten one-minute announcements which were to be played on the island radio stations, telling the homesick GIs about the rewards of reenlisting. He was out of character, felt like a hypocrite, and got ample opportunity to feel contrite. The redeployment schedule was slowed and Jack was left behind with the rest of the men to curse the syrupy words of Jack Paar, recruiter. The Army had had the last laugh.

Jack Paar Comes Home: The Big Break and the Big Letdown

While Jack Paar was famous in the South Pacific at the end of World War II, he might have been just another unknown on his return to the United States—if it hadn't been for Sidney Carroll.

Sidney was a war correspondent in the Pacific theater who kept hearing about Jack's brash anti-officer act. Carroll caught up with Jack at a field hospital in New Caledonia.

Carroll was awed by the thin, calm, unhurried, pipe-smoking youngster's laugh-getting power and called him a "demigod" in an article he later wrote for *Esquire* magazine. "He was every unknown soldier's wish fulfillment. . . . That was why his little troupe could follow the biggest Hollywood stars the USA had to send. . . . He was one of [the GIs]. He said all the things they wanted to say."

When Jack arrived in the United States to look for a job as a radio announcer, the *Esquire* article was on the newsstands and the networks and the movie studios were clamoring to sign the wonder boy. Called to Hollywood, Jack wrote his own script for an RKO audition, playing a casting director interviewing Jack Paar for a job. The write-it-yourself approach was practically unheard of. RKO signed him at $300 a week and he promptly sank into a Hollywood limbo, making three B movies for RKO and, on loan to another studio, another picture with an unknown named Marilyn Monroe. He hated every minute of it.

As for RKO, he remembers spending most of his time on tour, promoting movies he wasn't in, riding through midwestern towns in an open car with a motorcycle escort while townsmen ran after him shouting, "Who the hell are you?"

One afternoon in the spring of 1947, the West Coast producer of a popular radio show got an urgent telephone call from his mother. She told him about a young man who had rented half her two-family house with his wife and wanted to break into radio. The "nice young soldier" had mowed the lawn, run errands for her, and even fixed things around the house. The lady asked her producer son to do something for the young man, but he didn't get around to it. Then one day, his mother called to say, "You don't have to worry about that nice soldier anymore. He just got the Jack Benny show for the summer."

Pat Weaver says that when Benny was preparing to go on summer holiday, he had no intention of letting his arch rival, Bob Hope, fill in and perhaps replace him in the fall. Jack Paar didn't know it then, but Hope's unacceptability was to be Paar's opportunity. Shortly before then—in 1947 —Jack Paar's doctor had introduced him to a fellow patient named Larry Marks, a comedy writer who had worked for Bob Hope, Fred Allen, and, most recently, radio comedian Henry Morgan, whose acerbic style was not unlike Paar's.

Marks was then at liberty. He liked Paar's work and began cutting audition records with him. A lively half-hour radio variety show evolved which was sold to American Tobacco, Jack Benny's sponsor. But it was still up to Benny to decide on his summer replacement. In due time, a nervous Larry Marks and Jack Paar arrived at Benny's house to play the audition disc. Benny listened to it in pajamas and smoking jacket. After a typically long Benny pause—agonizing under the circumstances—the comedian said to Paar, "You got a nice show there, kid. Some of the jokes are yours, and some of them are mine, but I like it."

Benny's Amusement Enterprises, Inc., took over the packaging, and Benny put two of his writers on the budget at $1,000 a week each. They didn't write a single line, as everybody admitted later, Jack Paar with some asperity. Marks added three more writers, and when the show debuted on June 1, 1947, it carried one of the heaviest budgets in radio history.

To a degree it was worth it. A critic commented after the

third show that the summer replacement series was "short on originality" with a format borrowed from Henry Morgan, but even so the material had "more verve" than most variety offerings. There were sharp, irreverent topical satires, movie parodies, and advertising burlesques—just like what Morgan had done. Derivative though it was, the critics liked it. The audiences were less kind—even those who actually came to the studio.

In those days, it was traditional for the star of the show to warm up the studio audience. But when Jack did it he was so condescending that the attitude in the auditorium became "Okay, smart-ass, make us laugh."

Meanwhile, he fought with his writers. He was younger than they, but it seemed odd to Jack that he was paid less than Larry Marks, who, like the two idle Benny writers, got $1,000 a week. Jack's weekly stipend was $750.

The writers thought Jack resented them because he hadn't the time or talent to write the scripts himself. Jack even argued that the credits should not include writers. Marks hoped to break down the barriers and suggested that Paar get better acquainted—have lunch with the writers at the Brown Derby. Jack resisted, finally agreed, but was so ill at ease the meeting was a fiasco.

Jack had taken to telling the writers that if they were unhappy they could quit. This offered a Hobson's choice. To quit was to forfeit future payment under the contract. The only way the writers could be paid in full was to get fired, and Jack wasn't about to accommodate them.

Finally, after a violent disagreement over a movie parody, Paar threw the quit line at the writers again, and one rose to shout, "Who needs you?" Three of the four writers left. Larry Marks sat in embarrassed silence awhile and finally joined the others.

In the aftermath, Arthur Stander, the writer who led the walkout, was fairest to Jack. He says, "The whole thing developed very subtly. We were unaware that in our minds [we saw it as] our show and not Jack's. What we did was override him on material he didn't like. We'd say to him, in effect, 'We know what's good, take our word for it. You're just a kid.' In a sense, this was an intolerable spot for any star to be in—whether he's been a star for ten minutes or ten years. We pushed him unknowingly to the point of anger."

When the summer ended, so did Jack's Hollywood career. He had made lots of enemies there, partly because of unbending attitudes and, his critics say, his unwillingness to show humility.

An executive on the Coast who remained friendly with Jack summed up the feelings of many, saying, "The thing that really bothered a lot of people out here was the way Jack took the biggest break a kid could get in this business as something that was coming to him and not as something he ought to be grateful about. You must remember the timing of this thing. For a young fella to come out of the Army with no real experience and fall into a spot like the Jack Benny summer replacement show was fantastic. Any other guy would have been humble as hell."

Jack was learning humility the hard way. But it would become a part of his personality. He was to become, by turns, humble and arrogant, recognizing his own shortcomings and, at the same time, guarding his talent, fully aware of the willingness of others to trifle with it.

Jack hated the phoniness and the insincerity of the entire Hollywood show-business community. He remembered what Fred Allen had once said to him: "All the sincerity in Hollywood you can stuff in a flea's navel and still have room to conceal eight caraway seeds and an agent's heart."

Miriam Paar is no women's libber. And friends say Jack Paar has always treated Miriam with a benign male chauvinism that nevertheless reflects a deep devotion. "Come on, Mother, where's lunch?" he chides when the hour to dine has slipped by as Miriam sits engrossed in Jack's remarks to a visiting writer. She jumps up and serves lunch immediately. But Miriam is no patsy. Rather, she is a full and complete partner in everything Jack does—and she always has been.

After the Benny summer show, Jack sat on the West Coast waiting in vain for the telephone to ring. Meanwhile, Miriam had carefully husbanded the family resources. The Paars did not go hungry. But Jack needed to work, and it was clear he wasn't going to in Hollywood. Finally, after a year of waiting, Miriam sensed that it was time for a move.

A friend says, "She has ESP with Jack and knows what is right for him. She is an amazing woman. She wanted him to go back to New York because she thought it would be good for him to get away from California. Finally, she suggested it—and at the precise moment, too. Jack can be very glum—when she suggested going to New York, he smiled for the first time in many months."

Within a week, Miriam and their infant daughter, Randy, flew east. Jack left by car and upon arriving in New York found a fan.

Jack O'Brian, powerful columnist for Hearst's *Journal American,* thought Jack's fill-in for Benny had been marvelous. "He was so good and he could say such goddam things and you didn't know he had your head until you shook it and it fell off. I thought I'd see if I could get this guy a job.

"Every day I would mention Paar [in the column]. Repetition makes reputation. About the fifth day he was hired for the CBS *Morning Show.*"

O'Brian says that Paar sent him an Olivetti typewriter with a note saying something to the effect, "I hope you appreciate the fact that I am grateful and that you are deductible." O'Brian, who says he generally sends gifts back, nevertheless kept the Olivetti.

The Morning Show was CBS's answer to NBC's *The Today Show.*

Out and In Again: Paar Lands The Tonight Show

The Morning Show did reasonably well—Paar says that the audience went up to 4 million viewers daily, an increase of 140 percent over the previous format, but that sponsors proved elusive. In fact, Paar was regarded as uncooperative with sponsors and once refused to do a commercial that would have had Paar say he had discovered why his wife was more attractive of late—looking in her boudoir he found the sponsor's lipstick.

He states, "Not long after the incident with the lipstick, CBS emancipated me from their dawn patrol"—this *Today Show* competitor eventually was scrapped in favor of a straight news format—"and gave me a half-hour program each weekday afternoon. It was a pleasant show, with Edie Adams, Martha Wright, and Jack Haskell, but . . . there were so few people watching us it would have been cheaper to phone them."

These experiences did hone Jack's skills. Soon he would be ready for *The Tonight Show*—if only he could land it.

Then came that telephone call from Earl Wilson, who, on departing from the dying *America After Dark,* had urged NBC to resurrect *Tonight!* with Jack Paar. Jack waited impatiently until NBC finally rang him up. After some sparring, he got NBC to agree to let him do the show his way—with a free-and-easy format. The debut was, in Jack's own words, "a disaster"—and the reviews were terrible.

He recalls, "On the show I grappled with a heavyweight wrestler, threw vegetables at the audience, and fed catnip to a lion. However, none of these incidents were as dangerous as the conversation on the show. The talk was sort of a verbal barroom brawl with the cast using words instead of pool cues and beer mugs. We didn't perform; we just defended ourselves."

As one critic was to observe, "Jack Paar is the only bull with his own china shop."

But the show quickly caught on. Beginning with 62 stations, a small audience, and two sponsors, Jack explains that "before long we had 154 stations, an estimated 30 million viewers weekly, and so many sponsors I felt guilty when I interrupted the commercials with the program."

The Tonight Show with Jack Paar as host was about to become the most talked-about show on television.

Paar's Shakedown Cruise

Once Jack Paar was clicking on *Tonight*—and it was clear to Jack in two days that he was clicking—he was convinced he was set for as long as he wanted to stay. It wasn't clear to anybody else.

One man in particular found it difficult to accept the fact that Jack Paar was molding the show in his own image and that it was working. The man, who was an important enough member of the troupe to give advice to everyone but Paar, exercised the prerogative at will. For example, he would advise Dody Goodman, saying, "Never mind what Jack says, do what I say."

Jack found this intolerable. "This man was causing trouble with the cast. The show was a delicate balance. I was living on my nerve endings. If someone was giving advice, forget it."

The man became increasingly intrusive—but, as Jack Paar notes, "Never with me." And he started taking credit. That hurt. Jack states that it is true the man suggested hiring guests by the week, and "We did that for a while. First we hired Stanley Holloway for a week at the scale $800." That saved the poorly budgeted show money, because otherwise a guest cost $320 for the first night and well over $200 a night for the rest of the week.

But there were other suggestions that simply did not work. Jack, who had done his similar show on CBS for over a year, felt he knew exactly how to use his talent and how to use the nine hours a week the show was on the air. In those days, Jack did his fifteen-minute monologue for the local audience first and an additional hour and a half for the network.

The guests were interacting well with Jack, and everything seemed to be working. Then one evening after the show, Jack and Jose Melis got into the Carey Cadillac which took them home each night and graciously took along the intrusive staffer, who had been drinking.

Suddenly, to Jack's astonishment, the man started flailing his arms. "He hit me two or three times, and Jose too."

For the moment, there was nothing they could do. It was not possible to pull over on the West Side Highway for a number of blocks, and the man continued his flailing and began frothing at the mouth.

Finally, the chauffeur pulled into a recess for disabled cars and announced that he had been a medic in the paratroopers in World War II. The man was having an epileptic seizure, the chauffeur said, and asked for Jack's handkerchief, which was, of course, clean, and proceeded to stuff the cloth into the epileptic's mouth. In recollection, Jack says, "God is so good to me. It was sheerest luck that the chauffeur was an ex-medic."

They waited until the seizure had subsided and then

wondered what to do next. The man couldn't talk and they didn't know where he lived. It was nearly 2:00 A.M. "We knew he was from Connecticut, but we didn't know where —not even the town. Finally, I telephoned someone who found his wife and the chauffeur took him home."

But that nightmare was only the beginning. Jack Paar didn't want the man fired. But he persisted in interfering. And the man was tense.

"He would scream and shout, making fast decisions on guests, for example, saying, 'We don't want him . . . yes, get him,' and so forth."

The man was supposed to be on pills, but he didn't always take them. And he wasn't supposed to drink, but he did. When the tension rose above his low tolerance, he would be driven into fits. Then Jack or members of the staff would have to put the hankie in his mouth and wait for him to stop foaming and striking. Sometimes he would hit Jack's wife, Miriam, and occasionally he hit Jose Melis.

But that was only part of the problem. Paar would arrive home after the show, go to bed, and fall fast asleep. The telephone would ring at 3:00 A.M. Jack would awake, and pick up the telephone, and it would be the epileptic's wife calling to say, "You son of a bitch, you drove my Ralphy into a fit!"

Ralphy at least would apologize. Jack said, "Every time after a fit, he would send in a handwritten note. They were sad, sweet notes."

Finally, Jack could deal with the problem no longer. Running the show meant a heavy personal involvement for Jack, who was constantly facing scores of decisions. But every time he said something critical in Ralphy's presence he had to worry that the staffer might throw a fit. In despair, Jack told an NBC executive the story and the staffer was moved laterally into a windowless office and given no responsibilities.

Ralphy never forgave Jack. Many years later, he gave an interview to a newspaper saying the idea for the show—the format and all the rest of it—was his idea. Jack Paar, he said, forgets his friends.

While Jack was dealing with Ralphy's fits and his indignant wife, he wanted to put the whole thing out of his mind. And he might have, too, but for that "Jack Paar forgets his friends" interview Ralphy gave the newspaper.

Paar Hammers Out a Format for Tonight

Dick Cavett, in his book, *Cavett*, said:

"Jack in all his work let his own quirks, neuroses, suspicions and dislikes play freely on the surface, along with his enthusiasms, instant reactions and emotional knee jerks. Even for those who didn't like it, it was compelling, and you had to admit that it appealed, if only to a voyeur instinct. There was always the implied possibility in his manner that he would explode one day, and you might miss seeing a live nervous breakdown viewed from the comfort of your own bedroom. No matter who the guest was, in a two-shot your eyes were on Jack. . . .

"He instinctively asked and said things that you yourself, if you were not inhibited, would like to ask and say. Which is to say, here was someone who went through with things that many self-respecting people denounced as somehow 'not done.' Yet those same people watched him nightly and loved seeing him do those things. When attacked unjustifiably and in some cases cruelly by some cheap columnist, Jack would give as good as he got, with humor. The fact that he also did this when he was criticized reasonably just made him that much more fun to watch. . . ."

It is paradoxical that as Jack Paar made his debut and settled in for a long run on *Tonight,* the public was to become embroiled in a sterile, long-running debate over the question "What is Jack Paar really like?"

For within a few months—and almost before the debate got under way—Jack clearly knew what he was and what he

was not, and how to use the best of what he was on *Tonight.*
As Cavett has pointed out, he also used something that
Paar regarded as a major failing—his emotions. Paar freely
admits that he simply couldn't control his feelings. But he
undoubtedly had a much bigger impact as a result of his
"shortcoming."

Jack himself has revealed his emotional dilemma with an
anecdote that helps explain the extraordinary fascination
he had for viewers.

During World War II, Jack Paar had a top sergeant he
despised. Jack vowed that somehow, someday, he would
even the score. A few years passed, and by sheerest coincidence, the now famous comedian spotted the sergeant in
a hotel lobby just as the sergeant spotted Paar. "Hey, Paar,
Jack Paar," the sergeant said, and Paar's emotions, flowing
as freely as his tear ducts, caused him to share a rough,
manly embrace with the sergeant. Like long-lost buddies.

Soon Jack was fully exploiting his unique personality,
and doing so to the exclusion of the usual performer's
devices. In his early experiments with format, he did blackout sketches and wore funny hats—like his predecessors,
Steve Allen, Jerry Lester, and Morey Amsterdam. But Jack
hated and mistrusted every minute of that sort of tomfool-
ery for himself on *Tonight.* Unlike Steve Allen and Johnny
Carson, who obviously believe themselves to be convincing
in character and costume, Paar knew it was wrong for him.
Thus, after he had been doing the show for about six
months he drew aside his writer and close friend Paul Keyes
to say, "Kid, I've made a decision. No more sketches.
. . . From now on, I go on with a monologue about my wife
and child. Any laughs I get will be from the point of view
of the first person singular."

Paar told Keyes that in his view this was the only safe
approach. While he told funny stories in his monologues
and joked with members of his permanent panel on the
show each night, Paar, to a far greater degree than Steve
Allen and Johnny Carson, made a point of interviewing

serious people, and he was good at it. He talked with the Kennedy brothers, for example—JFK when he was a senator and Bobby when he was attorney general. (Paar's talent coordinator, Bob Shanks, believes that the Kennedys were the first to recognize the power of *Tonight* and other talk shows as free political gravy. He makes a case for Rose and Robert Kennedy's having used the talk shows, particularly *Tonight,* to get John elected.) Over time Paar also interviewed a number of other outstanding public figures like Mrs. Eleanor Roosevelt and Albert Schweitzer.

To Jack it would be more than just inappropriate after such serious segments to wear motley. He told Keyes, "We are going to be destroyed if ten minutes later [after a serious interview] I am wearing a police outfit or sailor suit. They are never going to believe both Jack Paars. I am going to stay with the honest one—the Midwest Presbyterian."

(Jack had had an awful experience with police outfits. In a guest appearance on *Candid Camera,* he had posed as a traffic cop and had stopped a motorist and ordered him out of his car. The man protested, but Jack insisted roughly. So the man opened the door and pulled himself out, his two wasted legs wobbling under him as Allen Funt stood off camera frantically sliding his finger past his throat in a fruitless effort to "cut" the segment while Paar stood there in helpless horror.)

The Formative Years with Jack's Tonight Show Family

The anti-character decision was, in Paul Keyes's view, the most important one Jack ever made. Paar stuck to that decision religiously, but his concept was a bit broader than he implied in speaking of his wife and child as the focus: he also included in his monologues and comments members of his "larger family." Regular panelists and members of his staff with whom Jack had established a kind of familial relationship were used in his commentaries in the same manner as his wife and child. Some intimate aspects of the cast's and crew's personal lives were to become familiar to *Tonight* viewers.

Miriam Paar was, of course, scandalized when Jack told America about Randy's milestone first bra. Mitzi Matravers, Jack's secretary and—on jokes and bits of business planned for the show—his court of first resort, was similarly embarrassed when Paar, prompted by a friend of Mitzi's, told America that Mitzi was about to become engaged. Paar had called Mitzi to the stage from the studio audience while doing the show and made Mitzi tell the world—even before Mitzi had had a chance to inform her parents, and, even more important, while Mitzi was still vacillating over the engagement.

Incidentally, Mitzi was so caught up in the effulgence that was Paar to his friends and associates that she wondered if somehow she had been disloyal to have had enough of a personal life to become engaged. Jack didn't see it that way at all, and quickly made it clear to Mitzi that her romantic liaison and later marriage didn't mean leaving the show or the nest. Mitzi was and still is a member of Jack's "family," like so many other intimates of Jack's when he was doing the show. This was nothing new with Jack. He has always believed in keeping alive old friendships. Jose Melis, Jack's musical director, a friend and associate since Army days, was thrust into *Tonight* by Jack as eagerly as one might don a rediscovered pair of old slippers. Sidney Carroll, the writer who put Jack on the entertainment map after World War II with the article in *Esquire,* is also still a friend, to mention just one more example of Jack's fidelity.

Like Mitzi, talent scout Tom O'Malley was drawn reluctantly into the Paar vortex on several occasions when he might rather have been left out. While on the *Tonight* camera, Paar once spotted O'Malley in the audience and asked him before his millions of viewers why he wasn't out scouting talent for the show. O'Malley acknowledged sheepishly that he should have been on the prowl, but added that he had trouble tearing himself away since he found Paar more entertaining than anything he would see on the nightclub circuit.

O'Malley recalls in rueful amusement another day when he was discovered in the studio audience—the night actor Sam Levene was on *Tonight*. He explains, "I had interviewed Levene for his appearance. He was deadly. I couldn't pull anything out of him. I knew that he had worked with Henry Fonda, Bogart . . . but in the interview he was absolutely bereft of humor. I didn't realize it, but he simply wasn't in the mood to be interviewed. I wrote the notes for Paar and said, 'Take Levene and get rid of him quickly. He has no stories, is not funny, and has no memory of anything. Get him on and let him plug his [Broadway] show and dump him.' "

O'Malley continues: "I was standing in the back when Sam Levene came on. Within sixty seconds he got four huge laughs accompanied by applause. . . . One rollicking bon mot after another. Paar turned to him and said, 'I thought you were supposed to be boring, pal. O'Malley said I was to dump you.' "

It was vintage Paar, and quite typical: the kind of spontaneous devilishness that Paar had used from early in his radio career when he used network breaks to issue verbal valentines to a certain someone—his actress sweetheart as she traveled with a road company. It was this sort of thing that forced *Tonight* viewers to stay with the show until Jose Melis raised his baton to direct the final theme.

The night of O'Malley's travail, Paar set up Levene with a straight line to see what Levene would do with it: "O'Malley said you worked with Fonda." Levine grabbed it and, working the gag, said emphatically, "I never worked with Fonda in my life." At that, Jack had the house lights turned on and said, "Where's O'Malley? Get O'Malley up here!"

O'Malley recalls: "I ran by Paar and around the band and

out the back door. I had to escape! After the show, I went up to Paar and said, 'Thanks a lot for the plug, Jack,' and he said, 'It was sensational, pal.' "

O'Malley remembers still another public airing of his relationship less fondly. O'Malley had a drinking problem at the time, and, reluctantly, Jack fired him for it. Jack could be a bit paranoid when he felt crossed. Thus, when *Newsweek* had a somewhat disparaging piece shortly thereafter about Jack, Paar concluded, erroneously as it turns out, that the story had been inspired by O'Malley. He went on the show and, at his sarcastic worst, told viewing America that the source of the piece obviously was a "Judas" he had fired, a man Jack said he had picked up out of the gutter. While Jack didn't mention O'Malley by name, he referred to him as a former television critic and offered other clues that made it clear O'Malley was the perpetrator. Tom was horrified that his fall from grace was exploited on the air. Perhaps viewers didn't love Jack at that moment, but they were fascinated, as usual, particularly because he also gave *Newsweek* a piece of his mind.

Time passed. In 1959, O'Malley, who had kicked his bad habit, was booking guests for ex-schoolteacher comedian Sam Levenson. Tom had cooled off, and he still admired and liked Jack. He wanted to bury the hatchet. Tom wrote Jack about Frank Fay, the actor famed for his portrayal of the pixilated Elwood P. Dowd in *Harvey,* the play about the six-foot invisible rabbit. Jack had tried unsuccessfully to book Fay for *Tonight* for years. Fay had appeared on Sam Levenson's show at Tom's behest. Fay was "simply great," O'Malley reported in his letter to Jack, and "I suggested he go on with you and he said okay."

Paar wrote a handwritten "Dear Tom" reply on O'Malley's own letter: "This was very kind of you and thanks." Jack added, in a burst of solicitude, "This is my only letter to anyone all year." Later, Paar rehired O'Malley for $1,000 a week.

Young Man with a Talent: Writing for Paar

The Tonight Show offers a keen challenge for the comedy writer. It is a superb place to hone skills and offers one of the most cherished credits in the business. Anyone hoping for a career in television presumably wants an opportunity to pen jokes for *Tonight*.

Not Dick Cavett, Yale, class of '58. In 1960, the young Nebraska native was an unemployed actor and was stop-gapping as a copyboy at Time, Inc. While copyboys are usually crackling like well-stoked campfires to become writers, Cavett was not smoldering to move ahead at Time, nor was he hot to become a writer anywhere.

Understandably, he was bored silly with his errand-boy duties at Time. One evening when ennui was at its zenith he sent an empty beer can clattering through that august organization's pneumatic tubes and became a living legend with his peer group.

If Cavett was at all inspired it was in his determined efforts to avoid his chores—except the one that periodically sent a copyboy to the airport to pick up or deliver photographs. Cavett told the author he liked that detail because he could charge $7 for cabs against a bus-and-subway round-trip cost of $1 and thus bolster his small take-home pay.

Mostly, though, he spent his hours at Time hiding in the library, out of earshot of writers yelling "Copy!" or "Boy!" as he read the files on Buster Keaton, Stan Laurel, and other silent-screen comedy greats.

Cavett had fallen in love with an actress significantly more successful than he in reaching a common goal—Broadway. Carrie Nye, his bride-to-be, was in excellent company—that of Shirley Booth, Jean-Pierre Aumont, Nina Foch, and Cathleen Nesbit—but in a turkey of a show called *Second Fiddle,* and Dick felt that, without being cast, he had the title role.

What turned Cavett's attention to *Tonight* was the thought that the stopgap of comedy-filler writer was preferable to the stopgap of pastepot filler at Time, Inc. This after he read a newspaper item that Jack Paar worried constantly about his *Tonight Show* opening monologue and was constantly looking for more and better material.

Cavett mulled this over for some time and finally sat down at his desk thinking to type a few jokes, present them to Paar, and, if he was lucky, get to meet Paar and enter show biz through this ploy. What followed is almost, but not quite, a show-business cliché. He wrote a few pages that his ear told him were Good Paar and then stuck them in a plain envelope. On second thought, he figured that he might as well pry open the door with a stout stick and resealed the gags in a Time, Inc., envelope.

Having nosed around *The Tonight Show* before, Cavett headed for the back elevator at 30 Rock, punched 6, endured the ascent, then dutifully disembarked and wandered about the corridor Paar had to walk to get from dressing room and bathroom.

Voilà! Paar appeared around the corner, spotted the Time, Inc., envelope, and assumed, as the copyboy had hoped he would, that Cavett was a reporter for what had long been America's most powerful newsmagazine.

Cavett pressed his luck and said to the star, "*Time* is thinking of doing a story on you." Cavett remembered that Paar had been nursing a cold and added, partly to let Paar know he'd been watching the show, "That's just what you need on top of your cold." Paar laughed.

Cavett waved his envelope and said, "I wrote you some jokes you might be able to use." Paar looked a bit skeptical but took the envelope, thanked Cavett, and left for his dressing room.

Cavett, who is seldom at a loss, was nevertheless a bit bemused about his next move until it occurred to him to head for the studio and sit with the audience "to hear my jokes." He didn't really expect to hear them, yet when Paar appeared to do his monologue and took a folded piece of paper out of his pocket, Cavett was suffused with a sense of destiny and mentally wrote his own soap opera.

In his autobiography, *Cavett,* it goes like this:

"I knew what was about to happen. He would say, 'Everything I am going to tell you now is true. A kid just came up to me out in the hall and handed me a monologue that's funnier than the stuff my own writers give me. If anyone saw which way the kid went, let me know. Meanwhile, here are his jokes. . . .'

"But in fact what he had pulled from his pocket was a prepared bit that had nothing to do with me. I began to get a queasy feeling and to eye the exit. Suddenly I heard one of my lines used as an ad-lib. Then another one. Paar was working them deftly into the show. I began to emerge from my collar again and sit up. At the end of the show, I managed to get into the same elevator with him, and he spotted me and said, 'Thanks, pal. You should do that again sometime.'

"I graciously let a week pass, did, and the second time resulted in my getting a job. . . ."

Not that Cavett had given up on the idea of being an actor. It was just that "I thought the Paar thing was right for me, somehow, and would open up vaguely defined doors to who knew what?"

Needless to say, it did. After a stint as a talent coordinator for Paar, he went on to write monologue material for Jack and later for Johnny Carson as well—trapped, as it were, by his own talent.

Jack Paar's Singular Appeal

Paar's hold on his public—and his staff—obviously reflected his intense human qualities. Clearly, Jack had gauged his own personality correctly in choosing first-person-singular anecdotes and comments about members of his intimate "family" as his format.

It wasn't necessary to guess about Jack's popularity as a

performer. His accomplishment was especially impressive in that he started virtually from scratch, since nearly all viewers and advertisers had abandoned *America After Dark*. NBC, which had planned to cashier Jack at year's end, hastened to renew just months into the Paar run. As the show moved into its second year, Jack had an estimated 5 million fans, was seen over a record 115 stations, and, as that many stations on line would suggest, already had a higher rating than Steve Allen attained.

Even more important, he had as many as thirty-eight sponsors and would soon be sold out, though Steve Allen never was. At its best the Steve Allen version of the show was four-fifths sold.

It was clear that Jack's appeal was nearly universal. Everybody, it seemed, peeked in on the show at least some of the time. For two years, week after week, the pollster Albert Sindlinger sampled opinion and found Jack Paar to be the most discussed person in the nation.

Clearly, in integrating the best ideas from his prior unsuccessful television shows, Jack had found the winning formula. He had called it right more or less from the beginning of his *Tonight* experience.

The show began, of course, with Jose Melis's original theme—which, though musically sound and tuneful, was, lyrically speaking, hardly a harbinger of the kind of literary quality Jack liked to get into the show itself. You could sense Melis's Cuban-Americanism in the "1" and the "F R." It went:

I M 4 U

S I M

S I M

G I 1

2 B 4 U

4 F R

Enter Jack with opening monologue.

As Jack structured the show, it more or less hinged on that opening monologue—a device that set the tone for the evening; when it was unsuccessful it cast a pall on the rest of the night. Not that the audience held a poor monologue against Jack. Rather, it was Jack's perception of disappointment that hurt the show. Paar depended on the monologue to get things rolling, and he held it against himself when it went wrong.

(Curiously enough, for something so important to the star, the opening monologue went only to the local viewers in the early months. Jack went on for WNBC, the local New York station at 11:15 P.M., and the network didn't tune in until 11:30. This so exasperated Jack that he quit doing his monologue for a time. Instead, he let others warm up the studio audience and the viewers in metropolitan New York. Jack went back to the monologue again some months later when the live show was dropped for magnetic recording tape. The first fifteen minutes were also dropped at about the same time.)

Jack put painstaking effort into the writing of this opening number. And, once the show was over, he wasted no time getting to work on the next monologue. He began thinking about it almost before he climbed into the Carey Cadillac limousine with Jose Melis to motor back to his home in Bronxville, a posh suburb thirty minutes out of Manhattan.

Shortly after awakening the next weekday morning at 6:00 A.M.—Jack still rises compulsively at about that hour even though he has chosen to retire—he would begin thinking about that night's monologue and calling staffers to try out ideas. Jack felt he needed absolute solitude to work out the monologue, and he would motor down to an office suite in the Algonquin Hotel (where the famous *New Yorker* writers had gathered at the "Round Table" a decade or so earlier). Jack chose that hotel because it was only a block from the Hudson Theatre.

Secretary Mitzi Matravers would work at her chores

nearby as Jack wove personal things that had happened to him, Miriam, and Randy into his routine. He invariably was able to turn such episodes into amusing bits for the show.

There were, of course, references to the day's news, which were, by and large, prepared later by Jack's writers. In the beginning, they, too, found that Jack could be insensitive. More than one has said he left Jack's office to the sound of his work being wadded up and thrown into a wastebasket. "Later," says one in rueful recollection, "Jack learned to wait until we were out of earshot before he crumpled and disposed of our handiwork."

But it was the personal references—not the topical references—that viewers remembered most. Jack quoted Randy on one occasion when she was about eight years old as saying after a ride on the subway that the generally unsmiling passengers "looked like people who had played the game and lost." In another, more elaborate story, he told how Miriam used little tricks to memorize names of people she met. For instance, he said that when Orville Dryfoos, the late publisher of *The New York Times,* hosted a dinner party for the Paars and introduced himself as "Orv," Miriam asked Mr. Dryfoos if "Orv" was "Orville," as in the Wright brothers. Mr. Dryfoos said yes. When they left the dinner party that night, Jack told viewers, he said, "Goodnight, Mr. Dryfoos," while Miriam, who liked everybody and spoke warmly to all, took her leave with the more personal words "Goodnight, Wilbur."

There were anecdotes involving Jack's announcer, Hugh Downs. "The best Tonto I ever had!" Jack was to call Downs at a farewell party years later, and he says that he never had a cross word with Downs. Paar also regarded Downs as a leveling voice and good contrast. Paar marveled at Downs' erudition and often fascinating explanations: "Ask Hugh what time it is, and he'll tell you how to make a watch." Paar told listeners about Hugh's minor operation and how Downs was in a private room in the hospital when a priest entered the room by mistake to say final prayers for what the priest believed was a dying penitent. Paar said that Hugh told the priest, "I think there is some mistake, I'm only here for a little while." Said the priest sympathetically, "Son, we are all only here for a little while."

When the show was traveling abroad, Jack told an English audience of the hazards of being an American without foreign-language skill in Europe. In Venice, Miriam had wanted a couple of cheap dresses to pad out her wardrobe. After shopping at several places, she saw six beautiful dresses in the window of a small shop. She entered and started examining the clothes, asking the clerk if each dress in its turn was available in her size. "Do you have this in size ten?" she would ask in English. The Italian shopkeeper would grab the dresses back each time. It turned out, Jack explained, that the store was not a dress shop, but a dry cleaner.

In another monologue, Jack explained that he and Miriam would register as Mr. and Mrs. Primrose Magoo when they traveled—so that he wouldn't be mobbed by fans. He was in a hotel, he said, that had telephones with blinking lights to let patrons know that the desk had a message for the guest. Paar's light blinked, and he called the desk to say he was Mr. Paar. "You have a message for me?" he asked. They seemed baffled and said no. Paar muttered that there must be some mistake and hung up. Shortly thereafter, said Paar, "The desk called to say, 'Mr. Paar, this is rather indelicate, but is there a Miss Magoo living with you?' It was for Miriam."

In the same monologue, Jack went on to say that Miriam then returned home and he wanted to get in touch with her but could not remember his unlisted telephone number.

He asked the hotel to get him information in New York. Put through to the operator, Jack told the audience, he said, "Now, honey, this is Jack Paar and I kid you not and I'm the guy on TV and I don't have my phone number and I know it sounds pretty crazy but would you give me my phone number?"

The operator shot back, "That's what they all say."

"I said, 'I swear . . . don't you know my voice?' and 'Would you call back and ask for Mr. Paar?' But then I know that's not going to work because she would have to ask for Mr. Magoo. 'Please, I swear, I swear, my wife and baby . . .' "

Operator: "How do I know whether you have a wife and baby?"

Impatiently now, Paar demanded, "Give me my number!" She wouldn't. "Well, I admire that . . . that's what you are supposed to do. Well, I'll call my secretary. My assistant who calls me all the time [at home] knows my number."

Mitzi Matravers was still in the hotel, as were the rest of the *Tonight* people. Jack picked up the telephone to say, "Hello, operator, would you connect me with Miss Matravers, please?"

Operator: "There is a do not disturb on her phone until 11:30."

"I said, 'Now, operator, she works for me and she is sleeping because of me and you can just jolly well jingle her little line and tell her that the boss is on the line, Mr. Paar.' She said, 'She doesn't work for Mr. Paar, she works for Mr. Magoo.' "

Jack was concerned enough about his opening monologue that he would memorize it before air time. This required high concentration. Once he broke a rule, interrupting his concentration to stop and say hello to a guest, his friend Suzy Parker, the model. Suzy looked devastated and said to Jack, brimming with tears, "I'm getting a divorce."

Jack was stunned, and totally forgot his monologue. When he stepped before the cameras he couldn't think of his monologue at all. After standing there a few seconds in the terror known best to public speakers who have lost their notes and performers who have suddenly and inexplicably lost their train of thought, he composed himself and said simply, "I've been drinking." Fortunately, he managed to score heavily by following through extemporaneously on that theme.

It wasn't the only time that Jack experienced difficulty in concentration before the crucial opening monologue. Jonathan Winters, who has never become a great star—partly because of his own short attention span—was always a threat to Jack's concentration. Jack always managed to help Winters be funny when he was a guest on the show, but it was a trial. There was no pre-show isolation, no chance to concentrate, when Winters was a guest. Jack would be trying to get his act together, so to speak, and Winters would nag him constantly.

Winters is, as they say, "always on"—always doing characterizations, improvising. He can be funny with almost any bit, but like many other performers is quite unsure of himself. Once Paar was concentrating on his monologue when he saw Winters wandering around in a fog and Paar felt obliged to ask, "What are you going to do, Johnny?"

Winters said, "Be a fag fireman. Get me a fireman's helmet." Jack interrupted his endeavors and gave orders for someone to get a fire helmet. But suddenly Winters came up to Paar again to say, "I'll be Richard Arlen and you be Clara Bow."

Manfully Paar got through his monologue, only to be startled when Winters came out carrying a bunch of pussy-willows and saying sweetly, "I'm the breath of spring."

The Special Appeal of Jack Paar's Regulars

Paul Keyes believes Paar was the only one of the three major *Tonight* hosts who had an impact as an interviewer of significant figures, including the heavily armed Fidel Castro, days after he emerged victorious over Batista in Cuba. In Keyes's view—Keyes is now a highly regarded television producer on the West Coast—such segments did not detract from but rather added to Paar's appeal.

There was the risk, of course, that Jack would fall into the trap that helped undermine Steve Allen as a funnyman in his post-*Tonight!* television career—boring viewers with heavyweight ideas in the wee hours. Midnight America was ready to laugh, not think. Too much politics and viewers might roll over and fall asleep.

Jack was sensitive to that danger, and thus he was to set off serious segments with counterpoint from such permanent panel zanies as Dody Goodman, Elsa Maxwell, Hermione Gingold, Genevieve, Zsa Zsa Gabor, and Cliff Arquette. It was Jack's panel that wore the funny hats and said appropriately silly things—Cliff as Charley Weaver, Genevieve as the Parisian with a delightful mismastery of English, and Dody Goodman as, well, Dody Goodman.

Dody had danced in *Call Me Madam, Wonderful Town,* and *High Button Shoes.* She was also in a Broadway turkey called *My Darling Aida* in which she played a cooch dancer sporting a large black diamond in her navel.

When Dody first met Jack it was at an audition in his office—the day after he opened on *Tonight.* He thought her more a bird-brained housewife than a ballerina. He recalls, "To answer a simple yes or no, she would twist her mouth into a knot, scratch the end of her nose, and open her large blue eyes to the size of fried eggs. She began to tell me a long rambling story about a Cary Grant movie she and her mother had seen in her hometown of Columbus, Ohio. The story had no perceptible point, but her Midwest twang and hesitant, naive manner were highly amusing in a baffling sort of way.

" 'Look, honey,' I finally interrupted. 'Just answer me one question. Are you for real? Or are you putting it on?'

"She twisted her mouth, patted the top of her pink hair, widened her eyes, and said, 'A little.' "

Jack put Dody on the show the next evening, and she so beguiled viewers that Paar made her a regular. He soon noticed that Dody never seemed to try to be funny. "She just stumbled into it. The things she said really weren't particularly funny, but as she talked, fidgeting, fluttering her hands, and smiling happily, she achieved a wackily endearing quality."

Dody was, in short, the kind of improbable regular "guest" that made the Paar show unique in television. She was not a star or an author plugging a picture or a book or one of the "beautiful people" with that plastic sort of sex appeal for which Hollywood is notorious. Real or not, Dody was far more genuine than most of the regulars on talk shows—then or since.

Like other naturally funny people, Dody came at things from an oblique angle, and her unexpected remarks were to nudge funny bones from coast to coast. Jack had a habit of saying, "Give them enough rope. . ." To that line one evening, Dody suddenly quipped, "And I'll skip." Once, about a week after New Year's, Dody said goodnight thusly: "Goodnight, and a Merry Christmas to all. I know it's too late to say that, but I just thought of it." Dody was proud of her little dog, and once Jack asked her on the show what breed it was. "He's a little m-u-t-t. I spelled it in case he's watching."

Sometimes things that happened to Dody in real life were so odd that it was easy to believe she never made a conscious effort to be funny. While shopping at Macy's she found a wallet on the floor, which she promptly turned over to the floorwalker. Dody told Jack, "He opened the wallet to see who it belonged to. It was mine."

On another occasion just before both were to go on, Dody said to Paar, "There's something on your eyelash." Jack couldn't see anything but dutifully batted his eyelashes. "You still didn't get it," she said, brushing at Jack's left eye. Again, Jack couldn't see anything amiss. "Oh, mercy," she finally said, touching her forehead, "it's on *my* eyelash!"

Dody seems to have inherited some of her zaniness from

her mother. Before Columbus viewers could pick up the Paar show on their sets, Dody's mother used to ride to Cincinnati to watch the show on TV there. But she became so tired by the ride that she fell asleep and made the round trip without disembarking. Once Paar was at Dody's mother's place at a party during his run on *Tonight*. Dody's mother danced with various young men and, Paar insists, the mother finally whispered proudly to one, "I'm Dody's mother!"

"I know," said the young man, "I'm her brother," a line that sounds suspiciously like something Paar's bizarre writer, Jack Douglas, might have penned.

Paar did have a way of putting silly words into the mouths of his panelists when it suited his comic purposes. For example, Elsa Maxwell, the society news columnist and partygiver, was a mound of fat who rather resembled a small hippo. She is remembered for her response when Jack said, "Your stockings are wrinkled, dear. . . . But then you're not wearing any," a line for which Elsa got credit in the columns.

Elsa was certainly lively in her own right. She was given to making unflattering statements about people America had taken to its heart—like Princess Grace and Prince Rainier of Monaco, of whom she said, "But they're such bores!"

Elsa was born in Keokuk, Iowa, never finished grammar school, and, among other things, was a bit player with a starving Shakespeare troupe and played piano in a New York nickelodeon. She also wrote songs and, in another phase of a colorful career, was press agent for Monte Carlo. She became a famous partygiver at age thirty-five. Comfortably accepting her formidable girth, she called herself "the world's oldest and fattest mannequin." Paar played into this image. Once when Jack noticed she had some notes tucked away in her imposing bosom, he snatched at her neckline to show the concealed notes to the audience. Elsa reared back, and her bosom gave off tremors. "Be careful," Jack warned, "you might start an avalanche!"

Elsa may have been a bit nervous about making outrageous remarks about famous people. Genevieve remembers that she saw Elsa drinking from a small medicine bottle one evening before doing the show and asked if Elsa was ill. Said Elsa, "That's Scotch, dear."

Elsa feuded with fellow panelist Hermione Gingold, an English actress whose accent was so pronounced she recalls the answer of a stuffy English clubman to the question "Are you British?" "Am I British? If I were any more British I shouldn't be able to speak at all!"

At the peak of the feud between Elsa and Hermione, Jack asked Hermione what she thought of the many-chinned Elsa. "Just another pretty face," said Hermione gaily to what may have been the biggest laugh she ever got on *Tonight*.

Like Dody, Hermione came from an unusual family. She told Jack, "Rudyard Kipling was a constant visitor to my grandmother's house in London. He not only read her several of his splendid poems but he also gave her an extremely jolly Indian scarf with which she afterwards hanged herself."

Genevieve, the so-called Pixie from Paris, was to appear as a singer one summer night in 1957. But she was so adept at fracturing English that "Zhack" let her read commercials and the "bazeball" scores, during which she referred to errors as *faux pas* and boo-boos.

But it was Cliff Arquette as Charley Weaver who topped them all. (Jack likes to say that he could top Cliff as Cliff but not as Charley Weaver.) Cliff was an early radio performer in Chicago, the birthplace of many a fine broadcast talent. One night on the show, Jack was reminiscing with Fran Allison (of *Kukla, Fran and Ollie*) about those long-gone days and Jack mused, "I wonder whatever became of Cliff Arquette."

Cliff happened to be sitting in his San Fernando Valley, California, home watching the show and was so surprised he nearly dropped his Scotch. Cliff had retired after thirty-four busy but mostly anonymous years in show business—he was, for example, the voice of Doc in *Snow White and the Seven Dwarfs*. Next day, he sent Paar a wire saying, "Have old man suit. Will travel."

Paar explains that a few nights later Cliff as Charley Weaver came "slouching out on our stage, crumpled hat rolled up in front, his stomach lopping over his drooping pants, glassless spectacles perched on his nose. He fished a piece of paper from his pocket and announced in exuberant bucolic accents: "Hiya there, Johnny! I've got a letter from Mama."

Cliff was playing a character the versatile actor-artist had originally drawn as an unsuccessful cartoon. Charley Weaver was a wily but endearing old codger from Mt. Idy, an imaginary community of equally imaginary people like Elsie Krack, Grandma Ogg, Wallace Swine, and Ludlow Bean.

Charley, like Fred Allen, had a wonderful way with word pictures, which he used to convulse *Tonight* audiences. Charley once recalled meeting a man who had nine broken bones, two black eyes, and fourteen contusions: "He took a full swing at a golf ball in a tile bathroom." He also drew a neat word portrait of Grandpa Ogg, who drove into town from his farm in his new Rolls-Royce limousine. "The reason he bought a Rolls-Royce," he explained, "is because of the partition between the driver and the rear seat. He likes that, it keeps the sheep from licking the back of his neck."

One night on the show Paar and Cliff as Charley were talking about husbands paying little romantic attentions to their wives, like suddenly kissing them or hugging them by surprise.

Jack asked the panel, "Did you ever go up behind your wife when she's working at the kitchen sink and surprise her with a little hug or a tickle from behind?"

"I did that once," Charley said innocently. "Don't ever do it when she's cleaning a turkey."

Again, like the others, Cliff was not so much a rehearsed comedian as a naturally funny man. He once told Paar off the air that an elevator broke down in his hotel when he was hurrying to catch a plane. "I had to run down twelve flights of circular stairs. . . . I was running so fast in circles I nearly screwed myself into the basement."

Obviously, elevators fascinated Cliff. Paar and Cliff once entered an elevator together and Cliff quipped to the operator, "Four, if it's not out of your way."

It was as Charley telling about Mt. Idy that Arquette endeared himself to *Tonight* audiences. Paar asked about juvenile delinquency there and Charley said, "We put on a ballet for the kiddies at Snyder's Swamp. The boys dress as kumquats and the girls are draped in creeping nussman. In the finale, they all circle the swamp and then dance into it. Bottom's all quicksand. Have to replace the whole cast every year—but we don't have any delinquency problems."

The interesting thing about Jack's panelists was that they were talkers—and not always known entertainers. It was Jack's talent for discovering such people and recognizing their worth as engaging people that helped make the show a success. Zsa Zsa Gabor might be regarded as an exception, for the Hungarian beauty was an actress and was much married to famous men, including the late actor George Sanders. Zsa Zsa got her start in television by accident when she was invited to be on a television program that dispensed advice to viewers. A woman wrote in asking what a wife could do about a husband who was running around with other women. "Zhoot him in the laig," said Zsa Zsa. She was also asked this question: "My fiancé gave me a car, a mink coat, and a stove. Is it proper to accept these gifts?" Growled Zsa Zsa, "Uff gorse not. . . . Zend back the stove."

Jack Douglas, Paar's most offbeat writer, was certainly not a known entertainer. He was a craggy-looking man— sort of a modern-day Ichabod Crane with an imagination

to match his odd appearance. He wrote twenty minutes or
so of scripted material for each show, and Paar kept looking
at and thinking about Douglas as a possible panelist. Eventually Jack decided to put Douglas on the show in person
from time to time. Douglas would speak of Joe's Bar and
Grill and Bar—a redundancy since taken up by Charley O's
Bar and Grill and Bar in Rockefeller Plaza. Douglas's
humor was weirdly amusing—as were the titles of his
books, *Never Trust a Naked Bus Driver* and *My Brother Was an
Only Child.* In the latter, he wrote the classic letter home
from summer camp, a takeoff from a sometime feature on
Tonight. It went:

> Dere Mom and Dead: One of the kidds feel in the
> lak and drown today Herbie weas bite be a rottle snake
> today We had aple pie today we dint have watter sking
> today because mister monhan brok both of one of his
> leggs
> so did melvin i hop i like the rist wach you bring me
> if you cum up to see me soon my coonseler is a fagg
> can i be one ? i dont thimk it cost enything xtra
> yore sun Louis

When Jack originally interviewed Douglas as a potential
writer for the show, he asked for a little background. Douglas volunteered that he had been a part-time smoking in-
structor in a boy's camp and said that he had been
drummed out of the Boy Brownies for refusing to salute
Gaylord Hauser, the health-food enthusiast. Jack promptly
hired Douglas.

When Jack first met Douglas he was living in a rustic but
nonetheless exclusive suburb of Hollywood where he had
a hog barn that contained an elaborate electric-train set.
Jack asked why he had electric trains in the hog barn and
Douglas said, "I just like electric trains better than hogs."
Logical. And, as they say in the fashion boutiques, very Jack
Douglas.

On that first visit, Douglas asked Paar if he would like to swim in the pool. The pool was filled with floating lumber and orange crates. Paar recalls that Douglas methodically threw the debris out of the pool so that they could swim. When they were finished he carefully threw it all back in. "If a squirrel or a rabbit should fall in," animal lover Jack Douglas told Paar, "they deserve a fighting chance, don't they?"

Both Paar and Douglas have a passion for privacy, and at Douglas's place, this was made emphatically clear by wacky signs along the driveway. The first sign said, "Danger—mad dogs." The second one said, "Bridge out—slow to 6o." And the third one, just this side of the house, said, "Have you telephoned these people?"

Douglas's fresh, macabre sense of humor offered many high spots on *Tonight*. Says Paar, "He delighted in jokes about his girl who took a wrong turn going to the ladies' room at the Radio City Music Hall and was kicked to death by the Rockettes, and funerals so cheap that the corpse had to ride up front with the driver."

Jack Paar's humor could be morbid too. Once while he was riding in his Rolls-Royce with a friend at the wheel, the formal funeral of Winston Churchill was being broadcast from abroad. The two men rode silently to the impressive sound of royal trumpeters. Finally, Jack said, "When I go, they'll probably get the Harmonica Rascals." On another occasion he was musing about death and said, "When the grim reaper comes for me I'm going to hold onto the arms of the davenport."

When Jack got mad at Douglas and fired him for putting too much effort into his books and not enough into the show, he judiciously hired three writers to replace him. Douglas then opened in a nightclub act. One evening thereafter a button popped off his shirt, and he was Douglas to a fare-thee-well in what followed. He got down on the floor and was crawling around looking for it. "I don't know what I'd do if I found it," he said. "I'm single and I have no one to sew it on for me. I do have a Filipino houseboy, but he's bleary-eyed by the time he arrives in the morning. He drives to work. From Manila."

One of the critical problems on *The Tonight Show* has been to make sure the guests give solid performances. The pay, in Paar's day $320, was minimal—far less than most performers command no matter what they are doing—and some tend to dog it. Most do rise to the occasion, realizing that to score on *Tonight* can do wonders for a career—even a successful one.

Jack was an expert at coaxing good work out of some performers, but was less successful with others. Jonathan Winters, who could be devastatingly funny or simply embarrassing, was one of Jack's biggest successes. Paar would introduce Winters by saying that if Winters were half as funny on camera as he was backstage where he convulsed the crew, he would be terrific. Winters ordinarily rose to the challenge.

Dick Cavett has commented on Paar's customarily effusive introductions and offers a make-believe but thoroughly typical intro for Winters: "He might say . . . 'Johnny Winters is pound for pound the funniest man on earth,' and add that before the show Winters was making the stagehands laugh harder than anyone in history.

"The amateur Freudians would say that what Jack is doing here is saying, 'This guy is capable of being great, he has been great all over the place in the past, and if he isn't tonight he must have something against me because eyewitnesses can testify that he can be if he wants to be.' "

Paar's feeling is that this kind of intro caused Winters to outdo himself. So did other Paar devices. When Winters was on, Jack would sometimes top him with a funny line ("He resents it when you score," explains Paar) and thus force Winters to try harder still.

Jack Paar, Talent Scout

While well-known performers were frequent guests, Jack was especially interested in "pure finds"—people who had never been on TV before—and he sometimes gave them even more impressive introductions than the stars.

Tom O'Malley guessed that Paar would warm to seventeen-year-old Trish Dwelley. "I heard her and she sounded pure. Jack didn't have a good ear for singers. He liked simple, straightforward vocalists. She was simple and pure. She sang 'Tammy' with Jose Melis.

"When she finished we looked around and tears were rolling down Jack's cheeks. 'Honey, don't change, wear what you are wearing now,' he said. 'We'll use a black background and Jose at the piano. Tonight, Trish will sing "Tammy." '

"We were flabbergasted. Twelve o'clock came and, typically for this little girl who had never been on TV, Paar gave her this enormous buildup. The camera went to center stage with Jose, and Trish was in sweater and skirt. She started to sing. The audience was transfixed, and we were too. Then Paar started to cry. He brought her over and said we would contract her and she would be on three times a week—all sorts of promises on the air.

"Actually, Trish Dwelley couldn't sing very well. Paar had mesmerized us all. She came on a few more times and she sang off key. Then the New York *Post* said that she had been part of a backup group for Perry Como."

Thus, she wasn't, as it turned out, a pure "find" after all. She has since faded into obscurity. But the wondrous thing in Tom O'Malley's view was that Paar had a quality of being able to sell America on so modest a talent—at least for a time.

But Jack couldn't sell America a young, bright improvisational comedy team known as Nichols and May. The two had impressed O'Malley and the others with

their set pieces and improvisations. O'Malley went to
Jack. "I said, 'This may be the greatest comedy team of
all time. They are brilliant.' Paar made the mistake of
letting them do just improvisations—no set pieces, and
with that crummy Hudson Theatre audience. The audience didn't come up with good things and Nichols and
May bombed.

"I was sitting in the control room and Jack rushed in.
'Oh, my God, pal, they were awful. That intro you wrote for
me was so glowing!' He was embarrassed not for them but
for himself. Jonathan Winters was on the panel. Jack turned
to Johnny and said, 'Show them you can ad-lib. I'll play the
passenger and you be the pilot.'

"Meanwhile Mike Nichols was grim in the dressing room,
and Elaine May, a tough lady, was almost in tears. I said to
them that we would bring them back. But Jack later said,
'Never. Don't ever bring up their names again.'

"So they went on to other big network shows—Perry
Como and Steve Allen on his Sunday-night prime-time
show. They were in the big money and very popular.

"Four months later, Mike and Elaine got a big spread in
Life. I devilishly put the magazine on Paar's desk, opened
at the spread story. Jack read it and said, 'Would Mike and
Elaine come and do the show?' I said, 'Oh, they are way out
of our price range now. They're making $5,000.' We were
paying $320. And he said, 'You mean, even though I gave
them their first break?'

"The irony is that we went on to a prime-time show and
they appeared many times and he frequently alluded to
their having had their first break on his show."

But as Dick Cavett has indicated, there was nothing dis-
honest about this sort of thing with Jack. He has a "quality
of blanking out unpleasant things [and this] can be a bless-
ing. . . . If Jack has been accused of lying, I think it is
because of this quality," says Cavett, who believes Paar
could pass a lie-detector test in such cases.

There was, as all this suggests, a spontaneous quality to Jack Paar's *Tonight* even in guest appearances. As *Time* commented: "Always, the high points were provided by the talkers—guided or goaded, driven or drawn out by Jack."

Jack Paar: Agent Provocateur

Even with more serious guests Jack had an amazing faculty for getting important people embroiled in fascinating conversational wars, and, in Jack's unique style, funny ones. Once Jack scheduled the monumentally unfunny Adolphe Menjou, an actor with an imperious manner who took inordinate pride in his conservative clothes and was outspokenly critical of anyone who did not dress as he did. Jack's old pal Hy Averbach had made a private crack to Paar about Menjou that caused Paar, hoping for a good dialogue, to put Averbach on the show with Menjou.

Menjou was wearing a weighty double-breasted glen-plaid suit and heavy foulard tie; his hair was slicked down and his mustache waxed as always. Agent provocateur Paar asked Menjou what he thought of the way Averback was dressed. Averbach was wearing a well-tailored suit with side vents. Menjou unhesitatingly picked it apart, saying it was "all wrong." As for the side vents, sniffed Menjou, "Those are for horseback riding!"

At that point, Paar turned to Averbach and said, "Tell him what you said." Averbach, as Cavett has so sagely remarked, was like the rest of the world's civilized people and declined to answer. Averbach did not have Paar's audacity. Paar then impishly made reference to one of America's most overdone automobiles, a squarish limousine with huge headlights balanced on its fenders, saying, "Averbach says you look like a Pierce-Arrow."

There was a tremendous laugh; the line was later quoted in the columns and a fuming Adolphe Menjou actually threatened to sue Averbach. Says Averbach, "Menjou was an irascible old asshole," and Jack had revealed that as only Jack could.

Time magazine spoke of Jack Paar's success in a cover story about him little more than a year after he got the show and was already a tremendous success. Jack states that that August 18, 1958, issue had the biggest circulation of any issue of *Time* to that point.

Time called Paar one of a "whole new class of TV-age entertainers—the just talkers. But his appeal has little in common with Steve Allen's brash sidewalk zaniness or Arthur Godfrey's somnolent saloon drone. When Paar first appears on the screen, there is an odd hesitant hitch to his stride. For a split self-effacing second he is a late arrival, worried that he has blundered into the wrong party. His shy smile—he has developed one of the shyest smiles in the business—seems to ask a question: 'Is this applause for me?'

"Then he remembers: he is really the host. Almost diffidently he pulls up a chair. What Paar calls his 'cute little Presbyterian face' beams puckishly. With his voice wavering between a whisper and a sigh, he begins to engage his guests in quiet conversation."

Like others, *Time* noted that Paar let himself be "topped" by visiting jokesters and that he was "all the world's straight man.

"And yet, Paar can hit. A caustic remark, a misconstrued question, a real or fancied attack in or out of the studio can provoke stinging repartee."

Joe Culligan, who organized the initial advertising sales campaign for *Tonight,* remembers that Jack admired the big cats he loved to make movies of and that he was very much like them—cagey, suspicious, and ready to pounce on an interloper.

Once, after the redoubtable radio gossip Walter Winchell attacked Paar for a misstatement by Elsa Maxwell, Jack swung his ax with abandon, guessing on television that Winchell's "high, hysterical voice" results from his "too tight underwear."

Paar, who never forgets a slighting remark, had previously demanded a correction after Winchell had reported in his column, "The comic Jack Paars have their pals depressed. She's the chawklit heiress." Paar, whose marriage to Miriam is as solid as the Bible, deeply resented the line, which he said caused great distress to himself, Miriam, and daughter Randy. Jack didn't know Winchell, so he asked a friend who did to ask for a correction.

Jack recalls, "This self-appointed general manager of the world sent back word that he could not retract the item but that the source which gave him the wrong information would be 'dead with him.'" Jack got no consolation from that and thus his cold war with Winchell became a hot one. He has called Winchell and another "gossipmonger," Lee Mortimer, who like Winchell is now dead, "angry old men of the keyhole."

But the feuds and the many pressures built over the years. *TV Guide* carried an untrue item about something Jack Paar supposedly said to Dody Goodman's agent during the period when Jack had stopped using Dody as a regular panelist on the show. Jack asked for a retraction, and when none was forthcoming, Jack began berating the magazine's owner, Walter Annenberg, on *Tonight.* He told stories about the seedy beginnings of Mr. Annenberg's father, stories that the former ambassador to the Court of St. James's has striven mightily to suppress. (Annenberg reportedly purchased every copy he could find of an unflattering biography written by Gaeton Fonzi of *Philadelphia* magazine, called *Annenberg: A Biography of Power.* A few copies are still in private hands; a prominent Wall Streeter lent me his copy.)

As Paar's attacks continued, NBC's Robert Sarnoff, who knew Annenberg and respected his power in television, told Paar he was "thin-skinned" and asked him to lay off. Paar refused.

Paar recalls that once he featured *Herald Tribune* television columnist John Crosby as a guest. Crosby had written derogatory articles about NBC's programing, saying that NBC had handed the schedule to Sonny Werblin, then president of MCA, at the time the biggest television packaging agency, and said, "Here, you fill it." Thus, says Paar, he was asked by NBC's president, Robert Kintner and Sarnoff to cancel Crosby. When Paar refused and used the critic over their strenuous objection, Crosby's face mysteriously was washed out electronically. Whether that was a result of an actual mechanical problem, the work of a brown-nosing Sarnoff underling, or reflected an order from higher up is unknown.

(Just recently, though, the electronic gremlins were at work again at NBC. Betty Furness was on *The Today Show* telling of a Consumers Union report on videotape recorders that, as luck would have it, ranked RCA's SelectaVision in the highest category along with a similar set offered directly by the Japanese manufacturer who made the RCA set. At this point, the words "RCA SelectaVision" were flashed on the screen along with the name of the similar set. Then Miss Furness mentioned Consumers Union's second choices, which included the pioneering Sony Betamax and the similar machine Sony made for RCA's archrival, Zenith. The names of these two machines then appeared on the screen—upside down.)

Paar persisted in his attacks on Annenberg. Finally, NBC asked Jack what he wanted to desist and he said a "full retraction," and he was promised he would get it. Then, while *Tonight* was visiting the West Coast and emanating

from there, NBC called to say that Annenberg had retracted and was Paar pleased? Jack looked at a California
copy of *TV Guide* on page 12 as directed and found nothing.
It turned out that *TV Guide* had retracted—but only in its
New York edition. The magazine's editors apparently
hadn't kept Paar's travel plans in mind. "They figured I
would never know," remarks Paar.

He has never forgotten the episode. In mid-1979, a producer pleaded with Jack to participate in a television special
to be called *TV Guide—the First 25 Years.* The producer,
Robert Precht, wrote Paar, "No coverage of television is
possible without Jack Paar. You are one of only a few who
truly made a major impact on the medium. I could go on,
but the bottom line is that we need to hear from you."

Jack wrote back that he had no wish to be on any TV
program ever again and certainly not one sponsored by *TV
Guide.* "I said, 'If I was so important, or contributed so
much, why didn't *TV Guide* say something to that effect
when I was alive [sic]?' "

In telling the author about *TV Guide*'s refusal to square
things, Jack Paar related a story about a London critic who
had maligned John Osborne's early works many times.
Then Osborne wrote *Look Back in Anger.* It was a smash hit.
Osborne went to the men's room and locked eyes with the
previously unconvinced critic, who was at the next urinal.
The critic said he was very sorry about what he had said and
that Osborne was indeed a genius. As Osborne prepared to
exit from the rest room, he said, "Next time malign me in
the men's room and apologize in public."

Jack Walks at Midnight

In the pristine years of television in the late 1950s when
Jack Paar was *Tonight* host, there were a few who believed
he was a bit too blue. Of course, a pass at the notes in Elsa
Maxwell's bosom could hardly be regarded as salacious
anywhere this side of a nunnery, but Jack did have his little

stories with mildly risqué overtones, as who doesn't? Nevertheless, Paar felt he was taking a bum rap when criticized on this ground. He was quite sensitive on the point.

No wonder, then, that he was outraged in February 1960 when NBC snipped a videotaped joke about a W.C. hours before his show aired. It was, as Jack would charge in his autobiography, *I Kid You Not*, damaging to his reputation, since the omission suggested that he had told a "smutty" story without submitting the evidence to the jury. He wrote: "I never approved of off-color stories, on or off the air. On the show, I have always tried to have our lady guests avoid low-cut gowns and wiggling behinds. I have frequently asked comedians to drop jokes which I considered risqué from their routines when they appeared on the program."

Jack had read the W.C. story during the taped show for February 10. He said that it had been given to him by a friend who had gotten it from his thirteen-year-old niece, whose teacher had read it to her junior high school class, then passed out copies to all the students. Not only did NBC clip the story out of the taped show, it refused Jack's request to show the censored portion of the tape the next night—to, as Jack argued, "let the viewers decide."

By today's television standards, certainly, the story—an ancient one, as Jack pointed out—would be regarded as weak tea, scatologically speaking. It went like this.

An English lady, while visiting Switzerland, was looking for a room, and she asked the schoolmaster if he could recommend any to her. He took her to see several rooms, and when everything was settled, the lady returned to her home to make final preparations to move. When she arrived home, the thought suddenly occurred to her that she had not seen a W.C. (water closet) around the place. So she immediately wrote a note to the schoolmaster asking him if there was a W.C. around. The schoolmaster was a very poor student of English, so he asked the parish priest if he could help in the matter. Together they tried to discover the meaning of the letters W.C., and the only solution they could find was Wayside Chapel. The schoolmaster then wrote the English lady the following note:

Dear Madam:

I take great pleasure in informing you that the W.C. is situated nine miles from the house you occupy, in the center of a beautiful grove of pine trees surrounded by lovely grounds. It is capable of holding 229 people and it is open on Sunday and Thursday only. As there are a great number of people and they are expected during the summer months, I would suggest that you come early, although there is plenty of standing room as a rule.

You will no doubt be glad to hear that a good number of people bring their lunch and make a day of it, while others who can afford to go by car and arrive just in time. I would especially recommend that your ladyship go on Thursday when there is a musical accompaniment.

It may interest you to know that my daughter was married in the W.C. and it was there that she met her husband. I can remember the rush there was for seats. There were ten people to a seat usually occupied by one. It was wonderful to see the expressions on their faces.

The newest attraction is a bell donated by a wealthy resident of the district. It rings every time a person enters. A bazaar is to be held to provide plush seats for all the people, since they feel it is a long-felt need. My wife is rather delicate, so she can't attend regularly.

I shall be delighted to reserve the best seat for you if you wish, where you will be seen by all. For the children, there is a special time and place so that they will not disturb the elders. Hoping to have been of some service to you, I remain

Sincerely,
The Schoolmaster

Jack was not prepared to take NBC's censorship without a protest. At the office the next day he wore a bemused expression. He almost gave himself away to Mitzi (Matravers) Moulds, who sensed in Jack's demeanor and a certain glance that Jack had plans—"Jack had a way of letting you know something was up."

When Jack went on that night, he was ready to spring his surprise. He explains, "It was nearly midnight. In less than an hour it would be the birthday of Abraham Lincoln—the man who freed the slaves. So I emancipated myself from the program. I explained to the audience what had happened and told them how deeply I felt about the matter. Then I walked out of the studio and turned the program back to the censors. Having been fired a number of times by networks, I finally fired a network."

There was an immediate and profound uproar. No star of Jack's magnitude had ever exited to a comparable reaction in the history of broadcasting. That next day, Jack Paar was headline copy all over the nation. He was gratified by the response—much of it favorable—and particularly pleased by a column written by the respected *New York Times* TV critic Jack Gould. It said in part:

"Mr. Paar is not the traditional trouper; he is a creation of television. If he began as a light humorist, his forte on his own show has been an outspokenness that has not alienated viewers weary of nice nellyism and self-appointed sacred cows who can dish out criticism but cannot take it.

"In this regard let Mr. Paar be champion, other faults notwithstanding. . . . During his farewell . . . he castigated the type of yellow journalism that pontificates on morality and then over its front pages splashes lurid accounts of sexual goings-on brought out in a murder trial.

"The Fourth Estate would be well advised to take heed and, in this instance, not dismiss Mr. Paar as a buffoon with inadequate references; he is echoing a point of view widely held by responsible and sensible people."

Whatever else had happened, Jack had found a powerful

ally in his attacks on the likes of Walter Winchell and Lee Mortimer.

Hugh Downs, caught by surprise as was the rest of the cast and crew, continued the show, of which only Jack's opening "monologue" had been completed. Comedian Orson Bean, a guest, felt obliged to defend Paar's stand. Like the others, Bean was in shock. For the rest of the evening it was difficult to talk about anything else.

The press jumped into the situation immediately, and in the madness that followed that night, Mitzi Moulds got telephone calls at her apartment "from all over the world."

At the time of Jack Paar's exit from *Tonight* a large motel complex was being erected in Florida by the wealthy Mackle brothers—two men with considerable holdings on the state's west coast.

The Mackle family was to step reluctantly into the publicity glare later when Barbara Mackle, a daughter of one brother, was kidnapped by a psychopath, Gary Steven Krist, who buried her alive in a box connected to the surface with breathing and feeding apparatus. She was released physically unharmed several days later. The world will not be denied a good story; later, there would be a book and a movie about the bizarre crime and its strangely fascinating perpetrator.

In any case, Jack and one of the Mackle brothers were friends. And it came to pass that Jack and Miriam arranged to occupy a room in the half-finished complex, though there were few amenities and no telephone. Jack and Miriam stayed in the barren motel for weeks. Substitute hosts continued the show during Jack's absence.

Somehow NBC learned of Jack's hideaway. Miriam Paar, with her sharp instinct for Jack's best interests, would have been the logical person to call NBC head, Robert Kintner. Kintner, who is now retired in Washington, does not remember how he got in touch with Paar. Jack didn't call him, he said, and Kintner does not remember speaking with Mrs. Paar. But in any event Kintner, once informed of Paar's whereabouts, hastened down to see him.

It wasn't easy, but Kintner finally persuaded Jack to come back. But first, it was agreed that Jack would take a vacation in Hong Kong to simmer down and get used to the idea of moving away from his hard-line position. Says Mitzi, "He really hadn't intended to come back."

Jack returned to the show on March 7, 1960, and he continued as host of *Tonight* until the spring of 1962. (Thereafter, he shifted, à la Steve Allen, to a Friday-night prime-time show in the fall of 1963.)

Jack took pains to see that the show was executed on a high plane and once complained when Paul Keyes complimented him on one of his funniest shows ever, "Yeah, pal, but it had no literary quality." Not unexpectedly, then, the censorship issue was no laughing matter. Later, when in London with *The Tonight Show,* he was asked to appear on the BBC.

"I was in the green room and they fed me some drinks. I don't drink before the show."

Almost as soon as Jack went on, one of the interviewers asked, "Didn't you once flounce off your show?"

Startled by the unexpected question and the insulting way it was put, Jack said, "They only do that in the BBC and the Admiralty. I didn't flounce, I walked." He adds, "With that, I walked off and left them with twenty minutes to fill."

Vengeance Is Mine

From a legal point of view, some of Jack's *Tonight* stuff was potentially actionable. For Jack Paar wielded great power and rarely hesitated to use it. As Paar explains the network attitude toward success, "Once you are a smash hit, they are great to you. It's the eleventh commandment. You are right—on everything."

Imbued with infallibility by NBC, Jack occasionally got carried away. A friend says there were times during Paar's heyday on *Tonight* when Jack could sit in his office and have a sense of being the most important person in the world. It was a sobering fantasy. Since Jack was and is quite sane —"only a carrier of mental disease," as Hugh Downs used to jest—he quickly returned to reality.

Despite those occasional extremes of euphoria, Jack knew that while he was by no means an average individual, he was no superman either. On the one hand he would puff himself up—when Miriam once refilled the guests' sherry glasses at home and happened to overlook Jack, he demanded, "And what is the matter with the king of comedy?"—and on the other he would say in describing an experience, "I'm just Jack Paar, I am nothing." By turns the king and the humble man. Part of his game. He was, by virtue of the confluence of his carefully nurtured talent with the explosive growth of television, a man who rose to power rivaling that of potentates and kings. But unlike some who have climbed to the top of the Big Rock Candy Mountain of show business, Jack Paar did not become a megalomaniac.

Jack certainly used his power effectively and well in his dealings with NBC. A friend has said that Jack "knew after two nights on *Tonight* that he had something unusual going and became very powerful from that moment on. He had an instinct about how to push the network around." Thus he once refused to go on until raises for his staff that NBC was blocking were put through. NBC folded before Jack missed a single bar of the opening theme on *Tonight.*

He was somewhat less successful in dealing with his critics. Since there was a danger that Jack would go off half cocked on *Tonight* and be sued for more money than he could afford, his personal savior, Miriam Paar, sometimes entered the picture. Jack told the author that when he outlined some heavy plan involving an attack on, say, *The New York Times,* or some other important and powerful critic of the moment, Miriam sometimes went into action. She would call Jack's old pal, writer Sidney Carroll, who, Jack concedes, could talk him out of ill-advised action if anybody could. But Jack adds that even Sidney rarely succeeded.

Once, says Jack, Ed Sullivan publicly called Jack a son of a bitch. "I knew he had been drinking, but he said it and had to pay for it." Sidney argued in vain that Jack oughtn't to answer the insult on the air, but, says Jack, "I did it anyway." And, as usual, he got away with it.

Anyone who has wielded great power knows that it is possible to turn it against one's enemies in subtle ways—and even against one's peers who may be friends but who are nevertheless temporarily out of favor.

Once Bob Hope asked Paar to go on the Hope show in an exchange shot—without pay on either side. From Jack's point of view, this was no bargain. The minimum price for an appearance on Bob Hope was $7,500, and the maximum was $10,000. The price for an appearance on *Tonight* was still $320, and that sum was paid by NBC, which owned the show. Since Bob Hope would avoid paying his usual fee out of his own production company's pocket, he would be making out at Paar's expense.

"Hope sent me a script and I had to fly to the Coast and work all weekend," Paar says. Hope clearly felt that Paar should be eternally grateful that he had been invited to go on the show. Hope had played little tricks—he had secretly booked Steve Allen as well. Says Jack, "I have nothing against Steve, but we were never pals."

The author heard this story at Paar's home in Connecticut, and Paar mused a bit about Steve Allen, who is famous for publicizing his many talents. "He discovered penicillin, etc.," said Jack wryly, and he then added, "I like Steve Allen . . . but not as much as he does."

Jack Paar learned something else when he arrived in California. Bob had decided that Jack would wear a Little Lord Fauntleroy costume, down to short pants, lacy white blouse, and fussy hat. True to his image of himself as a performer in the first person singular, Jack refused. Paar didn't like the opening bit either.

"He wanted the show to begin, 'It's *The Bob Hope Show* and here's Bob,' and I was to walk out. I refused. He threw his arms around me and he said, 'If you do this, we'll go to my house and have roast beef.'"

Paar was dumbfounded that Hope would expect him to be excited about a roast-beef feed at Bob Hope's—a promise one must assume Hope found to be an effective bribe with others he wanted to manipulate. Paar finally agreed to do the "Here's Bob" walk-on, but "after three days' rehearsal it was so bad we had to cut it." Paar thought about this a moment, smiled, and added, "I never did have roast beef at Bob Hope's."

Now it was Hope's turn to deliver. Paar explains, "We wanted Hope, but he said he wouldn't come until he did a picture [he could plug] and then he said, 'I won't follow Paar with a monologue.' He wanted to sit and talk for a $320 show."

At that point, Paar called Hope's office and said, "You tell Bob Hope to send me $10,000. I don't want him on my show."

Later when Jack had a prime-time show on NBC, he, too, booked major talents, and at a hefty $7,500 a shot. Milton Berle was to be on, and he told Jack in advance, "I'm going to needle you." Jack thought this risky in view of the special relationship Jack had established with his audience. They were sympathetic and inclined to laugh with Paar—not at him. "I said, 'I don't care, but will it work?' He wouldn't listen."

Berle came out and needled Paar as promised, and the audience just looked at Paar and didn't laugh—though Paar concedes that he did. Paar had a special camera he used long before Carson did the show on which Paar alone would appear to react to comments by his guests, their discomfort or joy. Sometimes he would simply look askance, or he might roll his eyes in disbelief. In Milton's case, he laughed.

After Berle finished, he came into Paar's office in his robe, looking, says Paar, "like a boxer."

" 'I died,' Berle said. 'Are you going to sweeten it?' I said, 'We never add a laugh to the tape.'

"He pleaded, saying, 'Milton wasn't [that] bad.' I said I'd leave it to the producer. I knew he wouldn't make a move without me. [I'll] let the s.o.b. die—it's not a bad entertainment.

"The show was taped on Sunday for the following Friday night. Milton used every ruse he could think of. Finally, he called and said he would buy back the segment for $7,500. [But] we had nothing to put in there. I said no—because he had refused to listen to me."

That Sunday, Uncle Miltie "died" on Jack Paar's prime-time show. It wasn't a bad entertainment, says Paar, but Milton clearly disagreed.

Coming Down

I have a recurring dream. . . . I dream that I've been fired—and I wake up in a cold sweat.   —Jack Paar

Although the specific incident that caused that recurrent dream occurred when Jack was little more than twenty years old and was working for a Midwest radio station, he has never gotten over that experience. This despite his superstardom and fame on *Tonight*. The traumatic events occurred before the Army, and—this is important—before he had any money to fall back on, and before he met Miriam.

Even when things went wrong during his *Tonight* years, causing Jack to overreact, he did so in part as a result of the rejection he experienced so many years earlier when that first radio station cashiered him so abruptly.

Jack Paar still has that nightmare, though he is now retired, with enough money to do anything he likes. Not long ago, he contacted Britain's Cunard Line and asked what was the grandest way to travel on the *QE-2* luxury liner. The best accommodations, he was told, were to be found in the penthouse over the bridge. So he and Miriam hired that sumptuous stateroom, sailed to Europe in style, and had a marvelous time.

It was through the adroit management of his financial affairs, for which Miriam Paar can claim much credit, that

Pat Weaver, the inventor of *Tonight*.

Vaudeville's gift to television—*Broadway Open House* host Jerry Lester.

Dagmar, who took late-night television by storm.

Milton DeLugg, musical director of *Broadway Open House*.

Steve Allen with Jayne Meadows, his wife and constant companion.

The men-on-the-street (clockwise, from top right: Tom Poston, Louis Nye, Don Knotts) and their leader, Steve Allen (top left).

Vintage *Tonight* with Skitch Henderson, Gene Rayburn, Steve Allen, Eydie Gorme, and Steve Lawrence.

Ernie Kovacs—the original zany.

Jack Paar and his writer, the inscrutable Jack Douglas.

Jack and Miriam Paar.

Jack Paar with Pat Harrington, Jr., Zsa Zsa Gabor, Hugh Downs, and a mystery guest.

The characteristic Paar perch.

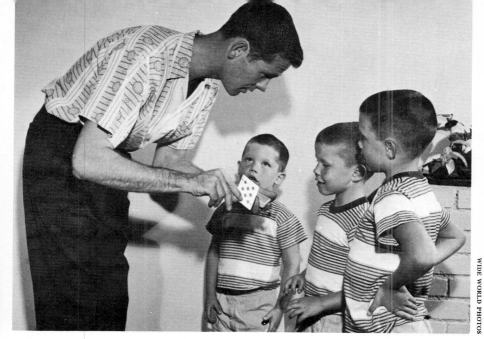

Johnny Carson, in 1957, beguiling his sons with a magic act.

Young Carson in action on *Who Do You Trust*.

The Rhinestone Cowboy.

Johnny Carson with Alice Cooper and friend.

Carson and NBC president Fred Silverman—in a light moment as Carson is named "Entertainer of the Year" 1979.

Carson and Burt Reynolds sharing an egg handshake.

Carson tells Racquel and the nation that he'll stick with the show.

Carson and "Heeeeeeeerrrre's Ed."

Doc Severinsen—veteran of Steve Allen's *Tonight* and still trumpeting.

Jack Paar wound up his career so well-off and contented. But it did not happen before he had an experience that once again called up those early feelings of failure.

He could have avoided the experience altogether. For Jack did have money—had earned plenty of it prior to his last show on television. In his final days on *Tonight* he was receiving $4,000 a week—four times his initial pay. Then, during the years on his Friday-night prime-time show, he was his own boss at "Dolphin Enterprises," for which NBC initially paid him $100,000 per show for a thirty-five-show season in the early 1960s. After all expenses—the production costs, the writers' and musicians' salaries—Jack cleared about $25,000 a week for his corporate self. Later, NBC agreed to up the ante, so that Jack personally would net about $30,000 a week. That's over $1 million a year. Gene Sheppard, the radio monologist, used to allude to "monopoly money" in talking about such compensation. While Jack's pay was a far cry from the millions Carson appears to rake in annually, it was enough to allow Jack and Miriam to invest in lucrative deals along the way. Not the least of these was a television station that was to become an NBC affiliate in Portland Springs, Maine, before the Paars sold it for what some say was a $1 million profit. (The Paars, who are so generous with what they have, do not talk about what they have.)

As for that final disappointment in the early 1970s, it was a recap of Jack Paar's NBC show, this time on ABC. For once, Jack badly miscalculated. He could hardly have had less going for him on a network show. Far from being the leading factor in the business it is today, ABC was by far the weakest in a broadcast world that television writer Les Brown used to say amounted to a two-and-a-half-network economy. ABC got the advertising leftovers while CBS and NBC sliced the whole pie more or less down the middle. ABC fared that poorly in part because its programing was weak and in part because it had far fewer stations than either NBC or CBS. In its frantic efforts to gain ground in prime time, ABC offered in the summer of 1969 the attractive personality Dick Cavett, three nights a week. Cavett won many awards, including an Emmy, for his urbane wit for ABC, and was thus persuaded to take over the network's late-night talk show that had been hosted with indifferent success by comedian Joey Bishop. Clever though Joey Bishop can be in ad-libbed repartee, he was not a capable interviewer. He was replaced by a man who is undoubtedly the most erudite interviewer at work today, a man who makes the guest feel as though Cavett is indeed a guest of the guest, as one observer has commented. ABC's late-night program was running five nights a week in ratings competition with high-flying Johnny Carson on NBC and tree-skimming Merv Griffin on CBS.

The critics, most of whom immersed themselves happily in Cavett's witty, intelligent conversation—a relief from TV's monosyllabic drone—liked the show a lot, and so did other influentials. Cavett promptly won a second Emmy with it. But hampered by ABC's limited network and the anti-intellectualism of the average television viewer, Cavett ran a poor third after Merv Griffin in the race for late-night TV ratings.

ABC was vexed, and finally, in December 1972, reacted in despair, cutting Cavett's nightly series back to one week in every four and only three days of that week. Two of the other weeks were devoted to varied programing, and in 1973 Jack Paar was persuaded to take the fourth week on the same three-day schedule and attempt a comeback. Jack says that at the time ABC wanted to drop Cavett, but that he refused to be a party to that and thus settled on the one-week-a-month slot with the understanding that his onetime writer would continue to do his one week a month.

But the setup defied television ratings logic. Viewers like to make a habit of the shows they favor, but this isn't easy if a show lacks a regular time slot. For ratings success, a show needs to go on at least weekly, and, in the case of

Tonight, as NBC has found when Carson is off, preferably every night.

Just how big a mistake ABC had made was soon obvious. Being on one week in four was confusing to everyone. Even Paar's writer, Jack Douglas, who wasn't living in New York, was balled up. He once called in bafflement, not having sent any material: "Jesus. They [just] told me you were on last week." Says Jack Paar, "My own mother didn't know when I was on."

Then there was the studio audience which Jack inherited from Cavett. The theater was near Lincoln Center in New York, but its particular street was a seedy one, drawing more than its share of drifters. Besides, Cavett's appeal was broad enough to draw hippies and other disaffected youths in that period following the Vietnam protest movement. The disaffected did not cotton to Jack Paar's Midwest Presbyterianism. He lacked the carry-over and reception he had had in the theater during the *Tonight Show* years. "I had a following—but not in the studio."

What's more, in a musical era dominated by hard rock, the pure, simple melodies Jack liked to feature baffled ears conditioned to roaring electric guitars. Says Jack, "I can't stand rock acts. I don't understand them. I can't introduce people in overalls. . . . Today comedy is shock, music is crap."

The results: humiliating. The once spectacularly successful Jack Paar did even less well in the ratings than the rapidly sinking Dick Cavett. (Cavett's current interviews on educational television are, again, highly regarded, and he is doing well with this, his natural audience.)

Jack Paar quickly recognized that he had failed to pull his old audience, and he thus announced in the fall of 1973 that he would not continue when his contract ran out in November of that year. Says a close friend, "He would have loved the ABC show to be successful, but it wasn't and it really hurt. He figured, 'Oh, my God, they don't love me anymore.' "

In a cruel and unfair article, Cyclops in the Sunday *New York Times* noted that he had written a number of nasty things about Paar in the past and went on to write his nastiest article yet. He said he hoped that Jack's emotional approach that sometimes led him to cry and had won him the nickname "Leaky Jack" was a thing of the past.

In a graphic demonstration of how Paar could move to excess those who didn't like him, Cyclops went on to draw an inappropriate analogy. He said that what had begun with Nixon's Checkers speech had been perfected by Paar, taught to television quiz cheat Charles Van Doren, "got a baroque embellishment" at the time of Chappaquiddick, and "achieved its apotheosis" during the Watergate hearings.

How a popular entertainer who was never seriously accused of either wrongdoing or faithlessness got mixed in with the disgrace of Richard Nixon, the lie-for-pay Charles Van Doren caper, and the deviousness of Edward Kennedy at Chappaquiddick was astonishing.

No wonder Jack Paar still has bad dreams.

Jack is sanguine about things now and steadfastly maintains that he has no desire to go back before the television cameras—though he is so entertaining in private company, so clever with an anecdote, that it is hard to believe he means it.

He does miss the adulation, obviously. In a rare appearance with Merv Griffin, he told a number of stories demonstrating how it feels to be an ex-star. In one he tells of a visit to an electronics shop near his home where the proprietor was trying unsuccessfully to record a message for his telephone-answering device. The proprietor accepted Jack's offer to help, and "One-shot Jack" quickly recorded the message in a single try. The proprietor was pleased and asked if he had been an announcer.

It is perhaps understandable that the proprietor didn't recognize the king of comedy of over fifteen years earlier, for there is little recorded history of Jack's years of controversy and triumph. There is no film or taped record of Jack's historic visit to Albert Schweitzer, whom Paar reached through the efforts of a bush pilot in a flight threatened by a poorly secured piano being carried as cargo over the trees of Africa. There is no record of Jack's celebrated visit to the Berlin Wall, where he tried to tell the story of the German people involved in that debacle, with the result that he inadvertently nearly caused an international incident. There is no record of his efforts to raise money for Castro's Tractors for Freedom, an effort on *The Tonight Show* criticized by Senator Barry Goldwater and Claire Booth Luce, who said it violated the Logan Act, which forbids interference with foreign policy. Mrs. Walter Reuther was involved on Jack's side, but few knew that Paar did the segment at the behest of John F. and Robert Kennedy, then the president and attorney general of the United States.

There is no record of Jack's many amusing stories, or those of his reborn celebrities like Hans Conried and Oscar Levant, or of the outrageous incidents so widely reported in the press.

There is no record of the extraordinary era on *Tonight* that was so uniquely Jack Paar, certainly the most human of hosts in the show's history, and the man who captivated millions at midnight for nearly five years.

Let it be noted that at one time there was a nearly complete record. Jack had films of all his shows, but like the filmed and taped records of the Steve Allen and Johnny Carson years, they are all gone now—except for the few films Jack gave to Margie, Alexander King's widow, and, among a few others he gave away, those he turned over to the Kennedys for their archives. Much of the record was dated, of course, and of little value except to historians of one of the most important media of communication in history.

Jack realized this. So, after storing the films for years, he finally decided he could do so no longer. He began tip-

ping his garbage man for picking up three films a visit.
Jack still had fans. One day, the garbage man stopped by
to say, "There was no sound on that last segment, Mr.
Paar." The garbage man was showing the films to his family
at home. His was perhaps the last family in America to see
Jack Paar in his vintage period.

Relative to Steve Allen and other big stars of yesteryear,
Jack Paar has experienced little difficulty in coming down.
He insists that he found it traumatic to do *The Merv Griffin
Show*—though he realizes he was a smash hit. He insists
he'd rather not entertain on the airwaves anymore and has
resigned from the union. Yet when he has company—surrounded by friends of a lifetime—he is Jack Paar, monolo-
gist, once again, ending the day as he did as a schoolboy,
given a period alone with his peers. Still electronically ori-
ented, he has rigged cameras high above his tennis courts
so that his guests can play, then watch themselves play.
Once in a while he will sojourn to that mecca of the successful, Palm Springs, and occasionally he'll travel to Europe.

But mostly he stays at home with Miriam. "Often I say to
myself, what a shame that I am so content. I don't need
anything."

Summing up his career, like the jesters of old, Jack Paar
jokes about death. Perhaps, he says, his tombstone ought
to read, "You've had your chance and now he's gone."

Jack and Miriam Share the Wealth

Sidney Carroll, the magazine writer who did the *Esquire*
piece that put Jack Paar on the civilian map after World War
II, has been a friend of the Paars ever since. He says Jack's
spending habits call to mind two guys who chanced to meet
after being out of touch for a number of years.

First guy: "What are you up to?"
Second guy: "I sell elephants. Can I sell you one?"
First: "Are you out of your mind?"

Second: "No, seriously—they make fine pets."
First: "My wife would kill me."
Second: "Give you two for the price of one."
First: "Now you're talking!"

Says Sidney, Jack is notorious for bringing home white elephants—two at a time. "Jack loves to shop, and he does it all the time. He comes home with the most incredible stuff, some of which drives Miriam up the wall. If he likes the looks of a thing, he'll buy it. He usually gets two because he gives away so much."

Sidney speaks from personal experience. For example, Jack once bought two fine emergency gas lamps. Sidney was the next friend Paar saw thereafter, and, predictably, Sidney became the owner of a fine emergency gas lamp.

Jack finds new mechanical devices so fascinating that he becomes transported. Once Jack's agent and manager was trying desperately to reach Jack at his Bronxville home concerning a hot major offer. Jack had just returned from a specialty hardware store that stocked so many unusual items Jack went to shop there practically every day. On this particular day, he had purchased a new sweeper that was supposed to be the greatest ever designed and he was using it in his new home on Pondfield Road in Bronxville to clean the sawdust off the floor. Jack's agent had telephoned again and again in an effort to get Jack to come to the telephone. Finally he relayed this message: "Tell him it is a matter of life or death and that I must know his answer immediately. He *has* to come to the telephone." At this, Jack exploded, saying, "No, I won't! Will you please tell Marty I'm vacuuming!"

Jack's sometimes whimsical attitude toward money may reflect the fact that he and Miriam have never been in serious financial straits. In the tough days when Jack was suffering career stall in California, Sidney, who believes Miriam was financially independent, says, "They would go to the cellar and bring up a bucket of money."

To Jack, money is a troublesome detail—an annoying

impediment to his spending plans. Once, during the period of *The Tonight Show* when Jack's name was on everybody's lips, he passed a Rolls-Royce agency in New York City. It is understandable that someone as impressed with superb mechanical equipment as Jack would see a car he wanted in the Rolls-Royce showroom. Characteristically, he wanted that particular Rolls—just as it stood on the showroom floor. The salesman, who must have just gotten off the boat, had never heard of Jack Paar. When Jack said he'd take the car, the salesman wanted a deposit. Jack had no money on him and was concerned that someone else might come in and buy *his* car. Then Jack remembered that he was carrying a check from his mother—her Christmas present to him. As a deposit, then, he endorsed the check and gave it to the salesman. The check was for the same amount his mother sent each year at Christmas for as long as she lived—$5.

Most of the checks that the postman dropped in the Paar mailbox during that period were for much larger amounts. Jack would go through the mail with such detachment that Miriam once found a check for thousands of dollars in the wastebasket where Jack had deposited the unopened envelope with the other "junk" mail. Needless to say, Miriam, who was as careful in running the household as she was dedicated to Jack, always rescued the junk mail for reappraisal.

Not that Jack is either careless or a spendthrift. He and Miriam expect value for their money and they plan their major expenditures as carefully as their Dutch ancestors—staying within a budget.

But that does not keep Jack from giving away items of considerable value that he has tired of, or from selling them at prices that enrich the buyer. Years ago, when Jack was living in Bronxville, one of his writers, Bob Carman, convinced him that he ought to have a stereo layout in his offices in the Westchester suburb. Jack said, "All right, pal, go to your favorite place and pick it up."

Carman did so, had the equipment installed, and states, "Jack liked it very much and became crazed." Jack began adding movie-making equipment, eventually assembling a complete 16-millimeter movie lab, bolting the equipment together, cutting and soldering every last wire himself.

Carman continues: "By the time I left Paar to go to *The Joey Bishop Show,* Jack had become an electronics genius. He had wired the stereo and movie equipment so that it would do every [audio and visual trick] you could think of, and with a skill that would have made a wizard envious."

Jack used the equipment for some time, employing it, for one thing, to edit movies of wild animals, but in time his interest flagged and he disposed of some of the equipment quite casually. For example, the basic stereo included a pair of magnificent turntables that, nevertheless, required more patience than Jack was prepared to lavish on them. Early in his electronics period, Jack called Bob Carman to his house. Carman had a teenage son and Jack said of the turntables, "Give them to the boy." Carman was to receive much more than that. "He laid a number of very expensive pieces of equipment on me and insisted that I not pay for them."

Mostly Jack's valuable castoffs went to friends, but sometimes he would sell to the first congenial person who came along. Sidney Carroll was an admirer of a beautiful station wagon Jack had some years back. Jack had ordered virtually all the options available for the car. One day, Sidney visited Jack and noticed that the car was gone. When Sidney asked about it, Jack said, "I wanted to get rid of it in a hurry, and so I took a couple of thousand for it." Says Carroll in exasperated recollection, "I could have killed him. I would love to have had that wonderful car."

Jack undoubtedly would have sold to Sidney had he been around, or, more characteristically, might even have given his friend the car had he known how much Carroll admired it.

Jack was extraordinarily generous for a man in a business

so uncertain that tomorrow's newspaper often tells of the demise of yesterday's smash hit. This sort of thing breeds stinginess, and thus Jack Paar's generosity was not only extraordinary, it was—and is—legendary. So was that of Miriam, who was just as giving as Jack.

Jack's generosity even extended to his career. The staff remembers wonderful gifts at Christmas, and lunches in between so lavish with wine that Jack would come back to the studio and ask, "What's wrong? Everyone seems to be going to sleep." Louis Nye remembers receiving a panic call from Jack once because Paar, in a mixup, appeared not to have enough guests for the show. But when Louis arrived, it appeared that there were too many guests—not too few. Jack was embarrassed and asked Louis, "Can you dance?"

Louis shook his head as if to indicate no, but said, "I can dance for, maybe, a second."

Jack indicated that this would be fine, and on the show he said, "Here's Louis Nye." Jose Melis, Jack's musical director, did "stop time" on the piano, Louis came out, "sort of tapped a little," and bowed, and Jack said with his usual enthusiasm for a job well done, "Thank you, Louis Nye!" And with that Louis shuffled off camera. Louis needed the money and says, gratefully, "If he had sent me away without an appearance, I wouldn't have been paid."

Paar is justifiably proud of his role in bringing Godfrey Cambridge to national television. But Godfrey, who was not known as a comic but from *Purlie Victorious* on Broadway, required the best audience for his jokes. Jack reasoned that the best setting would be a black campus, Howard University, so that Americans could see what blacks laugh at when whites are not around. Paul Keyes, who wrote for Paar, remembers that the crew got a lot of stuff with Cambridge and that Jack gave the audio to Cambridge, "which became his album." Says Keyes, of Paar's gift, "Most guys would have cut themselves in."

Paul Keyes, now a major producer on the West Coast, is

a major fan of Jack Paar, human being. He remembers that Selma Diamond, then a writer with Sid Caesar, was so funny in person that she was booked on *Tonight* repeatedly and a record company decided to make a sound platter out of her Paar shots. The company asked Paul to cut out Paar's lines, skillfully putting together a track which would include "the meat" of Selma's comedy. Paul was to search the unused material to find a verb here and a noun there that could be deftly inserted so that the record would sound as if it had all been done at one time by Selma and would have the continuity of a set piece. It was tricky, but by no means impossible for a skilled tape editor like Paul.

Paul told Jack what he had been asked to do, and the first time Selma appeared on *Tonight* after that, Jack called to say, "Your girl was awfully funny last night." Says Keyes, Jack was funny too—but not intrusively so. He adds that most men on camera will go for any and every laugh they can get, but Paar told Keyes, "I saw some chances to get in with some lines of my own, but I held back because I knew you'd have trouble getting them out."

Jack and Miriam's friends will never forget their generosity. A confidant says the Paars will surprise friends who they learn are in trouble with good, healthy checks. The confidant adds, "Maybe the Paars have never been in financial straits, but they understand it. One friend of the Paars was in desperate circumstances—about to lose his house in a foreclosure. He did not ask for money, or mention his trouble to the Paars; Jack and Miriam just smelled it out."

The hapless friend went to his mailbox one day and discovered a check from the Paars for $30,000—enough to bail him out. There was no note mentioning repayment, and neither Jack nor Miriam worried about whether they would get the money back. Rather, they were concerned about their friend and his problem.

The confidant who tells this story remarks, "I didn't hear this from Jack. I got word of the episode from the fellow in trouble. The Paars don't talk about these things."

Between the Acts

Mort Werner, NBC's programing ace, was not a man to fool around. Characteristically, when a conference of aides began to fall apart, he would make a sign like a baseball umpire waving the runner safe as he said, "Let's cut through the baloney." He would then proceed to sum things up and make a decision.

Werner often got bored with important meetings and left them early. Once he and an NBC programing chief on the West Coast were meeting with program packagers. The other executive had been holding forth and trying to make a point and so turned to say, "Isn't that right, Mort?" But Mort's chair was empty. The next the West Coast executive heard, Mort was back in New York.

But Werner had no intention of walking out on a meeting with programing executives from the various NBC affiliates at the end of the Paar years.

He had to convince them that a relatively obscure broadcast personality was the right man to succeed Paar. He chose a roundabout technique.

He reminded them of the first "failure" on the show as he put up a picture of Steve Allen, to a roar of applause. Then he reminded them of the second "failure," and up went a picture of Jack Paar. Cheers.

Then he said that he wanted the affiliates to meet another

failure—someone who had flopped in a lot of broadcast opportunities and who couldn't possibly make it with *Tonight.* Up went the photo of a boyish-looking man vaguely familiar to most of the executives in the room—a slim man with a crew cut. Johnny Carson, then the host of ABC's successful game show *Who Do You Trust?*

Carson was Mort Werner's choice, and in picking the young comedian, Werner was definitely putting his career on the line. Jack Paar had quit the show in March, and Johnny Carson wouldn't complete his *Who Do You Trust?* contract and be free to leave ABC for six months. *Tonight* could go down the tubes in the meantime, but Werner was so certain Carson could take over successfully that he was willing to take the chance.

The way Werner saw it, all three men had similar backgrounds in broadcasting, wide experience—and, most important, the ability to ad-lib.

In describing the needs of the show, Werner alluded to trains. He said that the man who ran the show had to know how to engineer the train. "He has to know when to stop for commercials, where to go when he starts up again, and how to keep the train on the track." Then he added, with some irony, perhaps, "All we ask is that he devote his whole life to the program."

Carson wasn't half so certain as Werner that he could step into the vacuum created by Paar's departure. He had argued against the idea with his agent, Al Bruno, and had even turned down a chance to become host years earlier— when the show was offered to Paar. This time he weighed his talents against the demands of the show and decided he had what it took.

But there were six months of guest hosts before Carson arrived on the scene. None of them caught fire—all knew Carson was set for the job, and this might have sapped their enthusiasm. The list of interim hosts was long and formidable. Among them were Art Linkletter, Joey Bishop, Bob Cummings, Merv Griffin, Jack Carter, Jan Murray, Peter Lind Hayes and Mary Healy, Soupy Sales, Mort Sahl, Jimmy Dean, Arlene Francis, Hugh Downs, Donald O'Connor, Steve Lawrence, Groucho Marx, Jack E. Leonard, and Hal March.

No question, it was Mort Werner's biggest gamble—and one he almost lost. Early in the summer the Carson *Tonight Show* was sold out to advertisers. But the show lost so much momentum during the dog days that half the advertisers canceled and the *Tonight* revenue base eroded badly. Carson had better be good or Werner might as well quietly leave the room without notice and fly all the way to his retreat in Hawaii.

The man Werner had picked to succeed Jack Paar is a complex and enigmatic individual whose public personality masks fascinating traits that are rarely revealed on television. As an aide has said tellingly, though tritely, "The Carson you see on the screen is just the tip of the iceberg." To understand Johnny Carson the man, it is worthwhile to examine the life of a farm-belt boy half a century ago.

Johnny Carson: The Early Days of a Television Superstar

There is a marked contrast between Johnny Carson the entertainer and Johnny Carson the man. His ambivalence is a little like that of Sid Caesar in a skit on *Your Show of Shows*. The character Caesar played was a hardened convict who had been a vaudeville hoofer. In the skit, the con was making a break. But just as he scrambled to the top of the wall, the tower spotlight hit him. Desperate though he was, he broke into a soft-shoe dance, smiling for his "audience."

Carson the entertainer owes everything to his audience; Carson the man owes nothing to the men and women who crowd around him on the street. He rarely has to mix with crowds and doesn't seem to enjoy it. He is well protected from the crowds who come to view *Tonight*.

Carson arrives at the Burbank studio in the afternoon driving in his own Mercedes 450 SLC, which he parks in the spot reserved for the star at the top of the pecking order —the stall nearest to the studio door. He is immediately squired inside by an NBC guard, who stays with him— holding any would-be buttonholers at bay—until Ed McMahon says, "Heeeeeeeerrrre's Johnny."

Then, spotlight warming his soul, Carson steps into a

standing ovation. Suddenly, he's television's down-to-earth boy next door, the town clown who keeps them laughing at the neighborhood tavern—totally accessible by implication and as familiar as meat and potatoes on a midwestern dinner plate. At the same time, though, he is the Big Star basking in the adulation of that special kind of crowd—an audience.

As the focus of audience attention, Carson is happy. He experiences a euphoric high. But let some well-meaning citizen approach him for an autograph or, worse, let a crowd of visiting firemen press in asking him to pose for a picture, and he feels restless and uneasy. As he told *Rolling Stone:* "I still feel uncomfortable in large groups of people. Not audiences, mind you. With audiences, I'm fine. I can go out in front of 20,000 people because I'm in charge. When you walk into a large group of people you're not in charge, and all of a sudden I sometimes feel uncomfortable."

Even as a child, Johnny Carson was shy and standoffish in a farm-belt household where interfamily responses were generally somewhat muted. His younger brother, Dick, has explained that the Carsons are "not an Italian family" and that "nobody in our family ever says what they really think or feel to anyone else." The late Al Capp saw the Carson reserve as reflecting fine manners. Carson's parents, to Capp, were "almost the definitive Nebraska mother and father. Radiantly decent, well-spoken." Johnny Carson himself hasn't revealed many details of his childhood—even to the few persons he regards as confidants.

Dick Carson had a warmer personality. He was more friendly and outgoing. So was the boys' older sister, Catherine. Johnny stood apart in a household that was strict, to be sure, but otherwise was not notably different from any other during the Depression years in the corn belt, where reserve was as common as a leather harness.

Like so many other families in America's farmlands, the Carsons were of pioneer stock. Author Alex Haley had the

Institute of Family Research in Salt Lake City prepare a genealogical chart of the Carson heritage for a Haley appearance on *The Tonight Show* in 1977 when Haley was promoting *Roots.*

The enterprising search company threw fifteen investigators into a frenzied two-day search of the Carson family tree —a chore that normally consumes two months. The earliest Carson ancestors turned up were on his father's side—the English Kelloggs. Thomas Kellogg was born circa 1521 in the village of Debdon, Essex. Daniel Kellogg, born roughly 1630, crossed the Atlantic with his wife, Bridget, to settle in Connecticut. Among Johnny's maternal ancestors we have Captain James Hook, who may have served under George Washington at Valley Forge and who, in a private quarrel, lost a thin slice of ear to a man who lunged at him with a knife. Captain Hook then seized his adversary's ear in his teeth and yanked, tearing off a larger piece than he had lost himself.

Members of the family later scattered across the Midwest, with representatives from Indiana to Iowa to Nebraska. Emiline of the Nebraska Kelloggs married Marshall Carson, Johnny's great-grandfather. Marshall, born about 1833, dug in vain for gold in western Nebraska, then moved to Iowa, where he died in 1922, just short of the age of ninety. That was the year his grandson, Homer Lloyd Carson, married Ruth Hook. In 1925, Ruth gave gave birth to the biggest name in American television history.

Johnny Carson's story began in Corning, Iowa, on October 25, 1925. (The birth certificate was filed later in Des Moines, the state capital.) His father, a peripatetic utility-company lineman, was highly thought of by his company and eventually was promoted to a supervisory job so that he was able to move the family to a big frame house in the middle of Norfolk, Nebraska.

Johnny was eight at the time, and Norfolk was a typical Midwest community of about 10,000 people. Johnny has a vivid recollection of that town, and he told a reporter: "I will never forget looking down on Main Street from a fourth-floor hotel window there, thinking how high up I was and marveling at so much traffic down in the street."

If it were known which room Carson was in on that occasion, the town fathers could be forgiven if they marked the spot with a plaque. For as one sophisticated New York writer put it a few years ago, "From all reports nothing of consequence has happened in Norfolk since Johnny Carson slept there."

In talking of his youth, Carson doesn't mention boyhood friends but speaks instead of fishing and skinny-dipping in the Elkhorn River with brother Dick, and of summers with the family at a lake in Minnesota.

Speaking more directly of his personality traits, he has often mentioned his shyness and that he used the stage early in life as a means to social adjustment. He says, "I'm a performer, but I'm not gregarious, and that's a *big* difference."

As a preteener Johnny picked up a copy of *Hoffman's Book of Magic* at a neighbor's house. In it all the standard tricks were described, along with instructions telling how to make some of the equipment. There was also an ad for a magic kit offered by a mail-order house in Chicago.

Johnny had already had a taste of the stage and was gratified by the laughs he got imitating the cartoon voice of Popeye in a school skit shortly after the family moved to Norfolk. Though shy and uncomfortable in crowds, he found that by getting up in front of an audience—by being different, calling attention to himself, and getting laughs— he got "a high, a great feeling." Thus, he was ready for magic, which, like humor, relies heavily on the unexpected for a warm response.

"I sent away for [the kit] and the stuff came, and I couldn't think about anything else but . . . working with the magic.

"I ordered every catalog advertised and read them from cover to cover, and spent every quarter I could get for more stuff. Finally, one Christmas I got this magician's table with a black velvet cover. I have never since seen anything more beautiful than that was to me. The next thing was ventriloquism. I bought a mail-order course, also from Chicago, for $15."

When did he first realize he wanted to be an entertainer? Some years ago when Alex Haley was doing a Carson profile for PLAYBOY, he told Haley, "I just can't say I ever wanted to become an entertainer; I already was one sort of—around our house, at school, doing my magic tricks, throwing my voice and doing the Popeye impersonations. People thought I was funny; so I kind of took entertaining for granted. I was full of card tricks, too. Around the house, I was always telling anybody I saw, 'Take a card, any card. . . .' "

As young Johnny Carson became more adept at card tricks and other feats of legerdemain, his mother booked him at her bridge club. He told Haley, "They thought I was great; and I felt great, making my mother so proud, you know?"

He might have become just another ordinary midwesterner, possibly an insurance salesman—like so many with a talent who started out on the high school stage, or as sidemen in the school dance band. But Johnny wasn't an ordinary spotlight grabber. While others were hanging out at the local soda fountain, he was turning his hobby into a paying proposition.

"I was fourteen when I earned my first fee for my act— $3 from the Norfolk Rotary Club. Then I began to get a fee like that at picnics, county fairs, 4-H clubs, service clubs, chambers of commerce. I was billed as 'The Great Carsoni,' wearing a cape my mother had sewed for me."

In high school, he was what they used to call "well rounded," seeking out extracurricular activities that brought him additional attention. Sports fame eluded him. He went out for football, but when he took the ball for the first time, he was hit hard and knocked cold. The coach recommended other activities, and Carson took the advice, devoting himself to "parts in every school play" and to a funny column in the school newspaper.

Other aspects of his early life were related to the entertainment world. Late in 1941, Carson was ushering at the local Granada Theatre when the manager interrupted a double feature to announce the Japanese attack on Pearl Harbor. He was halfway through high school at the time. He continued his classwork and his free-lance appearances as "The Great Carsoni." He told Alex Haley in PLAYBOY:

"By 1943, when I graduated from Norfolk High, I was making pretty fair pin money with my act. Funny thing, though, I still didn't have any intention of entertaining as a serious career. I was still very small-town in outlook. It would be another three or four years before I'd find out that the Catskills weren't a dance team. I was still playing with the idea of becoming a psychiatrist, an engineer, or a journalist."

But first, Johnny Carson—like millions of other young men—would go to war. The Second World War was raging everywhere. The tide had not been turned in Europe, though Mussolini was out and Allied troops had landed on the Italian subcontinent. Meanwhile, General Douglas MacArthur had started his island-hopping campaign to push the Japanese out of the Pacific.

Unlike most of those who were inducted, Johnny Carson was destined to do his duty as an officer. Obviously bright, he was tapped for the V-12 program, which would have led to a Naval Air commission. Awaiting induction, he hitched rides to California, bought a naval cadet's uniform, and turned up at the Hollywood Stage Door Canteen, where the stars were entertaining members of the armed forces. Carson managed to dance with Marlene Dietrich. Then he traveled to San Diego, where superstar Orson Welles was doing magic. When Welles asked for a volunteer from the audience, Carson rose and was pleased to be sawed in half by the master. Later, he was sent to midshipman school at

Columbia University, got his commission, and was assigned to the battleship *Pennsylvania.*

He carried his magic equipment with him, entertaining officers and men "every chance I got." Like Jack Paar, he specialized in knocking the officers in the patter that accompanied his magic. The enlisted men loved it, of course, but his notoriety was limited, and he emerged from the service a better magician but a show-business nobody. His closest brush with fame: he did several hours of magic tricks for Secretary of the Navy James Forrestal. Carson could roll quarters over his fingers, slip cards up his sleeves unnoticed, and throw his voice from here to there. He also developed prodigious memory powers, a skill that, years later, would help him remember the names of all ninety-eight contestants in a Miss Universe contest he emceed—not to mention thousands of jokes which, altered to suit the occasion, would add to his reputation as the fastest draw on the comedy circuit.

Leaving the Navy, he entered the University of Nebraska, in Lincoln. He tried but soon tired of journalism and so switched to radio and speech. Soon he got his first radio job at local station KFAB writing for a comedy Western called *Eddie Sosby and the Radio Rangers.* It was on three days a week and paid him $10 per week. Still in college, Carson had to get permission to come late to Spanish class.

In his senior year, Carson did a thesis on comedy, which included recorded excerpts of radio performances illustrating timing and sequence, building punch lines, recognition devices, and running gags. In his thesis, Carson included Fibber McGee and Molly, Jack and Mary Benny, Rochester, Ozzie and Harriet, Milton Berle, and Bob Hope. Like many would-be comedians, Carson was a serious student of the trade. Like Steve Allen, he became one of the rare ones who analyzed comedy techniques in writing.

Johnny graduated in 1949 and immediately took a full-time job at WOW in Omaha. His radio experience is strikingly like that of both Steve Allen and Jack Paar. For all three, small-time radio offered the perfect training ground. Johnny did a bit of everything—commercials, news, station breaks, weather reports, the works. His price in those halcyon days: $47.50 a week.

He drew attention to himself when he rebelled at the pseudo-interviews with stars that were distributed to small-town disc jockeys. The star's recorded answers were to be preceded by matching questions. In one instance, instead of asking the recorded Patti Page when she first started singing, he said, "I understand you're hitting the bottle pretty good, Patti—when did you start?" The taped response: "When I was six, I used to get up at church socials and do it."

The subrosa antics were the sort of thing that got Jack Paar fired several times in his early years. Carson was older and perhaps a little more deft. At least he didn't get fired, though he even took on sponsors, butchering commercials for comic effect. For Friendly Savings Bank, he counseled, "Drop in any time. At two or three in the morning is fine. Help yourself. Just leave a note."

That was on a disc-jockey show which he kept even after he got his own television show, called *The Squirrel's Nest.* His career fortunes were improving apace, and he raised his fee for magic shows to $25. His magician's assistant in college, Jody Wolcott, remained with him after graduation, and soon they were married. Not long after that, the couple had the first of their three sons, Chris.

Johnny's most notable effort on *The Squirrel's Nest* was in behalf of the pigeons that were defacing City Hall. A group was campaigning to rid the city of them. For no known reason other than to draw attention to himself, Carson called for "Equal Time for Pigeons," imitating the birds "cooing their side of the story," and the anti-pigeon campaign was dropped. It seems clear that Carson was not so much a pigeon lover as a radio comedian running amok.

In a natural progression, Carson went on to become a staffer at WOW-TV and was soon confident enough to

begin thinking about California and New York, where the
action was. He got a cameraman friend to shoot a half-hour
film of his best stuff and waited for his vacation. He then
loaded up his "beat-up Olds," added a U-Haul trailer, and
drove to San Francisco, looking like a latter-day refugee
from the dust bowl. It was the anyone-getting-ahead-in-
broadcasting-hits-California syndrome revisited. Carson
knocked on every radio and TV door in San Francisco and
got the inevitable "Don't call us, we'll call you." Finally,
Carson decided San Francisco was barren territory, gave
up, and moved on to Los Angeles.

Same welcome there. But Carson remembered a "childhood family friend" named Bill Brennan, who had gone
into radio sales in L.A. Brennan recommended Johnny for
a staff announcing job that opened up at WNXT, a local
station. He was hired and again did everything but sweep
out the radio studio in addition to his on-the-air responsibilities.

While the records were spinning, Carson would work on
an idea for a TV show—knowing that most successes in the
business had made their own breaks. CBS saw the idea and
liked it for a local Sunday-afternoon spot. The budget: $25
a week. The opportunity: unbounded.

Carson was writing and acting in his own scripts—and
getting "pretty fair" newspaper notices. Then, an inspiration: he had a friend rush past the camera while he was on
the air and announced, "That was my guest for today, Red
Skelton."

In California, where radio is as important to commuters
and the population generally as the throughways, Skelton
heard about the episode and really did turn up for one of
Carson's shows. That isn't exactly the way Steve Allen got
the guest stars to drop in on his early California show, but
the result was the same. Comedians are always ready for a
busman's holiday, it seems. Carson understood that as well
as Steve Allen. Fred Allen dropped in on Carson, and so
did others. But it was Carson's first bag, Skelton, who

opened the door for Carson to the big time. Skelton made repeated appearances on the Carson show and finally offered Carson a job writing for his show. Carson knew just what to do: "I grabbed it."

From High Perch to Disaster: A Star-to-Be Falls Hard

If Red Skelton hadn't slammed into a breakaway door that didn't break during rehearsal in 1954, Johnny Carson might have waited much longer for his big break.

But Skelton hit that door so hard he was knocked cold, leaving his live television show without a star on short notice—it was ninety minutes before program time. In a frenzy, Skelton's staff called Carson at his home and asked if he could fill in. It was a golden opportunity, and Carson, who not only wrote for the show but also acted in some Skelton skits, was ready. "I had always been doing bits and cracking gags around the office, and they wanted to know if I could make it to the station [in time]." Carson likes to prepare meticulously for his appearances. He practiced his best material during the 60-mile race from his home in the Valley over the mountains to the studio.

On the show itself, he delivered a humorous lecture on the economics of TV.

It was generally agreed that Carson was agreeable, funny, and appealing as a substitute host. The critics liked him—and so did CBS, Skelton's network. CBS programing chiefs were convinced Carson could carry his own variety show. Thus, in the old tradition of "stand-in wows critics,"

Johnny got his big break and, in a flash, became a hot property.

The Johnny Carson Show was the result, and the notices were good despite unhappiness in the Carson company itself. Over the next thirty-nine weeks, there were nearly as many directors (seven) as writers (eight) following each other in dreary succession. The show ended its rocky run in the spring of 1956.

Carson has commented in a published interview about the experience in a manner indicating that his developing instinct for survival had gotten an important boost: "That was my first *big lesson* . . . if you get too many cooks involved . . . if you don't keep control, you're going to bomb out, and there's nobody to blame but yourself. . . . It was primarily through my own naiveté that the show failed. I had built the show initially around a format of low-key skits and commentary on topical subjects—something rather like *The Tonight Show.* We got good reviews, but the network people felt the ratings should have been higher, and I let them start telling me what to do.

" 'We've got to make the show *important,*' they told me. How would they go about doing that? With chorus girls. They were going to make me into Jackie Gleason! I'd come rushing on in a shower of balloons, with chorus girls yipping, 'Here comes the *star* of the show, *Johnny Carson!*' And the rest followed in that vein. I let myself be a poor imitation, and that's sure, swift death for any entertainer. But I think if nobody ever fails, he never has successes. The show flopped—but to me only in the sense that it went off the air after thirty-nine weeks. I learned the hard way that you have to go with your own decisions."

At this point in his career, Carson was just another show-business has-been even before his career was properly launched. As might be expected in the unforgiving world of show business where a talent is only as good as his last vehicle, Carson waited in vain for a call from his agent. Nothing.

Taking charge in a manner characteristic of many of the successful show-biz talents, he visited the agency and said, "Look, I can get myself some kind of act together. Get a couple of writers to work with me." The agency said no, so Carson went home and wrote an act all by himself. Then he peddled it himself, finally landing a date in beautiful downtown Bakersfield at a place called the Maison Joussaud, at a respectable $400 a week. The family was secure again—at least for the time being. Carson now believes himself to have been naive in thinking some of the top agency people would come to see him. They didn't. Two junior members came, sat through the act, and left.

Strong Management to the Rescue

But soon he was to meet personal manager Tom Shiels. Shiels had started in the management business with classmate Al Bruno about 1940. They had been charged with finding an orchestra for the high school prom. The boys had been told they ought to see an obscure band in Bridgeport, Connecticut. They traveled there and heard a fine band with a distinctive sound using a clarinet lead or melody line. The band, recently formed, was called the Glenn Miller Orchestra. Its young leader was thrilled to get the prom gig for $350. After the ball, young Shiels was asked to become its manager. During World War II, Glenn Miller's plane went down and he apparently was drowned in the roiling waters of the English Channel. Shiels went into personal management, handling Glenn Miller's singing group, the Modernaires, and taking on additional clients as time passed. Shiels, who had settled on the West Coast, eventually persuaded Al Bruno to return from the liquor business and become his East Coast partner.

Personal management is career guidance for show-business personalities. It involves getting producers and network officials interested in the client's career and picking and choosing between business deals offered the successful star. Shiels had managed game-show hosts and comedians. Both Shiels and Bruno had seen and were impressed with Johnny Carson's work on CBS, including a second show, the well-received but unsuccessful *Carson's Cellar* on CBS local TV. Shiels spoke with Carson at length at a party, and was enthusiastic enough to sign him. He then pointed Carson in the direction of New York City, where Al Bruno— a Carson fan—awaited his arrival.

Representing struggling entertainers was hardly a new experience for Bruno. Bruno had specialized in putting stalled careers in high gear. A warm, earnest, round-faced man, Bruno was singularly effective in advertising the talents of his clients. Jimmy Dean entered Al's office a down-on-his-luck country-music singer with almost no following and so broke there were holes in his shoes. He emerged a major star. Dennis James, who was to gain fame with game shows, was also broke when Bruno took over his career. Dave Garroway came to Al after his tumultous break with NBC and *The Today Show.* The break resulted from Garroway's odd personality quirks which were exhibited both on and off the air after his wife's suicide. Later, Dave almost made a comeback under Bruno's tutelage with a Boston talk show the broadcast company somehow allowed to peter out despite its considerable popularity and excellent initial reception. Bruno would have more luck with his new client.

Carson's Big Break:
Who Do You Trust?

Johnny Carson was having a slow period—slow enough, according to Bruno, that an offer to host *Do You Trust Your Wife?* found him so broke he had to borrow money from a bank and his father to make the trip to New York.

Johnny wasn't joining a totally unknown show, though. ABC's daytime quiz show *Do You Trust Your Wife?*, which had been hosted by Edgar Bergen, was being transferred to New York from California. The show was so weak at the time it was in danger of cancellation. The network was renewing it on a month-to-month basis. Shiels and Bruno had landed the host's job for Carson and were convinced Carson had the talent to put it on track. Carson arrived in New York, checked in with Bruno, and took up the assignment as the new host.

Ex-song-and-dance man Art Stark was named producer. Stark was a logical choice. He was not only a song-and-dance man but, by coincidence, he had written for Jerry Lester and, to a lesser extent, for Morey Amsterdam on *Broadway Open House.* He, Johnny, and others associated with the show began fine-tuning the format. The new team decided that it was a trap to restrict the show to just husbands and wives. So they used any two people—but generally a man and woman, many of whom were of course man and wife.

One big problem that erupted shortly after the new team took over: they discovered the back mail, which included dozens of complaints from people who had won things on the show and never gotten their prizes.

It turned out the staffer responsible for sending the prizes was in love with a girl called Chickie. He gave her the best stuff and neglected to mail out the rest. The budget of the new company was strained for some time as Art Stark bought the necessary merchandise to deliver on the old claims.

The show was highly professional and carefully crafted after Johnny Carson and the new staff took over. Five researchers would scour the city, looking primarily for tourists in such popular meccas as Radio City Music Hall and Madison Square Garden. The researchers also called the newspapers for interesting stories, and others wrote in, telling of their backgrounds. Before they were chosen, the contestants would be interviewed in depth. During the interview, the researcher, if he thought he was on to something, would ring up Mary Dodd. Mary was associate producer, and a thoroughgoing professional with a sense of what worked on television. She would enter the room, sit, and listen for a few minutes to decide if the person would appeal to viewers. Then the associate producer would get the researcher's write-ups and Polaroid snaps of the candidates. She would choose three stories for each show. Ideally, the staff was generally two to three days ahead. At this point, the writers came into the picture. It was the writer's job to set the story up in dramatic fashion.

The contestant would get a script, a copy of which went to ABC's censorship department. In that script there would be a line saying, "Johnny will talk about [so and so]." What made the show both more successful and raunchier than most on daytime television was that, as Mary Dodd explains, Carson would get a special script—with all the punch lines to all the jokes the writer had set up in the contestant's script. Censorship did not get Carson's script and was unaware—as was the viewing audience—that the script even existed. Obviously, things didn't always go according to plan, but Carson's quick wit usually saved interviews gone astray.

Under the format, the male would be given the choice as to whether he would answer or his partner. There was a scrambled name at the end of the show—Art Stark's contribution to the format—and if the winning couple could unscramble it, they won a prize.

Prime-time audiences who never saw the daytime *Who Do You Trust?* would find it reminiscent of Groucho's *You Bet Your Life,* which was also scripted, except that Johnny was "much more mobile," as Art puts it. Already developing some of the gimmicks and techniques he would use to advantage on *Tonight,* Carson would allow himself on *Trust,* for example, to be laundered in a washing machine, and he would try out kooky new inventions.

The show was what John Denver would call "far out." There was a Jewish cowboy who was supposed to be a fast draw. Johnny challenged him to a contest, and every time the cowboy went for his gun, he'd drop it and then get down on his hands and knees and crawl around the stage looking for it.

Typical of the blue material that got on the show was an episode involving a husband who was inordinately proud of the fact that his wife, "a middle-aged bag" according to Stark, could stand on her hands and kick her head with her feet. Preparing to demonstrate, the wife took off her skirt to reveal a pair of baggy bloomers. When she stood on her hands facing the audience and began pummeling her head with her feet—going for the world record—the bloomers began gaping at the crotch for an unscheduled peep show. Carson broke up along with the audience, and to build the response he merely did takes as the studio crowd roared louder and louder. Finally—and mercifully—Carson stopped the show. That outraged the house, because Carson had prevented the hapless exhibitionist from getting her world record. One can only speculate as to how the entry might have read in *The Guinness Book of World Records,* but the performance was a self-contained gem in any case.

Who Do You Trust? proved to be a perfect mating of man and vehicle. Carson seized upon the possibilities for bedroom humor and quickly became a master of the well-delivered line. The show carried "the most prurient dialogue in television," if you believe Jack O'Brian, who was a strict Roman Catholic and thus inclined to take a dim view of such things.

Double entendre, of course, allows the closet roué to express thoughts to the cognoscenti that the prim set would find outrageous if only they could break the code. A legend grew around the program, and one writer said that host Carson could pull a double entendre out of a spokesman for the Methodist Church. Soon they were calling *Who Do You Trust?* the "camp" show of its time. It would be excellent training for *The Tonight Show,* which Al Bruno was already touting Carson for, figuring that Jack Paar eventually would make good his persistent threat to leave the show. Carson was to have five years of the most helpful kind of training for *The Tonight Show,* something any potential host might well envy.

Shortly after Carson became *Trust* host, the announcer on the show, Bill Nimmo, told Carson he was leaving to do a show of his own. Carson needed a new man, and he looked for someone who could be a foil for his jokes as well as the announcer for the show.

Ed McMahon, meanwhile, was laboring in one of the more important backwaters of broadcasting with announcing jobs and minor-league talk shows in his native Philadelphia. McMahon was hoping, without any special conviction, that he might someday have a job in New York.

Providentially, Dick Clark, whose Philadelphia-based *American Bandstand* teenage show was a big winner on early television, lived next door to Ed in suburban Drexelbrook. When Ed extemporaneously emceed a large party for the community, Chuck Reeves, Clark's producer, attended and found Ed's patter amusing.

Later, while in New York, Reeves learned that *Trust* needed an announcer and he thought of the ebullient Ed McMahon. In McMahon's autobiography, *Here's Ed,* he tells in detail how hard it was for Reeves to reach him in Philadelphia, because McMahon had an unlisted telephone number in his new digs, some distance from old neighbor Dick Clark. Clark tried unsuccessfully to reach him. Somehow, though, Reeves made the connection and, as Ed would have it, show-business history was spared a colossal blunder. Soon Ed was on his way to New York for an audition.

The meeting with Johnny Carson was disappointing. Carson said almost nothing. He and McMahon stared out the window at the Shubert Theatre, where a couple of workmen were putting up letters on the marquee. By Ed's account, the two men were fascinated by this mundane endeavor. Then Carson, every bit the taciturn Nebraskan, asked, "What have you been doing?" Ed indicates that he sketched out his triumphs as briefly as possible. Carson said, "Good to meet you, Ed," shook his hand, and McMahon was out the door. But Art Stark asked McMahon to hang around for a while. Then Johnny came out and he and Ed went on camera for about two minutes. The two "talked about nothing," Ed reports, and Ed got the familiar "Don't call us, we'll call you" instruction so familiar to candidates for speaking parts and then headed back to Philadelphia.

Weeks went by. Eventually figuring his "pleasant dream" of a big break in New York City was simply that, McMahon made plans to leave on a junket across the Atlantic. But the day before he was to depart, he received a call from New York. It was Art Stark. He asked when McMahon planned to be in Manhattan again.

"Tomorrow."

"What time?"

"Ten in the morning."

"See me."

Ed and Johnny's producer talked and talked, but Art mentioned no offer. Finally Stark asked, "Are you planning to move to New York?"

"I don't think so," Ed answered in some confusion.

"I thought maybe you'd want to."

"Why?"

"Well, I thought it might be tough for you, doing the show."

"What show?"

"Our show. You start Monday."

"*Next* Monday?"

"For Chrissake, didn't anybody tell you?"

Carson was, of course, already looking ahead to better things and while waiting figured he'd have to make some of his own breaks. He joined the Friars Club, a society of big-league comics and actors, and quickly established himself as one of the keenest of wits in that rapier-sharp gang of cutups. It was Jack E. Leonard, the master putdown artist, whom Johnny called "The Mean Mr. Clean," to the everlasting admiration of the other comics.

Al Bruno, meanwhile, was doing what personal managers usually do. They ride herd on everything concerning their client professionally. The fee is 10 percent with a small escalating percentage. The personal manager is not the "agent," and Al Bruno hired one who would negotiate for Carson once an opportunity arose and at the usual 10 percent fee. Bruno also arranged for William Lazarow to handle Johnny's tax problems. It's traditional and almost necessary, the way the business is structured, for the income of television personalities to be sliced several ways by agents and managers. It is also traditional for stars to feel they are being bled to death by percentage-taking leeches.

But since the networks generally limit their dealings to agents and prefer not to deal directly with talent, the talent has little choice. Stars are different, of course, and many rely on business managers to handle most of their affairs when they become established. As for the agent, he or she may wait until a deal is in the offing before taking up negotiating chores. Thus men like Bruno are needed to generate interest in the "property" by contacting producers frequently so that the client's availability will be known should an opportunity arise.

Meanwhile, Carson was about as much in demand for a big spot as every other game-show host, which is to say not particularly. Bruno was nevertheless convinced that Carson had great potential. "There are not too many communicators in this business, and I certainly thought he was one. At no point did I feel that I was mistaken in this view, and I felt he certainly had the talent."

In an insecure business in which panic is just below the surface calm, Carson was as anxious as the next, according to Phil Dean, who did publicity for Carson for a short while.

Bruno, who had asked Dean to take on Carson as a client, remarks that Carson was "very dedicated to us. He worked like a Trojan and was completely dedicated to his craft." Phil Dean sees the relationship between Carson and Bruno differently: "Every insecurity Johnny had, Bruno suffered. He's very Italian. He represented Johnny Carson a thousand percent. Everything Carson did was 'terrific; great, Johnny.' He totally devoted himself to making Johnny Carson a big star and treated him like the greatest guy in the world."

Onward and Upward: An Uptight Carson Tackles Tonight

NBC was certainly impressed with the top rating *Who Do You Trust?* got on daytime TV and even more impressed with its star, Johnny Carson. Moreover, Al Bruno had been touting Carson as a potential successor to Jack Paar if and when Jack finally made good on his continuing threats to leave *The Tonight Show.* Bruno says that he used every excuse he could think of to see network executives so that he could remind them of Johnny's talent and availability.

Actually, Bruno was fibbing about availability. For he was having little success in his efforts to persuade Carson to become *Tonight* host—if and when the job was offered to him. Bruno says Johnny absolutely refused to consider the idea. When Bruno pleaded, Carson would respond, "How can I follow Jack Paar?" And, more broadly, Carson would question how anyone could make a success in the wake of someone as sensational as Paar.

But shortly after Paar gave up *Tonight,* Bruno was able to convince Carson that the public was ready for a change to someone less frenetic than Paar and that Carson was the logical person to fill that role. Or as Bruno tells of finally persuading his client, "After two years [of coaxing] Carson finally bought it."

Carson may have bought it, but he was anything but confident.

When Johnny Carson moved to NBC and *The Tonight Show,* his friend and mentor Art Stark, who was still under contract to packager Don Fedderson, stayed on as producer of *Who Do You Trust?* at ABC.

Stark had his hands full as he attempted to make a star of Woody Woodbury in Carson's old slot. Woodbury, a talented and engaging performer with considerable promise, baffled *Trust* fans by appearing in a battered fishing outfit. Woodbury had had considerable success with this garb in a prior nightclub act, and the entertainer felt it was integral to his appeal.

Stark argued that the outfit was inappropriate for national television. Stark lost the argument and Woodbury lost the show. (Later Woodbury was to acknowledge his mistake and say he believed that if he had listened to Stark he would have become a big star.)

Carson's move from *Trust* to *Tonight* began in euphoria and quickly became traumatic. Despite success, Carson needed Stark badly.

The opening-night gala brought Groucho Marx in from the West Coast to introduce Johnny. There were other heavy hitters on hand. Joan Crawford—initially terrified without a script—so enjoyed herself that she wanted a show of her own. Old-timer Rudy Vallee—famous for college humor and his nasal-toned, ricky-tick vocals into a hand-held megaphone—was there, and so was the up-to-date nasal-toned Tony Bennett. Comedy writer Mel Brooks matched wits with Carson, and there was Johnny's second banana from *Who Do You Trust?*—Ed McMahon.

It was on that night that Carson stated, to his later regret,

"Jack Paar was king of late-night television. Why don't you just consider me the prince?"

The debut got good notices. Jack Gould, reviewing in *The New York Times,* wrote that the format was "unchanged" but that "Mr. Carson's style is his own. . . . He has the proverbial engaging smile and the quick mind essential to sustaining and seasoning a marathon of banter.

"At the outset he said he was not going to describe every guest as an old and dear friend, an indication of a refreshing attitude against prevalent show-business hokum. A healthy independence without overtones of neuroses could wear very well.

"A reportorial curiosity in what makes people tick is something of an essential on *Tonight;* the revelation of celebrities as they really are is probably the program's primary appeal. On his premiere Mr. Carson was very poised in talking with Joan Crawford, Rudy Vallee, and Tony Bennett, but some of his questioning was rather orthodox in publicizing their outside interests.

"In this regard Mr. Carson encountered a format difficulty that had also plagued his predecessor. The show often tends to be overbooked with talent or prearranged routines, so there is not always time to develop promising conversational leads. It was a particular pity that Miss Crawford had to sit mute and out of camera range while Mel Brooks went his strained way."

Gould went on to say that it would be "some weeks" before it could be told how Carson would run the program and how his personality and interests would influence the proceedings. Then, in an obvious reference to the tension of the Paar years, Gould added, "At least [Carson] began in an atmosphere mercifully free of impending crisis."

Elsewhere the styles of the two were contrasted, with Paar's deemed an anxiety neurosis and Carson's a tranquilizer.

More important for NBC than for the television audience was the fact that, as Gould reported, the show was "sold out commercially, which is fine for Mr. Carson but rough on the viewer."

But Carson had moved from a carefully crafted *Trust* environment that worked so well for him to a world of relative disorganization, and he was uncomfortable. On *Trust,* Art Stark had prepared a show that gave Carson sufficient scope to react and to do funny things within a structured environment. If things went badly Art Stark was there to help. "There were fall-back positions and places to fall," a member of the *Trust* staff comments.

The monologue, at least, was set and, some feel, was sharper politically in the early months than thereafter. Richard M. Nixon was defeated in his attempt to win the governorship of California in November, and Carson said, "But he's not giving up; now he's going to run for head of his family." Of youthful Massachusetts senator-elect Edward Kennedy at about the same time—he was thirty but seemed younger—Carson said, "He was the only candidate who made his acceptance speech while wearing Dr. Denton's."

Early Carson *Tonight* also featured popular Walter Mitty segments. There was Carson on the pitcher's mound at Yankee Stadium pitching to Mickey Mantle and Roger Maris, and another dream episode in which Carson flew with the Thunderbirds, an Air Force stunt-flying group— a whole series with Carson doing what every red-blooded American fantasized doing someday. These were high spots in an anxious period.

For the bulk of the show, good intentions were working but the planning apparently wasn't. One observer called the broadcasts loose, haphazard, and at the same time rigid. If there was a dull guest or one who failed to establish a rapport with Carson, the interview would slog onward because that was the way the show had been set up. One plus: the show was "billboarded" with important stars whose appearances were ballyhooed in advance in the newspapers. But as all *Tonight* fans know, this is no guarantee of a scintillating discussion. It was maddening for Carson. An interview allotted ten minutes on the schedule got ten minutes—even when the guest was dull as dishwater and Carson was dying out there. The format was that inflexible. It worked because the guest stars were important enough to draw an audience on curiosity value alone.

But more and more during such interviews Carson's eyes would wander as guests droned on. Shelley Berman actually went overtime and after much tedium said, "You know, Johnny, I was an overnight star." Carson's retort had bite: "Sure, Shelley, but not tonight." In other times of boredom he used his personal "react" camera to yawn and visualize his distress to viewers, too.

The pill-popping neurotic Oscar Levant said on a Jack Paar special that he thought Johnny "amiably dull." Told of the remark, Carson snapped during a broadcast that Oscar was "obviously sick." That same month Carson and a guest, tap dancer John Bubbles, got up and walked, leaving comedian Jackie Mason to finish the show Carson said Mason had taken over.

Other times he simply suffered quietly but unhappily. Carson, who acknowledged recently on *Sixty Minutes* that he can't handle alcohol and thus has been on the wagon for a decade, was bending an elbow not for enjoyment anymore, but out of exasperation and frustration.

All too often, the guests—or their topics, at least—were poor even though the staff set up pre-interviews with those scheduled so that they could prepare Carson for what was coming. In a skilled staffer's hands the pre-interview is a fine device for developing a solid topic of conversation. When a skilled and intelligent pre-interviewer gets a brilliant or provocative response to a pre-interview question, the guest is told to say it just that way on the show when Carson asks the same question. But many of the Carson *Tonight* pre-interviews in the first months were conducted by staffers who weren't good at it or who hadn't developed sufficient appreciation of Carson's strengths and weaknesses.

It wasn't a matter of incompetence, nor was anyone particularly at fault. The producers and staff aides simply didn't know Carson well or understand what it took to help him succeed. The staffers did sense that Carson needed full time to concentrate on the show, and they were able, despite contractual guarantees to advertisers that Carson would do the pitches, to substitute McMahon.

Despite Carson's concern, the advertising held up well. Shortly after Paar left the show on March 30, 1962, advertisers had begun signing up for Carson's debut, and by the middle of that summer the show was sold out. Limp pre-Carson interim hosts lost some advertisers during the summer through poor performances. (As one observer saw it —in somewhat overstated fashion, to be sure—"Guest plugs for books, records, motion pictures, and appearances punctuated the commercials.") But there was a full roster of advertisers when Carson made his debut. The ratings were good as viewers tuned in to see what the new boy would do with the show.

Carson, meantime, anything but happy, knew that what looked good on paper simply wasn't working well enough on the tube—at least not for the star of the show.

The Second Rescue:
New Direction

Within months of Carson's takeover on *The Tonight Show* the star was troubled despite his success. And he was a big success.

By February 1963—four months into the run—the Carson-hosted *Tonight Show* had grossed $7.5 million, and all advertising spots continued to sell out. Needless to say, Carson was a bargain at $100,000 a year and NBC quickly signed him to another full year.

But Carson was uneasy; something was lacking. He remembered his early experience on *Who Do You Trust?* When he'd joined that show, it was called *Do You Trust Your Wife?* and the low-rated show had just limped into New York City from California under threat of cancellation. The host, ventriloquist Edgar Bergen, had been dropped. The situation: grim. But soon after Carson joined the show, producer Art Stark came aboard and began tinkering. The show perked up quickly.

Thus, when NBC's staff producer left *Tonight* for other chores, Carson suggested Art Stark as his replacement. As luck would have it, the timing was perfect: Stark was no longer under contract to the Fedderson organization.

When he arrived, Stark found an essentially unstructured *Tonight.* The structure he settled on is still followed by

Tonight and has been copied by other talk shows too.

Stark felt that *Tonight* would be watched primarily for its entertainment value at the midnight hour. Stark, a round-faced man who is short, plump, and decisive, reasoned that after a half hour of heavy news at 11:00 P.M. people wanted to be amused and that they wouldn't brook much delay. If something on the show didn't make people laugh, he wanted the flexibility to go quickly to another segment. Thus while there was an underlying structure, it wasn't allowed to slow the tempo of the show or force it to move at a ragged pace. Stark was putting to work once again the lessons of Tamiment, the Poconos comedy-spawning resort where he had been director of comedy sketches for three years. The ex-hoofer and comedian of World War II USO days wrote and directed at Tamiment and was experienced at timing and pacing shows to hold audiences. More important, he had good comedy instincts.

The evening invariably began with Carson's topical opening monologue. Unlike Paar's monologues, which usually pinpointed things that happened to Jack, Miriam, and Randy, Carson's avoided his family life and instead stressed events in the day's news. Nothing too heavy—sheer entertainment was preferable to trenchant political commentary and certainly safer at midnight. That was Stark's approach, and Carson wholeheartedly agreed with it then and still feels that way. Yet, Carson's topical opener had bite. It gave the show a good send-off. It was and is so successful that it is regarded as a forebear of the genre on TV. It is taped live and without canned laughter and thus is refreshing if not unique in a television calendar of tired sit-coms and rehashed jokes.

Following the monologue there was a break for commercials, after which Johnny would do a piece either with the audience itself or with Ed McMahon. For example, he might read a series of wacky lines for Ed McMahon's and the audience's reaction. He might offer advice: "If you must smoke, don't do it orally," or, "If you want to add years to your life, put your pants on backwards."

Further commercial breaks followed—in critic Jack Gould's view, they followed ad nauseam—and then came the first guest.

Stark hadn't been happy with the guests or their performances prior to his arrival, and he thought better guests could be found than in the past—people who had something to say. Pre-interviewing technique was sharpened to seek out topics that would appeal more to the *Tonight* audience. And Stark checked pre-interview results. Employing a "hard-hat" approach, as his good friend Skitch Henderson describes Stark's executive style, Stark would tell the staffer flatly, "It isn't enough," and send the aide off to the prospective guest again.

It wasn't always easy to find something for a guest to say —particularly big stars picked for their billboard value. One of Stark's favorite techniques was to get the guest to say something outrageous at the outset. Carson, knowing the line in advance, might give his camera *that* look—or ad-lib a line that had occurred to him on the spot. A seasoned comedy writer, he often surprised his staff by coming up with better lines than the writers suggested for such spots.

He didn't always get that preset outrageous line, though. Often a female movie star, eager to score for television, would tell the pre-interviewer she was willing to say anything. But the moment she got in front of the camera and thought about the millions of viewers out there, her concern about image would prevail and she would fall into a cautious stance and avoid the stunner. That was bad news. Stark knew that guests who came to say they were doing a movie or playing Las Vegas usually ran out of conversation fast—particularly the Hollywood stars.

Stark felt that *Tonight*'s base in New York City was a major advantage. On the West Coast, the stars' universe tended to begin and end in their own celebrity. He believed that people in New York were more casual about their stardom. They were used to letting their hair down. This seemed to reflect the excitement of the city. New Yorkers usually had a variety of interests and tended to be provocative and exciting people.

But the most skilled performer can bomb, and when this happened Stark had a solution. He would rescue Carson by going to a commercial as soon as possible. This threat of sudden death was—and still is—a strain on all but the most confident performers. But Stark reasonably concluded that the show was the thing, not the guest and his ego. Robert Blake, the macho star of *Baretta,* has told PLAYBOY magazine of the terror of failure as it existed on the show then as now. Blake said:

"There is no experience I can describe to you that would compare with doin' *The Tonight Show* when he's on it. It is so wired, and so hyped, and so up. It's like Broadway on opening night. There's nothing casual about it. And it's not a talk show. It's some other kind of show. I mean, he has such energy, you got like six minutes to do your thing . . . and you better be good. Or they'll go to the commercial after two minutes. . . . They are highly professional, highly successful, highly dedicated people. . . . The producer, all the federales are sittin' like six feet away from that couch. And they're right on top of you, man, just watchin' ya. And when they go to a break, they get on the phone. They talk upstairs, they talk to—Christ, who knows? They talk all over the place about how this person's going over, how that person's going over. They whisper in John's ear. John gets on the phone and he talks. And you're sittin' there watchin', thinkin', what, are they gonna hang somebody? . . . And then the camera comes back again. And John will ask you somethin' else or he'll say, 'Our next guest is . . .' "

Even brilliant comedians will dry up. On his maiden voyage with Carson, drama critic Kenneth Tynan himself was expecting a question concerning a controversial play about Winston Churchill. It didn't help that the act he had to follow was Tiny Tim's "Tiptoe Through the Tulips."

Tynan explains: "Carson froze my marrow by suddenly asking my opinion not of Churchill but of General de Gaulle, and . . . from that moment on, fear robbed me of saliva, so that my lips clove to my gums, rendering coherent speech impossible.

"The fault was mine, for not being the sort of person who can rise to Carson's challenge—i.e. a professional performer."

From Stark's point of view, the tempo had to move. Carson would be aware when there was a lull but had no way of getting out of it unless Stark helped him out of it.

It was no accident that Stark's first guest each night was usually a zaftig female, because that was an easy way to keep things going. Like it or not, *Tonight* had and still does have male-chauvinist overtones. After all, there were Johnny and Ed and Skitch—all males, and a girl added a certain lift. Often Carson would sit there eyeing some well-endowed female guest, making double entendres, and doing takes after her sometimes innocent or inadvertently provocative comments. Not that the women necessarily enjoyed it. Some loved the role and some hated it. Actress Diane Keaton complained to *The New Yorker* following a Carson appearance that Carson "played off her"—put her down in his male-chauvinist manner. But it has always worked for *Tonight.*

Carson's first guest wasn't always a pretty girl. Once Stark used a man who believed in dry-freezing people with terminal illnesses. They were to be thawed when a cure was discovered for their disease. While this was thick stuff for an early shot, Zsa Zsa Gabor came on thereafter and Carson asked: "How'd you like to be frozen and come back?" The audience got humor out of the whole idea of Zsa Zsa coming back after a hundred years, and Carson thus worked something off the early pretentious bit.

Often a strong comedian would do the initial guest number but would do it as part of an interview with Carson—even using some actual laugh lines from a routine as he sat in the guest seat. Carson, really in his element in these segments, would spar with the comic, usually with highly amusing results. Joan Rivers would say, "A funny thing happened to me on the way to . . ." and she and Carson were off and running.

Carson had several natural attributes that Stark capitalized on with the guests. He was athletic, amusing in a demonstration, and dynamic when on his feet. Thus, Stark tried to get Carson away from the desk early in the show—whether to throw darts or to do sitting-up exercises with Debby Drake or other some other health freak. (Carson delighted most viewers but caught hell from some bluenoses in that era when he and Debby stretched out on separate mats and he cracked to the sexy Miss Drake, "Would you like to leave a call?")

Stark also capitalized on Carson's remarkable athletic prowess. For example, Johnny once outbowed a prize-winning archer after a few minutes' training on *Trust.* In a related talent, Stark found Carson to be witty in his reactions when someone taught him something on the show. Carson was even funny when someone taught him how to breathe. And he could rise to the occasion with a serious body builder. Once, when a muscleman-contest winner was on the show, he told Carson to remember that his body was the only home he'd ever have.

Carson came back with, "Yes, I know my home is pretty messy. But I have a woman who comes in once a week."

Stark always hoped that the first guest segment would stand for five minutes and serve to swing the show around the midnight corner. On a typical show, someone like Bob Hope might come on at about that time—an important star to hold the audience. Then a strong vocalist or instrumentalist would appear at 12:15 or 12:20 to break up the talk; then back to talk and perhaps to a cerebral item. Not an Einstein or an Oppenheimer, but an author like astronomer Sagan, or, more typically, one like *Exorcist* writer William Peter Blatty or Dr. William Nolen with a book on surgery. Something interesting to be played straight—possibly a human-interest spot. Something unrelated to show business. The audience was mellow by then and ready for something less strenuous and for the show to wind down.

Stark stressed several things to Johnny, and like any good performer with an appreciation of the role of a mentor with skill, Carson took Stark's advice. Stark stressed the underlying structure of the show and how it could save Carson. He was not out there "naked." He needn't be uptight, because the show did not air in the tense prime-time hour of 8:00 P.M. At midnight, Stark reminded him, the audience was relaxed, and it was therefore easy to entertain them. Give them fun, he said, arguing that they'd excuse anything because Carson would be coming back tomorrow and the next day. Ad infinitum.

The Stark Method Pays Off

By early 1963 the show was seen in 3.7 million homes and Carson was eclipsing Jack Paar's ratings, though Dorothy Parker thought Carson "plastic" and other critics were still trying to figure him out. One critic was to say of Carson's stance, "He almost looks nonplussed; he almost looks happy; he almost looks indignant." Al Bruno, Carson's manager and surrogate stage mother, had Johnny's appeal figured even before Carson got the *Trust* job. Elaborating on his thesis in connection with *Tonight,* Bruno was quoted as saying, "He looks good in all fifty states. He's an All-American guy."

Meanwhile, the stars were vying with each other for the opportunity to join the fun. NBC was to billboard the hottest performers of the day—Danny Kaye, Liberace, and Sammy Davis, Jr., the night he opened in *Golden Boy.* Carson featured comedians like the acerbic Woody Allen, and reaching back in movie history, he tapped dancer Eleanor Powell.

The New York Times's Jack Gould took another look at the show after Carson was settled in. Gould captured the flavor of the show in telling how Powell had resumed her career after her eighteen-year-old son persuaded her to streamline her matronly figure. Svelte and sparkling again, Miss Powell hit *Tonight* full tap. Said Gould, "Her feet fairly sang with infectious rhythm . . . supplemented by Miss Powell's quick twinkle of the eye."

Gould went on to delineate the appeal of the show, the skill and intuition of its host. "Out of the studio audience, under Carson's prodding, came John Bubbles completely unprepared and wearing street shoes. In a matter of seconds Miss Powell and the well-known member of the team of Buck and Bubbles went into a superb tap duel and the screen suddenly achieved that distinctive warmth of real 'pros' hugely enjoying an impromptu ball." Gould found the episode "characteristic of . . . the continuing appeal of *The Tonight Show.*

"Where [else] would one encounter first the revelation of the human being that lies behind every star and then see her act? Not only did Miss Powell send every viewer off to bed with a feeling of renewed youth but in the process her own personality came to the fore as it never did even during her long film career."

Gould went on to comment that "as Carson himself noted, the show does not always have it so lucky. In addition to Miss Powell, Woody Allen was on hand with his supremely funny routine."

Woody was a fine complement to Carson and had a wonderfully disparaging sketch about his estranged wife. He said she came in while he was taking a bath "and sank my boats." He showed a picture of his wife next to a house, and said, "That's my wife on the left—the one with the shingles." A talent coordinator comments that some Woody Allen jokes were so funny he didn't need but a few—"the audiences would laugh a full minute at some of them."

Gould left the Eleanor Powell–Woody Allen show aglow and concluded of Carson's *Tonight* generally: "The late-evening program over at the National Broadcasting Company, all in all, does wear remarkably well. The viewer finds himself living in hopes that are not always realized, to be sure, and when *Tonight* is dull it is extremely so.

"But Mr. Carson, sitting in the chair once occupied by the restless Jack Paar, has worked out a style much his own.

Chiefly, the program is a showcase for one of the quickest minds on the air. When a colloquy gets going he can come up with an inverted quip that is often hilarious. He leans to an impish quality and admittedly savors the double entendre, occasionally to his own disadvantage. But for light laughter his batting average night after night is extraordinarily good."

To a reviewer from *Newsweek* Carson was an "engaging fellow, quick of quip, with a modest, mild manner that lets him get off irreverences and double entendres which might seem crass from less boyish comics. . . . The president of the American Heart Association came on and, flustered, launched his speech with his back to the camera. 'Doctor, it's National Heart Month,' Carson said gently, turning him around. 'We have the wrong part of the anatomy.' "

Implementing the Stark Plan: Talent Coordinators at Work

It was the talent scouts—formally called talent coordinators—who booked for *The Tonight Show*. These individuals found that they had to lead secretive lives. One former member of the Carson entourage recalls that the fawning and red-carpet treatment were unbelievable for staff members in general and talent coordinators in particular.

"It was necessary to have an unlisted telephone and important that you never told anyone you were on the staff of *The Tonight Show*. If you were found out at a party, you suddenly became the focus of attention and inevitably some bore would say, 'I have a son-in-law who sings *very* well.' This [kind of thing] brought all of us very close together. We could only trust each other—we were the only people who didn't want to be on the show."

The salve of an appearance on Johnny Carson will soothe the most scarred ego and—not just incidentally—can add immeasurably to one's worldly holdings. Forgotten talents step into the *Tonight* limelight and land on stage in Las Vegas or on Broadway. That engaging cherub of the 1940s, hoofer Mitzie Gaynor, tapped her tootsies in Burbank a while back and thereafter effervesced again at high stakes in the gambling capital of the western states.

Tonight's non-entertainers can win big, too. Given a particularly scintillating Carson interview, authors of good books with dim prospects—and even writers of bad books that deserve to go nowhere—can suddenly become white-hot and earn fortunes by their pens.

The late Alexander King caught fire on *Tonight*, convulsing viewers with descriptions such as "a face like an inflamed armpit," among other striking word pictures. The former *Time* staffer was plugging his autobiographies bearing the arresting titles *Let This House Be Safe from Tigers* and *Mine Enemy Grows Older*. Presto! King sprang to stardom in the twilight of his time, even winning a talk show of his own on which the irrepressible old gentleman once presented his stagestruck young wife in a snare-drum solo.

Tonight truly means opportunity, and any would-be celebrity with half a wit can appreciate the notoriety that it can bring. In some cases far more imagination is used in landing the date than is expended on the act itself.

Standing behind home plate are the show's umpires or talent coordinators. These professionals are expected to audition acts—to know a fast ball from a curve and to identify bean balls before they can disable the star. They are not always successful. Once while Carson was doing the show from New York—where, unlike California whose psychos are generally unoriginal and passive, the crazies can be fun —a man called to say he owned the world's largest lobster. It happened on the show-business equivalent of a journalist's "light news day." The talent coordinators thought the big crustacean and its master might generate a couple of laughs during the waning moments of the show when it's time to mellow out. The man's motive: to sing on the show.

He arrived with a crate several times bigger than Steve Allen's bread box, and it contained a lobster as long as a bathtub. The man and his captive were ushered on camera and Carson conversed with him concerning the care and feeding of *Homarus americanus* and the presumed hazards of wrestling the beast over a pot of boiling water.

The man sang and left the stage. The segment recorded and in the can, he thanked the talent coordinator who had booked him. He was walking out when the staffer yelled after him, "Hey! You forgot your lobster."

"Oh, I won't be needing it now," the man shot back. "I got it today at the Fulton Fish Market—after you booked me on the show."

The talent coordinators decided to bend a strict rule against accepting gratuities—the lobster man didn't pause to mince words. And, through the wonders of videotape and a gas range, they watched that segment of the show hours later in a colleague's apartment, munching on the very lobster that moved so menacingly on the television screen before them. A small fraud on viewing America as well as on Carson, perhaps. But there certainly had been less entertaining episodes on *Tonight*, and it was an act that the talent coordinators, at least, could get their teeth into.

The coordinators thought twice about turning down such offbeat acts because they knew that Carson's ad-libs often made such things work—for the show as well as the guest. Consider the talking dog. The talent coordinators were avid readers of the show's fan mail because possibilities often turned up in the lines of such letters. One letter from a local viewer extolled the virtues of a verbal canine, and the writers also weighed this one. They reasoned that, even if the dog didn't talk, Carson's takes and his looks askance at the television camera would give viewers a good time. It might be funnier if the dog didn't talk than if he did.

So in due course dog and master were announced on *Tonight,* and the man came through the curtain, his best friend trotting along behind him. The man sat down, leaving the chair nearest the star vacant. His dog jumped into it, turned to Carson, and, clear as a carnival barker, said a quick "Hello!" And the house came down.

Animals are always good prospects, and a myna bird with a vocabulary of a hundred words seemed surefire. The sweet old lady who owned it was naturally distraught when the bird, made nervous by the lights and sounds of the studio at 30 Rock, said nothing at all. John Gilroy, then a talent coordinator, explains that the staff sympathized and suggested the lady leave the bird so that he or she (nobody checked) could get used to the tumult and the trumpeting. The sweet old lady was to come back in a week for a second try. Meanwhile, the temptation to do the obvious was overwhelming. Everybody on the show, it seemed, walked by the cage saying things like "How's your ass?" and "Stick it up your bird!" as the myna, its head cocked attentively, listened to these and other naughty ideas. By the time the poor woman returned, the bird had such a foul beak they couldn't put it on the show and the lady, now devastated, contemplated a suit against NBC over her ruined pet.

Animal acts could backfire for countless reasons. Once, Susan Hampshire, the British actress, was in New York to promote the Columbia picture *Living Free,* sequel to *Born Free.* The young lion cub that was to make an appearance with Susan was on loan from Lion Country Safari, the drive-through wildlife attraction in West Palm Beach, Florida, an enterprise as interested in a *Tonight Show* plug as was Columbia.

The cub had been brought to New York by a handler named Linda, who normally appeared on camera with lend-lease animals in a miniskirted safari suit. Columbia publicity people took one look at Linda and decided that to be upstaged by a cute lion cub was enough of a challenge for their star. Linda, an attractive blonde, was decidedly a surplus animal in Columbia's book, and the *Tonight* staff agreed to keep her off camera.

When Linda heard she was to be denied her usual moment of glory—a modest reward for a lot of messy kittysitting—she was furious. So, shortly before showtime, she glutted the cub with milk. By the time Carson picked up the baby lion it was growling at both ends, and almost immediately the young cat exploded all over one of Johnny's expensive suits. Carson had to tough it until the station break, when he went for a quick change that enabled him to remove the visible—but not the smellable—results of the debacle. While offstage, Johnny spotted Linda, wearing her miniskirt and an expression of studied innocence.

"How long will this smell persist?" he asked.

The culprit, smugly convinced that her guilt had gone undetected, deadpanned the good news: "Oh . . . maybe a week."

It was far longer than that before Lion Country Safari's cats got another crack at Johnny Carson.

It is the talent coordinator's responsibility to make sure that guests come off well—that they talk about interesting things in an engaging manner and not bore the audience with trivia. As Dick Cavett has explained, a good talent coordinator does a certain amount of coaching, saying things like "Tell that story just the way you told it to me . . . and say the line 'And I can never face those people again!' just the way you said it." Cavett went on to say that you had to assure the guest that his stories were not as boring as he thought (or claimed to think) and in some cases had to stay with him to see that he didn't get drunk before air time.

Actors—particularly those with stage experience—are sensitive and smart enough to mold *Tonight* interviews into cohesiveness either through attitude or a point of view. (Those who know they are incapable of this—the ones who can't order coffee without a script—are terrified and often refuse to do the show. "Good God, if he goes to a commercial after a few minutes, I'm finished.")

There is more to it even than that. Put the professional in the wrong format and he may soon be in deep trouble. Talent coordinator Shelly Schultz admits he made a mistake when John Glenn went into orbit around the earth— a first for an American. Shelly thought of Leo Delyon, who had a routine about an astronaut's father which was "really funny." John Glenn was still circling when Shelly called Delyon with what seemed like a good idea—at 2:00 in the afternoon.

"I said, 'Leo, why don't we bring you out in makeup as an old man, and you're this astronaut's father.' It was a little demeaning, but it was funny in staff meeting. So I contrived this thing and suggested to Leo that he come out and really play the part and Johnny would introduce him as John Glenn's father. So we did it. So Leo starts his routine and is making a shmuck out of the guy and he's calling him this and he's calling him that and 'Why don't you go to school?' and, I mean, the audience just didn't think it was funny at all. It was an oil painting out there and Leo is dying and he's too far in it to get out and he had to go through it. Remember that in the early days of the launches we were honest-to-God worried about those astronauts.

"Flop sweat gets picked up on the tube real fast. If a comic is [in trouble] in the middle of his routine you know because the vessels come up in the head, the eyes bulge, and the sweat starts to pour. Oh, it's awful when someone panics.

"Not only was it not funny, I tell you it absolutely ruined Leo's career and it was my fault. When he was through, he got off the stage and cried. He said, 'It's over,' and it was true, it was over, it was absolutely fucking over. Coast to coast. It was the worst death we had in all the years I was with the show.

"Leo was thirty-five then. He ended up being a piano

accompanist for some musical acts. I don't know what he's doing now—but he's got to be pissed off at me, wherever he is."

Not everyone panics. The more experienced and confident stars can make almost anything work. Glynis Johns, the British comedienne, came on once with a sly smile and didn't speak at all. All she did was nod. Guest host Joey Bishop: "You're just in from England?" Johns nods yes. Bishop: "Staying long?" Johns sagely nods no. Etc. The put-on was amusing for everyone—even an anxious Joey Bishop.

But that kind of thing in unskilled hands can lead to disaster. Jay Michaelis of NBC comments that anyone aside from an experienced comic who tries to be wildly funny with Carson is taking a dangerous chance. "If you are a real moron, it is safer to come off like a real moron."

The talent coordinators will worry in any case—especially if, as Robert Conrad did, the guest goes across the street to exercise his elbow and "explore the subtleties of gin."

Michaelis concedes that Conrad did well, was "bouncy and so forth," but the staff would rather the actor had been in the studio, sober and in makeup, a safe thirty minutes before he arrived bubbling with good cheer.

Obviously, the talent coordinators work strenuously to avoid awkwardness and the dead air that may result. They are paid to make sure guests have something fascinating to say—something more than when their next picture or series will debut or when they open in Vegas.

Nonperformers are even more worrisome. People like Dr. Edward Gross, a low-key University of Washington sociologist. No one needed to worry, though. Dr. Gross is studying why people get embarrassed, and he told a winner of a story about one of the most embarrassing moments he'd ever heard of.

Dr. Gross spoke of a man on the lecture circuit who looked down just before he was introduced to discover that his fly was open. He hurriedly zipped it up. Unknowingly, though, he also zipped a tip of the tablecloth into his fly. When he stood up and walked to the center of the speaker's table, he pulled the cloth, candlesticks, centerpiece, and dishes—everything—off the table and onto the floor. Things fell with such a crash that a number of passersby stopped to share the delicious moment. The speaker's embarrassment was only beginning.

The audience snorted—stifling laughter—as the victim worked feverishly at his crotch but found that he couldn't extricate himself. An alert individual left, came back with scissors, and carefully cut the lecturer free. But when the man stood to speak, a small, telltale bit of the cloth hung from his lap. Noticing the remnant—not to mention squeals from the audience—he dropped the hand holding his notes to cover his embarrassment. But every time he gestured, the white flag waved again. By this time, the crowd had exhausted itself in poorly suppressed laughter. Unfortunately, the speaker was not witty enough to use the funny event to his advantage.

Desperately he plowed on, the serious theme of his speech serving as ludicrous counterpoint to his predicament.

As if one evening's pain wasn't enough, news of the episode traveled by word of mouth. Lecturegoers who had heard about it would come to his later speeches, suddenly realize their speaker was "the one," and whisper details of the prior occasion to neighbors. The titters would begin again. The poor fellow finally had to give up his once-lucrative lecture tours and turn to another means of earning a living.

Dr. Gross said little else, but his appearance was a marked success—a talent coordinator's dream for the final minutes of any show.

Obviously, guests can't do it all. Carson sometimes does "blue cards," sheets of stationery passed out before the show for questions from the studio audience. The answers are prepared by the writers when Carson doesn't top their responses with a spur-of-the-moment ad-lib. One of the most famous was written years ago by Dick Cavett. It is now a wheeze that can be dusted off two or three times a year:

"Dear Johnny: I bet you don't remember me, but then again, maybe you do."

Carson: "I told you never to come around when I'm working."

Hazard of the Trade: An Agent "Buys" a Talent Coordinator

The airwaves belong to the American public, and the most serious implication of this little-understood fact, from a talent coordinator's point of view, is the very real possibility that an innocent act—eating a guest's abandoned jumbo lobster, for example—might be interpreted as an act of bribery and subject to stiff federal penalties.

The job itself was fun and well paid without extras—but invitations to see performers as guests of their managers constantly streamed into the *Tonight Show* offices. It was dangerous to accept such an invitation at the manager's expense. Shelly Schultz says, "I always paid my own way. It would have been foolish for me to become obligated, for a Chinese dinner and three free drinks."

Thus Shelly was not only shocked, he was horrified when an agent phoned Carson's producer, and Shelly's good friend, Art Stark, to tell him that Schultz had met the agent downstairs at the page desk at 30 Rock and accepted $500 to put the man's client on the show.

Confident of his associate, Art Stark asked the man to come to his office and tell the story in person. By prearrangement, a few minutes after the man arrived and was indignantly telling his story to Stark, Shelly Schultz walked in to say "Excuse me, Art, I have to ask you something."

Shelly then turned to his accuser to say, "Sorry to interrupt your meeting." Turning again to Stark, Shelly showed Stark a sheet of paper and asked, "Is this okay for tonight?" Stark said, "Fine." Stark then turned to the accuser and said, "By the way, do you know Shelly Schultz when you see him?"

"Absolutely," the man stated emphatically.

At that Stark pointed to his talent coordinator and said, "Well, that's Shelly Schultz and get the fuck out of here."

Writing for Carson:
Young Marshall Brickman at Bat

The Tonight Show once hired a man who had been to a school that taught comedy writing in Hollywood. Instead of putting down "It's so hot outside, the Hoboken ferry just took off its slip," he would put in the emphasis—as though Carson wouldn't know which words to punch—writing, "It's so HOT outside, the Hoboken ferry just took off its SLIP!" He lasted the required minimum for a hiree, thirteen weeks.

Marshall Brickman, who now co-authors movies with another refugee from television writing, Woody Allen, also prepared for a job on *The Tonight Show* in 1967. The show was still in New York then and he "trained" for a few minutes only and with Cavett, who was a client of Brickman's manager, Jack Rollins. In a brief encounter with Cavett, Brickman impressed Dick with his brilliance, learning more than the comedy writer who capped and underlined had in months of schooling.

Brickman took the initiative, asking Cavett, "Let me see some monologue pages the way you turn them in."

Brickman reasoned that if he handed Carson something foreign-looking, as some candidates had—say, a page chock-full of jokes all run together—Carson might be turned off even if Brickman's jokes were funny. Carson might think such a writer didn't know the business.

Cavett showed Brickman some monologue pages, and Brickman set up his jokes along the accepted format. He typed, "Johnny Carson Monologue" in the upper left-hand corner and, under that, "Marshall Brickman" as author. The date was typed in the upper right-hand corner, followed by "TOPIC" in caps, followed in turn by the subject matter, say, "St. Patrick's Day."

Brickman noticed that jokes were double-spaced with no more than four per page and that the margins were wide, and again he followed the format. Brickman wrote his jokes, submitting a couple of monologues in the prescribed formula. Shortly thereafter, Carson called him to the office and asked, "Want to try it for a while?"

"Sure," said the copycat with a flair for Carsonomedy.

Carson said there would be an opening in about three months and to come back then. Chances are this meant some clod like the Hollywood-trained jokesmith was on the way out.

That was fine with Brickman, who was finishing another project at the time. "I went off to Peru, to work on a little film." It was spring 1967. Brickman came back and, as promised, got a job starting at $400 a week—good pay for a young man still in his mid-twenties, and a superb opportunity to boot.

Starting day arrived, and Brickman walked into a room at Carson headquarters and found the other writers talking about a July 4 sketch. Brickman was young enough to be "very excited" at the prospect of working with veteran Carson writers Walter Kempley, a specialist in sketches; Ed Weinberger, believed by his peers to be the best monologue writer in the business; and David Lloyd, another top monologue contributor.

The writers puffed on cigars and were, in Brickman's view, "affectionately hostile. . . . I was the new kid on the block."

Brickman sat down and immediately began reacting like

a true novice. "I started to sweat and get dizzy. I thought it was an anxiety attack."

It wasn't.

Time: Hours later. Scene: A local hospital. Music: "Intermezzo." (Fade)

As our story begins, Marshall Brickman lies in a ward attended by a pretty nurse in starched white uniform who carefully pushes a thermometer between his dry lips. Minutes later, as she removes the thermometer from the young man's lips and glances at the glass rod, her eyebrows rise involuntarily. The mercury has climbed to 105. Marshall is seriously ill. It seems there had been a very bad strain of hepatitis in Peru and Brickman picked it up. The incubation period lasted about six weeks, and in Brickman's case ended in his very first hour with the Carson show.

Brickman was appalled by his bad luck and comments, "I thought, 'Well, I blew it.'"

To play it Hollywood-style, Brickman was not paid while he was in the hospital, which was typical of NBC's policy toward writers on *Tonight* at the time. But wait. Shortly after Brickman entered the hospital, Carson called to say that Brickman was not to worry—"Just feel better." Brickman did not expect to be paid and was pleased with Carson's "very nice gesture."

Brickman recovered, of course, but not before his thirteen-week contract ran out. When he realized that, he nearly had a relapse. Soon, though, he was back with the show, doing his "first real job ever" and quickly discovering what every writer with a deadline soon learns: "I was completely disabused of any romantic notions about 'inspiration.' We had to come up with the material. I learned to work under pressure."

Brickman's close friend Woody Allen, with whom Brickman collaborated on *Annie Hall, Manhattan,* and some of Woody's other movies, has described his television experience in similar terms. "You wrote a show to be seen at the end of the week, and there was no room for pussyfooting. You had to write something. And writing something is three quarters of the battle. Most people strike out by never writing anything. I can go into a room at nine o'clock in the morning with no ideas and come up with something. I can dredge it up. It may not be as good as when a terrific idea hits me, but I don't think you can spend your life waiting for that to happen."

Brickman didn't. Within eight months he had so impressed Carson that he became head writer. But it was a hectic pace—especially when the show went to the West Coast for visits. Once there was a musicians' strike and it was Brickman's responsibility to keep the show alive with additional material, sketches, bits. "I remember I used to carry my room key from Gene Autry's Continental Hotel at 4801 Sunset Boulevard so that when I had a nervous breakdown, they would know where to deliver me."

Brickman clearly knew how to write for Carson, and he stayed with the show nearly three years—until late 1970. He could have stayed longer. "I left because Cavett had a show and he was a friend and the idea of trying to make something work that wasn't already formed was a challenge.

"Tonight was like an ocean liner and Cavett a flimsy craft. I wanted to make that show work. Carson was upset, but he did let me go and he didn't have to. That was a much more mature thing that he did than what I did. He never got angry with me directly, but I was young and a little crazy. I don't think I would handle it the same way now. Carson was very nice. He offered me more money. But emotionally I had checked out."

The show that Cavett had was not in direct competition with Tonight, but it was compared to it nevertheless. It was a risky thing for Brickman to do, and for Cavett too, and they both knew it. Brickman explains, "I was a little more eccentric then."

Perhaps the viewer was too. *Tonight* thrived and Cavett didn't. The staying power of Carson's *Tonight* was proved once again—and in competition, however indirect, with two of the best writers Carson ever had.

Private Lives:
Carson's Stormy Second Marriage

Johnny Carson once said that second wife, Joanne, was so tiny there were Donald Ducks on her underpants. At five feet two inches and ninety-four pounds, tiny she was. Perennially youthful and pixieish, she looked like a carefree college coed in her Jax pants, bobby socks, and sweaters.

She was also headstrong and determined—qualities that would have an impact on members of the *Tonight* staff in time.

Joanne Copeland was born in San Francisco, the daughter of a man who worked in personnel. After her parents separated, she was raised in Catholic convents. At San Mateo College she was much envied as a cheerleader who went steady with the president of the student body. After graduation, she became a stewardess for Pan American. Later she came to New York to model her beautiful hands and to attend graduate school at Hunter College.

According to Al Bruno, then Carson's manager, Johnny and Joanne met in a singles restaurant called the Inner Circle, located in Johnny's building on York Avenue on the East Side of Manhattan. Carson agreed to give Joanne a professional evaluation of a contemporary's violin playing and so invited her to dinner. Carson, it has been reported, listened to the audio tape and said, "I think she should quit as soon as possible."

At the time Carson met her, he was suffering through his divorce from Jody Wolcott, his college sweetheart, who among other things had tired of her isolation in the Carson home in Harrison, New York, with the Carsons' three young sons—though she was not atuned to the swift life of New York City. According to Johnny Carson, the divorce was the worst thing that ever happened to him and certainly didn't help him financially.

The second time around, Carson had a wife who was comfortable in the Manhattan scene. Joanne Copeland had even appeared on television shows originating in New York —one of those pretty girls who brings the next guest forward on game shows. But it was as a home companion that she starred with Carson. Joanne worked hard at being Mrs. Johnny Carson—it was her consuming passion. At first they lived in three apartments Johnny leased in a U-shaped building at 450 East 63rd Street. Joanne put her energies to work there, decorating the apartments to her own taste. A friend says, for example, she lined one library wall with shelves, packing them with books organized in a novel manner—by color. The Carsons stayed at 450 East 63rd for four years, then moved into the posh new UN Plaza.

In 1967, apartments in the UN Plaza were for sale at $11,000 a room—high for the time. The building appealed to such wealthy celebrities as David Susskind, Truman Capote, and Robert Kennedy, among others. The apartments were spectacular and had views to match. One could see the East River and, in certain apartments, the United Nations buildings themselves. Many apartments featured working fireplaces. The heating-cooling system was regarded as a mechanical triumph. Hot water could be circulated in one set of pipes, and cold in another set. Thus, in those awkward periods between winter and summer, when most apartment dwellers are either too hot or too cold, the system could be fine-tuned for maximum comfort.

The Carsons paid $163,000 in cash for their spacious duplex. (Sold long ago by Carson, the apartment is now worth a fortune in the booming Manhattan market—somewhere around $750,000 to $1,000,000, a co-op expert guesses.) A representative of the management showed Joanne through a dozen of the already occupied UN Plaza apartments for decorating ideas. Joanne was planning to do the work herself. Eventually she painted some rooms a chocolate brown she and Johnny mixed themselves and called "El Greco Bronze." And she set to work improving the apartment. In some cases, extra closets were installed to house Johnny's many outfits. The extra closets in some bedrooms were so large they reduced the remaining space to maid's-room dimensions. Long after they moved in, building personnel were baffled to find that there were no countertops in the kitchen. Still, the Carsons rarely ate out —"In thirty-two days of the month, we eat home maybe thirty," said Joanne—and Johnny sometimes contented himself with milk or apple juice and popcorn he prepared himself. He also ate Sara Lee chocolate cake, "morning, noon, and night."

In an interview four years after her marriage, Joanne described the style of her marriage:

"Last night, we were here, and I'm doing the laundry and he's standing there popping corn. If I told you what we were wearing—I was in bikinis and a smock, he was wearing khaki pants. No shorts, no socks. I mean, everyone expects him to wear a silk dressing gown and me to wear feather boas. I'll wear Dr. Denton's as much as anything."

Sometimes Johnny played with one of his toys—his guitar, his drum set, his telescope, his projector, or his video-tape recorder, all of which were set up in a corner of the living room. That videotape recorder came with camera, and Johnny put it to many uses. Joanne said, "Sometimes he'll just tape the view through the window, or we'll do bits. He interviews me. I play different people, usually a girul from the Bronx who's just come to New Yawk. Or I say things like, 'You're such a big star. Can I touch you?' "

As Joanne described it, they were devoted almost exclusively to each other: "I have a ball. I love life. Johnny's the same way. We feel the same way about things, although I'm more vocal. I have this joy for living, like, I'll go out with my boots on and throw snowballs at the doorman. . . . Before I was married, I had lots of friends. I had somebody to talk to, somebody to go to dances with, somebody to go to movies with. I found that all in one person, so I didn't need anybody else. [Johnny is] a husband, a father, a lover, a doctor. . . . He fills my needs completely. I can't hold myself. I can't cuddle up to myself. I just need him to love me. The rest I can do myself."

Despite Joanne Carson's determined efforts to make him happy—efforts that included a large UN Plaza party for Carson at which a still very private Carson withdrew to a separate room with New York City Mayor John Lindsay for the duration, thus miffing the other superachievers in the building—the two experienced growing tension together. Carson was drinking, reflecting his problems at home and the pressures of seven and a half hours of network television each week. Something had to give.

According to columnist Harriet Van Horne, Carson's marriage to Joanne was always stormy. It was clear to the few who observed them closely that the marriage was in serious trouble.

In time, Joanne was to sue Carson for $125,000, as reported in *The New York Times,* charging that he broke a matrimonial agreement by ridiculing her on his TV program.

On June 21, 1972, the Carsons were divorced, after nine

years of marriage. Court records were sealed. The *Times* reported simply that Joanne charged Carson had been abusive. On September 5, she was awarded $100,000 a year in alimony and other cash settlements.

Storm Clouds: An Angry Carson Rebels Under the Strain

A couple of years after Stark applied his strong hand to the *Tonight* tiller, Johnny Carson's manner began to change. This reflected Johnny's realization that he was becoming enormously important. He was no longer host of a daytime television quiz show—that is, no longer one of television's glorified spear carriers. Instead, he was perceived by viewer and fellow entertainer alike to be a prince among performers. His was one of the most envied showcases for an entertainer anywhere—a five-day-a-week network television program. Dozens of talented would-be stars then working show-business backwaters coveted Carson's franchise as he rapidly became one of the biggest names in the world of show business. And no one perceived Carson's change in status more profoundly than Carson himself.

Had he any doubts about his growing fame and the value of it, they vanished when he opened in Las Vegas at the Sahara with a stand-up comedy act in 1964. Fifteen hundred fans came to see him nightly, some of them driving hundreds of miles. So popular was he in person that he broke the attendance record the show-business superstar Judy Garland had established two years earlier. Carson was euphoric and at the same time angry as he contemplated his six-figure salary at NBC. The Sahara management by contrast agreed to pay Carson $40,000 a week.

Everyone but the executives at NBC, it seems, realized Carson was worth top dollar even though his midnight audience was a fraction of those that top prime-time shows played to. The ad revenues on a smaller audience five nights a week eclipsed the revenues of popular once-a-week prime-time shows—especially so in that NBC was generally behind CBS in the prime-time ratings and thus operated, generally speaking, on a smaller advertising scale. The earnings from *Tonight* were already a measurable factor in the overall profits of parent company RCA. Even top Hollywood stars who appeared on the show knew Carson was important, and viewers were impressed—even appalled— as bigger-than-life movie personalities fawned over Carson shamelessly.

Nevertheless, in 1966, Carson's salary was a relatively modest $400,000 to $800,000 a year, or about $8,000 to $16,000 a week—depending upon which report you believe. Carson, still a taciturn Nebraskan, bristled at efforts to learn the true figure, arguing that he wouldn't think of asking anybody what they earned and demanding equal courtesy.

Says one man who dealt with Carson closely in the mid-1960s, "Within two short years Carson had become a real, honest-to-goodness star." For the staff, it sometimes meant dealing with star temperament.

To a substantial degree, Carson's short temper reflected exhaustion. Any performer would concede that Carson's on-camera hours were awesome. He told a reporter at the time that the schedule was "rough." Of the three major hosts, only Steve Allen, in a looser, more impromptu, and consequently less exhausting format, seemed to thrive under the load. Carson, like Paar, wearied and became irritable.

Carson complained to a *New York Times* reporter that for him "It's one of those strange shows where you're at work from the time you get up in the morning until you go to bed at night." In a jest to another he said that he was negotiating with the International Red Cross for a vacation.

Typically, he said, he got up between 9:00 and 10:00 A.M. and was not one to face the new dawn with zest, to say, "Hey, hey, another day!" Rather he would "just grumble and sulk for a while. . . . I don't really start to function until noon or afterward."

Carson would stay in his Manhattan apartment until about 2:00 P.M., when he left for the studio. By that time he had already read several newspapers—grist for his topical humor on the show. His pace picked up thereafter as he worked on his monologue, reviewed notes on guests, and huddled with his producer until the midnight hour when the show went on live.

Weariness leads to irritation, as everyone knows, and in a busy star—an individual who is likely to be high-strung and overstimulated much of the time—irritation can lead to rage. He answered with asperity when asked about his growing reputation for being defensive and withdrawn. "I'm friendly, aren't I? I'm polite, aren't I? I'm honest! All right, so my bugging point is low! I'm not gregarious. I'm a loner. I've always been that way. . . ."

NBC was not skilled in the care of stars—it lost Jack Benny and a host of top radio stars in 1948 partly because CBS pampered its stars while General Sarnoff, for example, had never bothered to meet Jack Benny. In the same fashion, Carson was just another employee. Whatever care was lavished on the stars came from the network vice-presidents. While they are well paid, the NBC vice-presidents don't earn a fraction as much as a star. They could hardly see why a star would need so much money and they forget that, as George W. Goodman ("Adam Smith") so aptly pointed out in *The Money Game,* money is the way the game is scored. Nor do network vice-presidents face pressures in any way comparable to those faced by Carson.

Carson became more and more irked that the network didn't understand or seem to care about his problems.

Finally, he hit them where it hurt the most. He took to making fun of commercials. He once interrupted Ed Mc-Mahon, who was in the process of demonstrating Smucker's butterscotch topping, by asking how long it would take the "ice cream" to melt. McMahon fidgeted uncomfortably, and when Carson pressed the point Mc-Mahon finally admitted that the "ice cream" was lard—necessary because ice cream would melt under the hot TV lights. Carson then called for greater honesty. In that connection, Carson went on to say that in the ad for a certain floor cleaner, graphite was sprinkled on the floor so that the mop would clean in a single swipe. This and other strokes were ominous—revealing an anger reminiscent of Paar before the walkout.

Ed McMahon was good at what he did, but his role was circumscribed. He knew not to stumble onto Carson's turf. In a climactic dialogue he did cross that line. Carson was telling how mosquitoes only went for really passionate people. McMahon later recalled ruefully, "Without thinking, I slapped my arm. It was instinctive. But it killed his punch line."

Ed McMahon sank reluctantly into the secondary role Carson so obviously wanted for him. The second banana recognized the show as his bread and butter, and he has not stepped over the line deliberately since.

One admiring talent coordinator says of McMahon's handling of the on-camera relationship, "He knows that man so well that the rise of a Carson eyebrow will cue him. He knows when to lay back and he knows when to help Carson. If McMahon says nothing but ten words a night, those ten words are what keeps the roll going."

Though Carson had resolved some differences with NBC, he continued to fume about his treatment by the network, and his displeasure was evident to the *Tonight* staff.

Bad days were even noticeable to outsiders. A writer for the now-defunct *Herald Tribune* visited the show in New

York on one of those days. The reporter, who had observed Carson's mood, was surprised at how well Carson was able to hide his testiness once he basked in the glow of the studio lights. The reporter said that as soon as Carson moved onstage to the host's chair he experienced a "chameleonlike change, becoming the pink-cheeked elf" viewers know and love.

"Under the camera's red eye, Carson seemed his usual dimpled, good-natured, imperturbable self. The viewer must have figured Ed was having a hangover or something when he muttered, 'It's not a night to disagree with you.' 'What was that?' Carson said. Ed's reply: 'Whatever you say is aces with me.' There was a special quality to the studio laughter—as if most of it was coming from the margins of the studio where the staff stands whooping it up. Carson did one of his cutesy-pie double takes."

If Ed had a hangover, Carson could sympathize. As Johnny told Mike Wallace on *Sixty Minutes* not long ago, the worst side of his nature came out when he was drinking.

Superagent Irving "Swifty" Lazar remembers Carson during that period as a "blackout drunk," as Kenneth Tynan reported in *The New Yorker*. Irving explained that "a couple of drinks was all it took. He could get very hostile." But he was a "brawler who couldn't lick a blind cat," according to one old crony.

It's a wonder Carson survived those early days, for he was vulnerable in the extreme as a result of his evening capers. The drinking bouts are proof, in the view of former Carson employees, that he was at the core "a seething lump of hostility," as Harriet Van Horne put it in a piece on Carson in the New York *Post* at the time Carson was threatening to quit. Miss Van Horne's deceased husband, David Lowe, knew this. He was a documentary producer for CBS, but he also moonlighted as director of *Who Do You Trust?* for ABC.

As Miss Van Horne saw it, Joanne Carson bears a share of the responsibility for Carson's drinking. From the begin-

ning, Johnny and Joanne were locked in mortal combat.
Miss Van Horne says he rarely sallied forth on one of his
frequent nightclub visits without either Art Stark or Ed
McMahon.

But when it came to the show, Carson was monomania-
cal. He gave of his best—laboring long hours over his
monologues. More than that, he is a superior wit, with a
marvelous sense of timing, and was thus a prize package for
NBC. And if something threatened the enterprise apart
from Carson's own conduct, Carson was quick to lop off the
ailing member—whether it was a writer, a producer, or
even a once-useful associate who also happened to be an
old, old friend.

In view of his enormous success, then, it is no wonder
that Carson, high-strung and proud, was vexed by the network attitude. He and his staff were equally appalled at his
treatment by NBC.

An NBC party marking his second anniversary, when the
show was an unqualified hit, seemed designed to bait him.
Shelly Schultz recalls: "NBC gave a party in a conference
room on the fifth floor. Well, you have not seen an angry
man until you've seen Carson. . . . There we were sipping
drinks out of plastic cups with some dead hors d'oeuvres.
I've seen smoke come out of a guy's nose before but I'm
telling you this was steam. He was pissed off. As I recall, we
all went out and got incredibly drunk."

NBC was to regret this and other slights in days to come.
Years passed and NBC continued to blunder.

In 1965, Carson became enamored of the idea of doing
a weekly television *Friars Roast* so that he could take it easy
—get away from the strain of a nightly television show. Al
Bruno tried in vain to change Carson's mind, though
Bruno reluctantly negotiated a deal with Anheuser-Busch
to sponsor the roasts. Carson was to package and produce
the show and to get a lucrative Budweiser distributorship
to boot. Bruno reports that after they made the commit-
ment, Carson became apprehensive, sensing perhaps that

what he was giving up was too important. In any case Carson told Bruno he'd changed his mind. Thereafter, the distributorship deal collapsed and Bud became just another sponsor of *The Tonight Show.*

But there were serious repercussions for Bruno. Perry Massey, who had been NBC's man in charge of commercials on *Tonight,* explains: "There was a period in Johnny Carson's life between the years 1965 and 1967 when he got rid of most of those who were closest to him." More than anyone else, Al Bruno may be said to have made Johnny's success possible. It was Bruno who campaigned relentlessly for two years to get Carson *The Tonight Show* and thereafter persuaded Carson to take it.

Bruno spent many off hours with Carson, socialized with him, and advised him in his personal life as well. In the end, this didn't help Bruno. In any case, Al Husted says that at UN Plaza Joanne knew the rich and well-known Sonny Werblin's wife. Werblin was regarded as a superagent and supermanager, and she and Johnny believed that Werblin would be good for Johnny's bank account. She persuaded Carson to hire the man who was later to become famous as the man behind the Meadowlands Raceway in northern New Jersey. Bruno, Johnny's longtime manager and confidant, was out.

Al Bruno had no warning. He believed he and Johnny were still close one morning in 1966 when he found a short telegram on his desk at 10:00 A.M. In a few words, the telegram said the relationship was being terminated. It has since been reported that Carson was displeased that a Miami cabaret booking Bruno had been involved in had gone badly; that the backstage crew had failed to handle the many sound effects Carson's act called for. Another source insists that Carson had been seething for some time before he fired Bruno. This supposedly reflected what some say was an inauspicious beginning of Carson's *Tonight* reign when he appeared to some at NBC to be doing poorly. Bruno, the story goes, had offered another client, one Mike

Douglas, to replace Johnny Carson. Al Bruno heatedly denies this story, and the solid ratings of the show in the early months do not support the theory. It is possible, of course, that the story was told by someone who for some reason wanted Bruno out.

Either way, when the telegram arrived, a bewildered Bruno telephoned Carson immediately for an explanation. While Johnny took the call and insisted he wanted to remain friends, he had no answer when Bruno asked, "How can we remain friends if you won't tell me why you're doing this?" The telephone call lasted about a minute and a half, Bruno told the author.

If Carson truly wanted to be friends, his reported conduct with regard to Bruno's clients thereafter is curious. Carson is said by Bruno to have complained when his producer, Art Stark, booked Bruno clients like Jimmy Dean on *The Tonight Show* thereafter. Bruno says that in order to save Art Stark embarrassment he stopped asking for *Tonight* spots. For this and other reasons, Bruno's career as a top show-business manager soon was effectively ended. He has turned to other business interests. He is not unfriendly toward Carson and still remembers him fondly.

He told the author, "It was delightful working with him. My client relationship with him was a lot of work and a lot of fun. I would not be telling the truth if I didn't say that." Bruno remembers the good times—that he and Carson spent much free time together, playing golf among other things, and that Carson kept a speedboat on Long Island Sound in New Rochelle and that they would commute to New York in it, through the rough East River waters where Carson, an ex–Navy man, was right at home. Says Bruno ruefully, "I'm a little disappointed that after all these years he hasn't ever tried to get back to me—to inquire or say 'Hello' or 'You son of a bitch' or whatever. I am sure it would be difficult to call me, but I think after all these years it would be easier. I'm still mad about that."

Carson's Take-a-Walk Revolution

If NBC had recognized Carson's contribution from the beginning, he might never have jeopardized *Tonight*'s future in a serious three-way competition. The fateful moment came in the spring of 1967. The American Federation of Television and Radio Artists—union of broadcast stars—struck all three networks.

Suddenly, the golden fountain of network revenues—easily one of the most impressive profit pumps in business—was seriously diminished as actors walked off the sets, donned their tailored blue jeans, and took up picket signs around 30 Rock and at the other network offices. Walking the line, these hardy star-entrepreneurs—in many ways the antithesis of unionism—looked like fashion-plate working stiffs. For once in the nation's history, strikers drew crowds of adoring fans.

The networks improvised, turning to reruns to fill the void. At NBC, *Tonight* was a natural for this rescue operation. For years recorded Carson shows had been playing every Saturday night—thus squeezing additional riches out of the best moments of *Tonight*.

But the minute NBC put on reruns of Johnny's shows, Carson sprang a trap. Acting out of the frustration of years of network indifference, the star of late-night television had his lawyers fire off a letter informing NBC that the network had breached the Carson contract and that it was therefore void. It does seem curious that NBC's top executives had never thought to court their human money machine as did the successful movie producers who ladled spoonfuls of sugary attention on their stars. But the top men in the black suits at NBC had neglected Carson, and the day of reckoning had come. While NBC complained vigorously at Carson's decision, their protest was in vain. He packed his bags and left to bask in the Florida sunshine as the NBC brass continued fussing and fuming in New York.

(While in Fort Lauderdale, Florida, Carson drew his own turn on the rack when he remarked that he was "just an unemployed prince." This allusion to royalty brought national ridicule in the newspapers. Carson, who had never liked the press anyway, was angry the reporters had forgotten that years earlier he had conceded on the air during his debut as *Tonight* host that Paar was king and he was just a prince.)

Carson's desertion couldn't have happened at a more inopportune time for NBC. Envious rival networks had been scheming to capture a share of NBC's midnight booty. Finally, they were about to offer serious competition.

There was an ironic footnote to the situation. Prior to the strike and Carson's departure, a top NBC publicity aide who had been worrying about forthcoming ABC late-night competition with Joey Bishop as host approached NBC's top man, Julian Goodman, with a novel suggestion. Why not have Carson stage a walkout and steal the headlines from the competition? The idea was rejected out of hand.

The actual walkout was a stunning setback, and NBC officials were understandably apprehensive when they read the letterhead on Carson's communication. Prominently displayed: the name of Johnny's top negotiator, Louis Nizer, a celebrated New York lawyer known for ingenuity, implacable bargaining methods, and surpassing awards for his clients. If NBC was lucky enough to get its star back, it was likely to be at a dazzling price jump.

Nizer was assisted in his endeavors by a show-business specialist—veteran lawyer N. Arnold Grant. Nizer plunged right in. He knew that he could never learn how much the traffic would bear until he found out how much advertising revenue NBC was earning on the show. This figure had never been revealed by NBC. But Nizer simply checked out Madison Avenue contacts whose agencies were buying time on the show. Nizer soon had a pretty good idea how much *Tonight* was worth to NBC.

Arriving to negotiate, Nizer pressed his argument hard with NBC. Says one NBC aide of the period, "I heard from a couple of the senior executives that Nizer was very difficult and that he got what he wanted. What Nizer tried to do—his bargaining move—was to say: 'Carson represents $25 million in revenues [or whatever] and look what he is making. He is entitled to a better percentage of the take.' That was when people first started throwing the million-dollar figure around."

According to one report, Carson was to be paid over $4 million in three years and that worked out to about twice what he had been getting if he was getting the top amount previously estimated. That is, his new salary was supposedly to have been $30,000 a week. (In previous negotiations his growing power had become manifest. He had already secured his thirteen weeks of vacation a year. And that annual vacation would stretch to fifteen weeks. With his 1980 contract—who knows?)

Though the contract was signed and Carson was prepared to return, Perry Massey detected an ominous note.

Massey, former director of commercials, recalls that, six months before the walkout, he'd been promoted by NBC and was to leave the program. That evening Carson had graciously interrupted his monologue and introduced Perry on the show. In the months preceding the walkout, however, Massey had been reassigned to be network executive on *The Tonight Show*.

Now he heard that Carson was angry with him. He

shrugged it off, thinking that whatever the problem it would pass. But it didn't. He was taken off the show and never told why.

Some of Carson's firings are better understood by those affected, for there were sometimes clear-cut deficiencies and the staff understood that those who let Carson down would be jettisoned. Merv Griffin has explained to this author the very real problem, saying, "In this business you either throw out your staff every three or four years, or you change networks and find new goals. I change networks; Carson fires his staff."

Carson Fires His Producer

At first, Art Stark was unaware that his career as Carson's producer was in jeopardy. Stark had known during the Carson contract negotiations that one of Nizer's demands, a demand met by the network, was that Carson would have the right to hire and fire all staffers. Stark had been apprehensive about that until Carson told him that the producer's job was safe. Reassured, Stark relaxed.

Nevertheless, no sooner had Carson won his demands than the climate changed. Stark, a veteran of many showbiz wars, immediately sensed trouble. Thereafter, on a grim, snowy day in Manhattan, Art Stark met Skitch Henderson as usual at 8:00 A.M. outside the Park Avenue nursery where both men's children went to school. Art asked Skitch—who worked for the network, not the star— whether Skitch had heard anything through his sources in the broadcast company. Skitch had heard nothing.

Skitch knew that every weekday there was a noon meeting on the forthcoming show, and Art would then call Carson at home at about 3:00 or 4:00 P.M. to report.

Stark said to Skitch, "There is something wrong. . . . The prince hasn't taken my call for a couple of days." Skitch, who years earlier had taken up on Carson's nickname and sealed it by serenading Carson with "Someday My Prince Will Come," could offer no clue.

Stark had reason to be apprehensive. He had always taken a strong hand with Carson, and some who overheard Stark's tough talk to Carson had asked Johnny why he took the rough treatment Art dealt out. Art couldn't have changed had he wanted to. Though he was and still is personally fond of Johnny, he had a strong personality and knew no other way to work with Johnny than to be blunt and decisive.

Skitch, who was very close to Stark, became apprehensive along with his friend on that cold, sad winter day. Says Skitch, "Stark was such a warhorse. He was scarred enough to have a sixth sense about protecting himself."

Stark's sixth sense was justified, and he didn't have to wait long for an answer. Carson abruptly summoned Stark to his apartment and stated that he wanted another producer—one who was not associated with NBC. Stark was flabbergasted and asked when he was to leave the show. "Right now," said Carson.

Neither Art Stark nor Al Bruno will speculate today as to actual causes of their terminations, but there were job-related factors at work in any event. A source close to the situation may have the immediate reason for Stark's termination. Just before his broadcast strike, Carson let his staff know that he would stay out and he expected them to stay out, too. A concerned Art Stark went to his lawyer to explain a dilemma. Stark had a contract with both NBC and the show itself. What was he to do? The lawyer advised him that he could be fired and rendered incapable of handling the show if he didn't go in. So he did go in—for a day. He then threw caution to the winds and joined the others who had stayed out. Carson, some say, weighed Stark's disloyalty in the balance when he decided to fire him.

It is also considered likely that Carson simply didn't want

Stark's strong hand on the *Tonight* tiller now that the show was solidly successful. And Stark's hand was strong.

Says Skitch Henderson, "He had everybody's respect. He had balls. He had discipline. He had almost a hard-hat approach, which was very helpful to Carson. Writers would bring in lines for Carson for Stark's reaction. He would go down the paper quickly and say, 'This works, this doesn't work,' etc. He was very skillful." Obviously some found this abrasive, and, Skitch adds, "He could be faulted for unnecessary roughness, perhaps."

Skitch also believes "the show would have gone down the tube without Art Stark."

When the blow came, Art Stark, though he had been apprehensive, was nevertheless unprepared for the swiftness with which the blow was delivered. It shattered him and he hasn't gotten over it completely even today. Skitch says that Stark came to his restaurant, Daly's Dandelion, opposite Bloomingdale's in Manhattan, to drink every day for two months after Carson gave him the ax.

Small wonder. Among other letdowns, Art Stark and his wife became social pariahs immediately thereafter. Comedienne Joan Rivers and her husband were exceptions—friends who stuck. They took the Starks to dinner the very next night.

When a Steve Allen drops a Jules Green or a Johnny Carson lets an Al Bruno or Art Stark go, the impact is likely to be severe both personally and professionally. The dropped aide doesn't just suffer temporary loss of income until the next assignment. In a real sense, it may be the end of the line in show business. Or, if not that, certainly a time to scramble; a time quickly to alter a style of life, including the sale of an expensive cooperative apartment in Manhattan and a home on the shore—a time to revert to a diminished style of life.

The lesson for the aide is that once he has served his role he must realize he may be jettisoned in favor of a new mentor in a new period in the star's life. If one would avoid this career hazard, one does it by not having that career in the first place—by never working for a star, as Bing Crosby once advised Skitch Henderson.

These days Art Stark's career is in low gear, and it has been for years. He has produced specials for the most part of late. Had he continued as Carson's personal business manager, Bruno would have become richer than he has become in other endeavors, but he is a successful business-man nonetheless and seems happy and well adjusted. His main regret is that his friend seems not to have cared about him personally.

I had long conversations with Al Bruno and Art Stark. Both were worried that any comment would be regarded as "sour grapes."

According to most reports, Carson finds it easier to be a friend now that he is a superstar and is married to his third wife, Joanna Holland. Joanna is by all accounts a strong, superior person and has given Johnny's life new meaning and dimension.

In any case, if Carson's friends include those who have done the most for him lately it is understandable. Stars are extremely vulnerable to opportunistic hangers-on and are understandably afraid that the golden flow of wealth will dry up and that their advisers meantime will have wasted or even embezzled their assets. It happened to Allen Funt and scores of other talents.

Certainly a television star's associates *are* in a position to hurt him. Sycophants are rife in television. Dick Cavett has said that once Carson gives up that show, "the same people who are sucking up to him now" won't bother to answer Carson's telephone calls.

Looking at Carson in the context of the jesters of the world, it may be a necessary quality of his personality that he remain cold and aloof. Till Eulenspiegel didn't get to be one of history's great clowns by good works. Carson is by the coldness of his nature superbly equipped to make cutting remarks. The cooler the jester, the more analytical he can be in humor—the more *devastatingly* funny.

The Survivors: Ed McMahan and Doc Severinsen

Ed McMahon

If Johnny Carson hadn't insisted that Ed McMahon continue as his announcer when Carson left ABC and *Who Do You Trust?* to host *Tonight*, NBC would have followed its instincts and replaced McMahon with someone else.

NBC was wrong and Carson was right. McMahon is a particularly effective foil for Johnny with his ingratiating laugh and because he fights the temptation to comment when Carson is building to a laugh.

It's been a rewarding assignment financially. Ed McMahon started modestly as a bingo announcer in a carnival at the age of sixteen. He states that holding a mike in his hand appealed to him from the first. But he spent some embarrassing moments at the bingo cage before he learned how to spiel. In bingo, the operator gets the money before the game starts. The art of giving a bit back calls for more skill than one might think.

McMahon discovered that the trick of calling bingo was to "get the rhythm going and finally heat up to something like the old southern prayer meetings where everyone gets caught up in the swing of the thing."

Eventually apprenticed to a carnival master—one Whitey

McTaag, whom McMahon repected but didn't like—Mc-Mahon practiced the man's rhythms, inflections, and pronunciations. "I mimicked the way he'd pick each little numbered ball out of the cage, hold it up dramatically for a moment, and then, even more dramatically, call the number on it."

McMahon was also a boardwalk pitchman in Atlantic City and was by his own account an expert at conning "marks" out of a dollar or two. Cynics would call this ideal training for a TV pitchman.

Clearly, Ed's youthful job experience was colorful and rewarding for a streetwise kid who was ready to go all the way. For example, even before he knew how, he grabbed an opportunity to earn extra money driving the semitrailer his bingo unit used to travel between locations. He was the kind of "main chance" player who always seemed to find that unusual opportunity. It is perhaps understandable, then, that he became a Marine pilot during World War II.

Before McMahon was assigned to a warship, the United States dropped the atomic bomb and the Japanese sued for peace. McMahon wasn't always so lucky. When the Korean conflict erupted, he was called back and his broadcast career in Philadelphia, where he was well known and successful, was truncated for a time.

Eventually he returned to Philadelphia and climbed the ladder, even having a talk show called *McMahon and Company* that followed the Jack Paar *Tonight Show* in the schedule for a time. Then came that telephone call from Johnny Carson in New York, and soon he was to begin a career as Carson's foil.

Under his contract with NBC, Ed gets eight weeks of paid vacation and a six-figure salary. A compulsively active man, McMahon earns a lot more announcing commercials for Alpo Dog Food and Budweiser Beer. Occasionally he even gets a shot at a feature film.

He has also been involved in a variety of business ventures. Some of McMahon's enterprises from the early period seem to have modest potential for profit. One produced industrial films and designed exhibits for public and trade shows, including the Vatican Pavilion at the New York World's Fair in 1964–65. Another manufactured paper products—among them, artistic postcards, fancy stationery, and decorative spice plaques to hang in kitchens.

In the mid-1960s McMahon's outside activities were getting considerable publicity on the show as a conversational filler. At one point he had three moribund companies—Parthenon Productions, Delphi Productions, and Corinthian Productions. McMahon had a Greek fixation, it seems. In his autobiography, *Here's Ed,* McMahon sees himself as a thoughtful man and wonders if in a prior incarnation he might not have walked the streets of Athens in the Golden Age of Greece with Aristophanes, Plato, Aristotle, Socrates, Euripides, Euclid, "and that bunch."

"But the great era I was part of saw the twilight of the Golden Age of radio and the dawning of television and I was so busy helping it dawn that I didn't have time to make the Athens scene."

McMahon occupies a small but important place in the history of broadcasting, and the fifty-seven-year-old native of Detroit is painfully aware of the fact that, without Carson, he might have been just another struggling staff announcer. As he has said, *"The Tonight Show* is my staple diet, my meat and potatoes—I'm realistic enough to know that everything else stems from that."

Professionally, McMahon is the straight man, the second banana. "I'm the backup guy. I must be there when he needs me and off when he doesn't need me. Sometimes we get five minutes out of nothing. I supply filler material that gets us from one place to another."

McMahon prides himself on the fact that he reads the newspapers thoroughly and often is able to come up with a bit of information when Carson or a guest on the show is stumped for a fact in a topical reference.

Overall, the assignment encourages an exceedingly close relationship to the star, and for years that was exactly how the two men were—exceedingly close. In the beginning, Carson avoided interviews on many occasions, just as he does now. It was not uncommon for Ed to answer the questions and for Carson to sit there listening. But the personal relationship between the two has changed dramatically from that of a frequent companion and confidant during the early years to an impersonal off-camera acquaintanceship today. It was a change Ed McMahon obviously had some trouble adjusting to. It has helped that McMahon now has a degree of notoriety in his own right —particularly for his feature films. Today, there is almost no contact between the two apart from the show itself.

"I only see Johnny for maybe a minute before we start taping. Once the show is on and Johnny is talking away, my hardest job is to determine whether I'm in or out of the conversation. If he suddenly tosses me a question, I have to ask myself whether it's rhetorical or about something that's happening right now. I try not to get in the way of conversation between Johnny and guests. I'm like the catcher in baseball. I can help the pitcher but he's the one who has to throw the ball."

McMahon has perfected the art, and while on camera the two are as close as a team of tactical cops during a drug bust. And for good reason on a show in which the danger can be more than simply a moment of embarrassment before millions of viewers. For example, on one of the many shows featuring wild animals, Johnny was to feed ice cream to a jaguar. To Ed, this particular cat looked especially formidable and threatening at the end of the trainer's chain. Ed was perhaps thinking about disasters that have occurred in publicity stunts with wild cats. More than one human prop has been seriously mauled when a presumably tame cat suddenly went berserk.

While Carson was getting out the ice cream, McMahon happened to glance at the trainer and in an obvious reference to the cat said, "Johnny, I don't think he's hungry." Surprised by the remark, Carson looked at McMahon questioningly, and Ed pointed to the trainer's hand.

Blood poured from three long, deep scratches, as the intrepid trainer said evenly, "He won't hurt you, Johnny."

Carson looked at the blood and said, "Yeah, you may be right. He's probably not hungry. Anyway, it's too late for ice cream." Exit trainer with ferocious beast.

Carson needs a McMahon—someone who can anticipate his moods and reactions, someone who shares his sensitivities. Once after McMahon had returned from a visit to Mexico and an informal restaurant there, he explained that to put male customers at ease, the maître d' would walk over and cut off their ties. Carson was skeptically satiric: "You're not serious. What if you happened to be wearing one of those expensive dollar-and-a-half cravats you get at Tie City?"

"Makes no difference. It gets cut off a little below the knot. If I had a pair of scissors handy I'd show you exactly where."

"Well, I'm certainly glad you haven't," said Carson, adopting the manner of one of his favorite slapstick stars, Stan Laurel.

Producer Freddie de Cordova sensed the comedy potential of the situation and picked up a pair of shears from the prop table, handing them to McMahon.

"This is about how far down on the tie they cut," said McMahon, reaching over to sever Carson's $22 Pucci tie at half mast.

This was the kind of joke that built naturally as the studio audience anticipated the inevitable. McMahon knew what Carson would do as he laid the scissors on the desk, and grinned at Carson à la Oliver Hardy. Carson cut off the ends of McMahon's tie, dusted his hands like Stan Laurel, and laid the scissors down again.

Next McMahon clipped bits from Carson's collar and put down the shears to await Carson's next move. Carson then clipped chunks from McMahon's collar and so forth until neither had collar or tie.

But as McMahon lifted the shears to cut a piece off Carson's sports jacket, he got an unspoken message. While Carson had plenty of clothes and, of course, endorses an entire line, the jacket he was wearing had sentimental value and he didn't want it ruined for the sake of a laugh. At the same time, McMahon said, it crossed both men's minds that lots of people were then out of work and couldn't afford to buy clothes.

McMahon explains, "Just how Johnny communicated to me the thought he had about the bad taste of what we were doing, I can't for the life of me say. But he has often shown that consideration for others is more important than a quick and easy laugh."

McMahon's talent for guessing Carson's moods and sense of propriety is as important as any he possesses on the show. It calls for tact and no little humbleness before the star.

Severinsen

When Carson took over *Tonight* in 1962, Jack Paar's close personal friend and musical director Jose Melis was dropped from the show and Skitch Henderson returned to lead the band.

Doc Severinsen also joined the band then, and this meant a reunion for Doc just as it had for Skitch. Among other assignments as a member of NBC's staff band, Doc had worked with Skitch on *Tonight!* in the Steve Allen years. After Skitch Henderson abruptly left the Carson show, Severinsen became musical director, and he may be regarded as even more of a survivor on *Tonight* than Ed McMahon. A near lifelong association is unusual for any jazz musician, but Doc clearly has what it takes, for even as a boy Doc played the trumpet with distinction.

Young Carl Severinsen of Arlington, Oregon, was the son of a dentist known as "Doc" in that northern cattle town and Carl naturally became "Little Doc" to the locals. The boy began taking trumpet lessons at age seven and two years later was named best trumpeter in the state.

In those Depression years, Oregon was an under-populated state to be sure, but Doc was no minor-leaguer. At twelve, he blew the roof off the audition hall in a national contest and became a Music Education Contest winner.

By the time Doc was sixteen, the nation was dancing to the music of its big bands, and Doc—already formidable enough on brass to hit the road—left high school to tour with Ted Fiorito's orchestra. He stepped off the bus a year later in time to graduate from Arlington's high school. In the war years, the Army made a typical "We don't care what you did in civilian life" placement and Doc spent his service in the Finance Division. It was taps for Doc's trumpet for the duration.

But the horn came out of the bag immediately thereafter as he joined and starred with the highly regarded Charley Barnet, then played briefly with King of Swing Benny Goodman before joining Tommy Dorsey, a man Doc regarded as a mentor and the greatest brass player of them all. Like so many top talents, Doc soon had his fill of one-night stands, and so became a "studio musician," a member of the NBC staff band, playing for, among others, Skitch Henderson on Steve Allen's *Tonight!*

Doc joined Carson in 1962, the year Carson took over. NBC dropped Jose Melis at the time to recall Skitch Henderson. (He himself was a tradeoff, Henderson says. Carson wanted John Scott Trotter but agreed to take Henderson when the network accepted Johnny's brother, Dick, as director. Incidentally, Dick Carson proved to be excellent.) Doc was to become Skitch's assistant, but basically he was first trumpeter.

In an early standard routine—borrowed from the Paar years—Carson played "Stump the Band." Carson would ask members of the audience for titles to sometimes nonexistent tunes. Skitch was to improvise melodies for them, and when Skitch was stumped, Doc would pipe away in a twanging country-western tenor, and bring down the house. But basically, Doc was a trumpet player.

For a man of Doc's variegated talents, *Tonight* was rather limiting. At Basin Street East, a New York club where Doc fronted a band in the mid-1960s, his virtuosity was apparent. Said *New York Times* critic John Wilson, "He moved through the most extravagant ranges with incredible assurance, soaring through 'Malaguena,' 'If I Had a Hammer,' 'In a Little Spanish Town,' and Bunny Berigan's old theme, 'I Can't Get Started.' "

Said Wilson of the Basin Street East performance, ". . . he is also a banterer with a wry, hip-hayseed delivery that gives an extra dimension to such comments as his introduction of the musicians in his [sextet] group—'I met these guys at a whip-in in Greenwich Village last night.' " At the same time, he proved to be, said Wilson, "an enthusiastic and extravagantly sincere hillbilly singer."

To some who have followed the jazz scene, Doc seemed the quintessential jazz musician, right down to the marital problems that plague musicians who spend much time away from home. At his Essex County, New Jersey, divorce in mid-1976 Doc agreed to give his wife, Evonne, their nearby quarter-horse ranch, $70,000 for her share of a Texas ranch, shares in a Florida business, life-insurance policies worth $168,500, a Cadillac, a Bentley, and $75,000 a year in alimony. *The New York Times* quotes Severinsen—amusing even *in extremis,* as quipping to marital judge Frederic G. Weber, "Thank you for your kind consideration during all this."

Perhaps it's that even quality under fire that has kept Doc alive while working on *The Tonight Show* since Steve Allen.

External Conflict: The Rivals

The Bishop-Paar Combine

When Carson returned with his impressive new contract after the strike, it was to a new and dangerous competitive situation. For when he hosted *Tonight* once again on April 24, 1967, he was to face Joey Bishop—aided by Jack Paar —on ABC. Meanwhile, Merv Griffin was appearing over many important television stations at midnight in a show syndicated by Westinghouse. On that first night Carson's strength was obvious. Carson, still catching headlines as a result of his celebrated walkout and contract negotiations, drew the curious as well as his longtime fans. That first night he drew over 40 percent of the midnight TV audience. Meanwhile, ABC, limping along with eighty fewer stations, pulled 12 percent. Merv took 16 percent of the audience with his Westinghouse syndicate. (Other stations continued to run old movies.)

Bishop's style was more relaxed than some of his fans were accustomed to, and his guest list was sprinkled with Hollywood stars. Bishop thoroughly enjoyed the L.A. scene, owned a Beverly Hills home and a Rolls-Royce, and regularly paid a barber $50 to come over and trim his hair at the house. In addition to featuring ever-present West Coast entertainment personalities, Bishop liked to get involved in the big issues of the day. He invited public figures to be guests and, understandably awestruck, he questioned them with a blend of amateurism and naiveté. He once said, "I think the guy at home can identify with me because I ask questions about the same way, usually stupid, that he would."

One critic wrote of Bishop's show that he was a sucker for downtrodden performers who needed a break. His emotional love for his fellow man, the critic said, "sometimes obscured his image as a tough Jewish comic from South Philadelphia—to the chagrin of many who liked him that way." Still, he was a strong ad-libber and had a talent for rescuing particularly saccharine moments with deft one-liners.

But on Bishop's midnight debut he was outclassed by his handy helper, Jack Paar. Paar told tales of people who had made appearances on Paar's *Tonight Show.* Paar cracked that he didn't know Mickey Rooney was drunk until "I noticed all the fruit flies around his head."

Paar used his old "ask the outrageous and watch 'em squirm" technique in asking Bishop about his friend Frank Sinatra, leader of the Joey Bishop–Dean Martin–Peter Lawford–Sammy Davis, Jr., clique—Hollywood's "Rat Pack." Bishop was hardly prepared to talk about Sinatra, a hypersensitive, extremely private man who is unforgiving of friends who cut through the curtain of privacy. Paar asked Bishop about Sinatra's young bride. Were they happy, Paar wanted to know, and did Bishop think it would last? Bishop dissolved into an embarrassed silence. Paar scored against Bishop, but the two didn't score against Carson. For one thing, they were seen on so few stations they simply didn't have a chance.

Soon it was back to the drawing board for the hapless competition. Carson had won the midnight hour—at least for the present. No doubt, he was already primed to ask for even more money. After all, he was worth it.

The Merv Griffin Thrust

Griffin made little progress against Carson after the AFTRA strike, in part because his syndicate simply wasn't large enough to compete effectively. But CBS was convinced Merv had the magic to beat Carson. He was to get his big chance two years later, in 1969.

CBS's affiliates had continued to preempt the network, using midnight hours for movies. CBS got none of the revenues, since local stations sold the commercials directly. CBS thought it knew just what to do. Griffin was approached to take on Carson, and CBS persuaded him through sheer money. CBS had always stoked its stars lavishly, and Griffin was no exception. CBS nestled its star-to-be in Broadway's Cort Theatre at a reported rental of $250,000 a year. One source insists the Shuberts, who owned the theater, would have accepted $100,000 gladly. In line with CBS's Tiffany image, the network poured $2 million into the Cort, thus converting it into a posh, intimate television studio. Griffin, deeply impressed, called the Cort his 500-seat security blanket.

Merv later insisted that he was paid at least twice what Carson was, as CBS programing executive Mike Dann delivered on an order to get Merv, period. Meanwhile, *Newsweek* estimated that CBS paid Merv about $25,000 a week and added that this was "roughly the same as Carson's reported salary." On a fifty-two-week basis, $25,000 per amounts to $1.3 million a year.

Whatever, the two stars were both among the highest-paid individuals in the nation, and no wonder. By this time the advertising stakes were enormous. In August of 1969 when Griffin made his debut, potential nationwide midnight advertising revenues were estimated at $50 million a year. As we have seen, NBC was already grossing over $25 million. ABC, despite its poor station lineup in those years, was reportedly billing a worthwhile $11 million a year.

Individual sponsors were paying $17,500 a minute for spots on what was now called *The Tonight Show Starring Johnny Carson* and $7,500 a minute on ABC's *The Joey Bishop Show*—indicative of the fact that *Tonight* continued to out-draw Bishop by a margin of two to one. CBS, capitalizing on its affiliate parity with NBC, asked $10,500 a minute for Griffin—a sum that would have to be scaled down drastically if Merv failed to give Carson a run.

Prior to Griffin's debut, *Newsweek* predicted that Carson's "intelligent brand of humor" would survive Griffin's "folksy" challenge. Merv's style had been described elsewhere as naive and breathless—gee whiz and golly gee. To wit, "Golly, Doris, I can't believe you've been a star for twenty years. Gee whiz, I was in high school when . . ."

Meanwhile, NBC checked out the competition and decided to take no chances. The senior network called in its ratings champ, Bob Hope, to be Johnny's initial guest. Bishop, in a shrewd move, yet characteristic of his save-the-down-and-outer philosophy, gave the Smothers brothers their first shot at network television since CBS had fired them for being too controversial with off-color segments and, more important, for their disparaging view of the Vietnam involvement.

As for Merv, he had a serious disappointment when his choice for superguest, Jet star quarterback and Super Bowl hero Joe Namath, failed to show up at the opening. Wrote *Newsweek*, "He would have helped. After a nervous but passable beginning, Griffin had some bright moments with Woody Allen. (Griffin: 'You've become a sex symbol.' Allen: 'Yes, but which sex?')"

Newsweek continued: "But then the show floundered through interviews with an uncommunicative Hedy Lamarr and a smugly evasive Ted Sorensen, who ducked questions he had agreed to answer in his pre-show interview. And Griffin, normally a pleasant foil for his guests, seemed unable to salvage the duller encounters the way Carson so often does."

Merv had curiosity going for him, anyway. He won 49 percent of the viewers and Carson just 39 percent. Bishop posted a poor third with 12 percent. But by the end of the week Carson was back on top again—and that's the way it stayed.

The three-way competition was soon finished. ABC never really built on its 1967 post-strike showings, never really challenged; Bishop limped along and was finally canceled. Things were grim at CBS, too. Affiliate defections soon reduced the airing to 150 stations, while NBC's full 200-plus network continued to tune in and share in NBC's *Tonight Show* revenues. Since Merv wasn't represented in some important CBS markets, he simply couldn't win. Soon Merv's ratings had flagged so badly that he dropped his Cort Theatre security blanket and fled to a CBS studio on the West Coast. CBS, which normally took financial setbacks in stride, counted its losses and for once was stunned. As for Merv, things did not improve dramatically on the West Coast. Perhaps it is true that CBS didn't help in demanding that Merv, who had became somewhat involved in the Vietnam controversy, balance out doves with hawks. Since Bob Hope and John Wayne were the only hawks left, Merv complained that he couldn't find enough hawks to strike the balance CBS demanded.

Carson emerged triumphant in the midnight wars and has been unbeatable ever since. On Vietnam he remained blissfully above the battle, barely mentioning the war that had sparked the most divisive national debate in many years. When challenged by the press, he argued that viewers wanted entertainment, not issues, and that he was maintaining a policy laid out at the outset. Carson was an entertainer and not a social commentator. Viewers clearly agreed with Carson's noninvolvement policy.

It wasn't courageous and Carson certainly didn't win the Smothers brothers' fans, but he didn't need them—nor serious controversy of any sort now that his ratings were cooking the competition. Carson can be accused by some critics of copping out on the most vital issue of the day, but Carson survived. Despite the spirited challenge, he emerged stronger than before.

Merv limped on in Hollywood and was canceled on February 11, 1972—when that fabulous contract he still insists paid him $10 million ran out. Nothing daunted, Merv went on to rebuild his syndicate, which he eventually sold to over a hundred stations—at 8:30 P.M. Prime time. He has lived happily ever since, but Carson has stayed on, no longer as prince but as king of midnight television. There was really no contest.

Says an NBC publicity man of the time: "One of my best friends was producing Bishop, and I knew the publicity people on CBS. We would get together and talk about it and there was no doubt that they were just trying desperately to get some of the money that was flowing into NBC for *The Tonight Show* and they didn't quite understand how to do it. They would have given anything to find someone who could handle the show like Carson. But the [underlying] philosophy was wrong."

The Style of Carson, King of Midnight Television

When David Letterman was on the show recently, he reminisced with Carson about the halcyon days, a little more than a decade ago, when the most innocent cuss word was thought to be strong enough to corrupt America. Even "damn" was out then, he implied.

Letterman noted that these days the naughty word "pee" was no longer zapped electronically and told how singer-actress Bernadette Peters had used it on *Tonight* one night when Letterman was guest host. Bernadette, who is as wholesome as fat-free yogurt, indicated to Letterman that her dog was lovable but not so couth as she. "I never pee on the furniture," she explained. In explaining his reaction to this line, Letterman told Carson that the fact that this idea had even "crossed her mind" was really more than he wanted to know about Bernadette's home life.

At the midnight hour, Letterman's "pee" sailed easily over the censor's head—just as Bernadette's had—and the studio audience had a good laugh. Presumably, so did the relatively blue crowd that views Carson at midnight.

What has surprised the NBC censors over the years is the fact that Carson has developed a wonderful sense of how far he can go. For example, he got a big friendly response from the studio audience recently by a welcome "to the show that comes into your bedroom and asks the burning question, 'Shall we do it now, or wait till Tom Snyder?' " His calling it "NBC's answer to foreplay" also left them laughing.

It is easy to go too far and turn off millions of viewers. Says Bob Kasmire, who as NBC vice-president in charge of corporate affairs had overall responsibility for censorship, "Guests come on—show-business comedians who are not used to working in television—and it is Liberty Hall. They go blue and Carson has to get them off the blue kick. Sometimes he does it with a look, and sometimes he does it by coming up with a joke that tops them and underlines the fact that they have stepped out of line.

"NBC didn't think up the restrictions. It is the viewing audience that complains. It took me a long time to realize that Carson had a sense [of what is appropriate].

"When the show is being taped an editor is watching. He is immediately responsible. If he has some problem areas, words used, a joke, an apparent and flagrant thing, he would talk to the producer and if the producer said, 'We are leaving it in,' it would come to me and nine times out of ten I would say, 'Leave it in.' . . . I learned over a period of time that you could trust him."

That doesn't mean Carson never consciously uses blue material. Kasmire explains, "When the show is being taped, sometimes Johnny will make a blue joke or encourage a guest to do one—do something that in the ultimate judgment shouldn't go on the air. It gets taken out. Carson doesn't care. He is working before an audience, and if the audience flattens out, he knows he can wake them up with a blue joke. He needs that audience badly."

Herminio Traviesas, a quiet, cultured man who was the last-stop censor on the show for many years, adds that to get the audience "back to life" Carson was capable of "outrageous vulgarisms." As those who have been in the studio audience know, he may say, "Aw, shit." Traviesas comments, "He knows it will be bleeped and wants it to be bleeped. While the conventional thinking is that Carson must be very difficult, quite the opposite is true."

But double entendres are important to a late show, and Carson, "like all pros," watches other shows—particularly *Saturday Night Live*—and asks, why them and not us?

Once, Carson as Carnac—the character who supplies questions for answers—got the "envelope," removed the "answer," and it said, "Bitch, ass, and horny." The question, Carnac said, was "What three words can they say on *Saturday Night Live* and not on this show?" This led to a confrontation.

Says "Travie," as the NBC censor is affectionately known, "All my people are well-liked adults. Ted Cordis, who was about twenty-eight when this happened [around the end of 1977], told de Cordova quietly but firmly, 'You'll have to take it out.' " Travie continued: "Fred de Cordova said, 'That's not going to go down easy.' And Ted said, 'Fine, I'll talk to Carson.' Now, Carson is always very calm in such confrontations—not like some stars who hit the ceiling."

Ted got together with the star and Carson asked, "Why are you taking it out?" Cordis told him these *were* taboo words for the show, and then had a brilliant thought. He added: "Besides, it's not funny. Only you and I will know what it means." Carson turned to Fred and said, "Take it out."

Says Travie, "Cordis had the nerve to tell him that, and because he was right, Carson went along with it."

It wasn't the first time there was a fight over the word "ass." Travie, who makes himself available at all hours for final arbitration in questions of taste, received a telephone call in New York one evening at 10:30 P.M. local time. That put the telephone call in the hour-and-a-half interval before air time on the East Coast—the last opportunity to make changes. The caller was an editor on *Tonight.* He told Travie, "I want the word 'ass' out and they are fighting me and so I'm appealing it to you."

A movie star was telling a story and Johnny Carson asked what would happen if whatever the star was talking about didn't work. The movie star said, "I'd go right out on my ass."

Travie comments, "I said to the editor, 'I am going to be arbitrary and take it out because otherwise they will say s.o.b., etc., and cite this as precedent.'"

With that Travie turned to his wife and said, "I just made a momentous decision for NBC. I took the word 'ass' out of the show."

There was this postscript. When President Carter was quoted in the newspapers as having said that if Senator Edward Kennedy ran against him in the primaries, "I'll whip his ass," Carson worked the quote—and its taboo word—into his monologue. Since "ass" now carried the presidential stamp, as it were, the reference passed the censor. Travie, for one, detected a twinkle in Carson's eye as he said the magic word, and Travie thinks that twinkle was for the censorship staff.

Travie has noticed that Johnny Carson loves to play with a new censor. "He knows we'll warn a new man. Yet he has managed to get in blue jokes several times."

You win some, you lose some. Carson once booked Judith Lowry, an aged actress who played the mother on the Cloris Leachman show, and asked her what she thought of the new morality. The fight on her answer went all the way to Bob Howard, then president of NBC. Carson's argument was that Ms. Lowry was such an old lady she ought to be able to say "It is bullshit" and not be shushed. She was, though, and Travie, who was away at the time, said that if he had been available, "I would have supported my people."

Words are, of course, the big problem, but occasionally flesh is a bigger one. No one insisted that Shelley Winters remove her fur coat after the earthy actress hinted that it was all she was wearing. She reportedly proved this to a substitute host by flashing off camera as she left the show.

But accidents will happen. Luscious Ann-Margret wore a shawl during a guest appearance because she was on her way to a party. The shawl fell down and her dress was cut so low, the studio audience thought she was naked to the waist, and the newspapers so reported the incident. The mishap with the shawl did not appear on camera. Rather, Carson "did a great react to the audience's react."

That was easy. But when Lola Falana, the singer, bent over while doing the show, one of her breasts just "fell out," says Travie. It was tricky, but NBC was able to perform an electronic mastectomy and the wayward bust appeared on the tape as a black spot.

Even the most sophisticated censor can be fooled by terms unknown to the average person. Once Steve Martin made reference to "scum bags." NBC's young censor was immersed in West Coast culture, where swimming pools are more common than this slang reference to condoms. He thought the phrase was a reference to a tool with a similar sound that is used to clean the pools. There were repercussions at the NBC switchboard, but the young censor could hardly be blamed for ignorance of a crude expression rarely used in any but the most raunchy society.

Even Travie could be fooled. He got his start following retirement from the advertising business after seventeen years when he was asked in 1967 to go to the West Coast for NBC and be in charge of censorship at the Burbank studios. His first assignment was a formidable challenge: *Laugh-In.* "We would read *Laugh-In,* my editor and I, going through the script page by page and marking it with paper clips. I'd say, 'Go to page thirty-three,' and he'd say, 'What about twenty-two? . . . Travie, don't you know what that is?' "

Like Kasmire, Travie believes it is the audience for the show that determines what should go and what should stay. And he believes the *Tonight* audience is older and more sophisticated than the *Saturday Night Live* audience. Thus he draws the line differently for the two shows. Nevertheless, when *Tonight* calls to ask, "Who says [something] is in bad taste?" Travie would say, "I say it is in bad taste," even if the item would pass muster on *Saturday Night Live.*

The *Saturday Night Live* audience is young and likes the kind of humor it gets, he said. He noted that show makes fun of deformities, and he finds that distasteful. In fact the entire program was so distasteful for Travie that the first show "drove me up the wall and the second one did too." He adds, "We get the scripts first and you should see what comes out of the scripts." But *Saturday Night Live* is "an emotional thing with me. I am not in synch with it."

Noting once again that it is the *audience* for a show that is the determining factor, he adds that therefore he cannot use his taste as the judgment factor. "We were getting the teenage audience with *Saturday Night Live,* which we had never got. It got good critical notices and the stations loved it."

So Carson will have to continue to make do without three little words. If something off-color is well done, the NBC censors will probably leave it in. But Carson knows that Travie and the other NBC censors don't like constant double entendre.

Blue notes are not always intentional. It's probably fair to say that nothing that has been written for the show has come close to getting the response the famous and inadvertent Ed Ames gaffe got years ago when the show was still being broadcast in black-and-white.

From *Tonight*'s point of view, Ed Ames's appearance on the show would be another attempt by NBC to plug a network show, and there was some reluctance to booking him as a guest.

Ed had been with the Ames brothers, a black singing group of the 1940s. But the group disbanded and Ed turned to acting, winning the role of Mingo, an Indian, on NBC's *Daniel Boone* series.

Ed squeaked past the *Tonight* bookers because he sang unusually well. His talent might not set the pioneer world afire, but at least no one expected him to be a bad guest on *Tonight*. Finally, he told the booker he could throw a tomahawk—not like Cochise, maybe, but well enough to embed the head in a target. The staff said okay—at least it was better than nothing.

So Ed came out, sang a number, and moved to the guest seat. In due course as they talked *Daniel Boone* Carson asked Ames to demonstrate how he handled a tomahawk. The staff brought out a silhouette of the human figure, and Ed took aim and threw the tomahawk at the figure. The tomahawk landed with a "plunk," its head embedded and handle pointed upward right in the pelvic area. The reaction was one of shocked disbelief and uproarious laughter. The inadvertently off-color episode got the biggest, longest laugh the show has ever gotten. The rerun of that moment in television history has become the highlight for every subsequent anniversary. It was parodied by *Saturday Night Live*. One of the comedians hacked away at the silhouette's crotch until it was kindling. A pretty good putdown of the now shopworn *Tonight* episode.

Ed Ames, whose popularity as a singer had faded with that of such groups as the Ames brothers generally, was suddenly popular again. He became a frequent guest on *Tonight*. It turned out he not only sang well, he had interesting stories and anecdotes. But he would never top his first appearance. At least Ed Ames would never want for an entrée to do the show, once he buried the hatchet with the *Tonight* staff.

Carson the Court Jester: Mean but Effective

That old vaudeville lead-in "A funny thing happened to me on the way to the theater tonight" has a history as old as stand-up comedy.

The medieval jesters often played tricks on those they met in their travels, hoping to generate some amusing tale they could tell their sponsors upon arrival at court. In short, funny things were often caused to happen so that the king would not be disappointed.

The tricks often weren't nice, but the jesters knew that people love to laugh at another's discomfort—as in the classic example of "better him than me" humor when someone else slips on a banana peel. In that tradition, comedians like Don Rickles make other people look foolish in ways that audiences find funny. Steve Allen would use that kind of comedy on *Tonight!* many years earlier. He would make milder thrusts at people on the street who peered into the show's hidden camera—and, in a different comedy vein, even at his peers. When it was the vogue to use book titles for humor, he once cracked that a modestly successful Jack Paar daytime TV show then on the air was *Death in the Afternoon.* And we've seen that he could defend himself as well as anyone with pointed ripostes. As for Paar, he was a prime practitioner of a related comedy approach —self-deprecation. Both approaches are popular and, when well handled, surefire.

Historically, Till Eulenspiegel was a master at provoking funny happenings. But he flubbed when he reacted to an inn hostess's remark that she was not acquainted with Till. Not recognizing the clown, she told Till she had heard the man was a thoroughly bad lot. Next morning, Till carried the sleeping hostess to some hot cinders he had collected and laid her naked back on them, saying, "See, hostess, now you can well say that Till Eulenspiegel is malicious."

Cruelty is not unknown on *Tonight.* When Kenneth Tynan was waiting to interview Carson for his extended piece on the show for *The New Yorker* magazine's February 20, 1978, issue, he found Carson scribbling an idea he had had for the night's monologue. Convicted murderer Gary Gilmore had just persuaded the state of Utah to go through with the death penalty despite a heavy campaign by those opposed to capital punishment to thwart his execution. Under state law, the condemned man is allowed to choose his own fate, and once Gary won the argument on his right to die, he opted for the firing squad. That squad had just carried out the sentence when Tynan met Carson for the interview.

Tynan explained, "Carson's comment on this macabre situation takes the form of black comedy. Since justice must be seen to be done, why not let the viewing public in on the process of choice? Carson proposes a new TV show, to be called *The Execution Game.* It would work something like this: Curtains part to reveal the death chamber, in the middle of which is an enormous wheel, equipped with glittering lights and a large golden arrow, to be spun by the condemned man to decide the nature of his fate. For mouth-watering prizes—ranging from a holiday for two in the lovely Munich suburb of Dachau to a pair of front-row seats at the victim's terminal throes—members of the audience vie with one another to guess whether the arrow will come to rest on the electric chair, the gas chamber, the firing squad, the garrote, or the noose."

But on *Tonight* that evening, the only reference to Gary Gilmore's execution was a terse "Capital punishment is a great deterrent to monologues," which seemed clearly to suggest that Carson was overruled—either by the network or by Carson himself. That Carson thought of the idea in the first place is indicative of a willingness to make light of society's cruelest adjuncts. Yet, the monologue was clever and made a strong case against capital punishment. Comedy in the service of humanity, if you will.

It is fascinating that many of the episodes Carson brought back for the seventeenth-anniversary prime-time two-hour special had cruel overtones.

Sally Fields was on one clip recalling to Carson that she and her boyfriend of the time, Burt Reynolds, had squirted shaving cream at each other with Carson on an earlier show. She then proceeded to foam up Carson's ears—one at a time. A comic sight. Then Sally sat. To this viewer and a few others, Carson seemed genuinely angry at the affront

—even though he chose to replay the tape on the anniversary show. He then sallied forth to—as they say in college dorms where foamy wars are as common as water-gun wars were thirty years earlier—"wipe out" Miss Fields with the same foamy cream. In the process he squirted a generous quantity at Sally's bust.

Carson also resurrected the episode in which he and Ed McMahon demonstrated a number of Christmas toys. Among them was a robot that was supposed to pitch a basketball through a hoop. Apart from the little-boy argument that ensued between the two grown men over whether Ed was entitled to a third attempt to match Carson's three misses, the episode was not kind to the manufacturer. After basketball, Carson demonstrated a small cannon which fired half a shotgun shell's worth of powder with a boom so loud both men jumped. He then put a fully loaded shell in the chamber and with a remark to the effect "Won't make baskets, eh?" proceeded to blow the dummy's head off. The toy's, not Ed's. So much for free plugs for toy manufacturers.

Then there was the anniversary-show film clip in which Carson discovered what he termed, in humor one assumes, "a broken heirloom"—a wooden cigarette case that had graced his *Tonight* desk for years. Don Rickles, who had guest-hosted the night before, had broken it, Carson was informed. In this clip, Carson got up and, followed by a camera, walked off his set and into the neighboring studio, ignoring the warning lights indicating the cameras were rolling. Barging in on a nonplussed Rickles, producer, and crew taping an episode of *C.P.O. Sharkey,* Carson complained pointedly to Rickles about the breakage, to the vast amusement of the audience—the visit was obviously unplanned—and to the disbelief of Rickles, his producer, et al. They laughed, of course, but were visibly shaken.

Of course, if Carson were kinder, he might instead be hosting a kiddie show opposite Captain Kangaroo. One of the givens for a top *Tonight* host appears to be the willingness to get tough. Without it, there would be no Carson; no laughs for the rest of us on *Tonight*. Bitter laughter plays well at midnight.

Johnny Carson as Mythmaker: An Assessment and a List

The American Heritage Dictionary says that a myth is any real or fictional story or recurring theme that appeals to the consciousness of a people. A myth, the dictionary says, embodies cultural ideals and gives expression to deep, commonly felt emotions.

As much as anything, myths are created by people. And few mythmakers are as effective and have as much impact as a nation's court jesters. They mock the politicians, deride the nation's legends, and attack pomposity in every field. More than any group, they provide insights into the national experience as well as defining it.

Thus, when Carson sensed disenchantment with President Carter and verbalized the discontent, he defined public sentiment. The feelings of the populace toward their president found expression in his gibes. And the alarmed president would become a laughingstock in Carson's hands.

Indeed, Carter's entire family would be grist for Carson's mill. As he once remarked: "And that family—Billy, Miss Lillian—they're not real, they've got to be from central casting."

The Tonight Show and its hosts may in fact be the most

important molders of America's perception of itself today. As a vehicle for creating myths, defining the American *Zeitgeist, Tonight* is unrivaled.

Moreover, *The Tonight Show*'s tentacles reach out. It has launched myriads of imitators—Mike Douglas, Merv Griffin, Joey Bishop, Dick Cavett, David Frost, Tom Snyder, and many others. *The Tonight Show*'s ability to generate revenue has encouraged all the other networks to develop similar shows, and they have multiplied like lemmings.

As a result, its progeny—and their progeny—have spread throughout the media. It has acted as a catalyst to the entire communications and entertainment business. It establishes personalities and celebrities of communications. Like a centrifuge, it spins them out into the world of media, where they—like the Carson, Paar, and Allen of *Tonight*—in turn create the American mythos, define our attitudes toward ourselves and our culture.

If the mythmakers of old turned people into legends— that is, into personalities who transcended daily existence, who became the figures ordinary mortals looked up to— who are our legends? Who are our comic legends? Our sex legends? Our legends of sports, art, and politics? Where were they spawned? I would submit that more than any communications vehicle, *The Tonight Show* has created and developed these larger-than-life personalities, has been the seedbed of our contemporary mythos, our American Dream.

A quick look at a handful of the personalities promoted by *Tonight*—our legends, if you will—should demonstrate the impact the show has had on America, to say nothing of those thousands of other personalities established by *Tonight*'s spin-offs. Look at the list and then imagine what America's entertainment life would be like, and would have been like, without these people, without these clowns, singers, and artists. What other forum would have given us . . .

Don Adams
Woody Allen
Shelley Berman
Joey Bishop
Robert Blake
David Brenner
Marshall Brickman
Albert Brooks
Mel Brooks
Lenny Bruce
Carol Burnett
Godfrey Cambridge
Truman Capote
George Carlin
Peggy Cass
Tim Conway
Rodney Dangerfield
John Davidson
Selma Diamond
Phyllis Diller
Paul Ehrlich
Harry Golden
Eydie Gorme
Buddy Hackett
Pat Harrington, Jr.
Skitch Henderson
Buck Henry
Milt Kamen
Gabriel Kaplan
Robert Klein
Don Knotts
Steve Lawrence
David Letterman

Rich Little
Paul Lynde
Miriam Makeba
Steve Martin
Elaine May
Pat McCormick
Bette Midler
Liza Minnelli
The Muppets
Bob Newhart
Mike Nichols
Louis Nye
Tom Poston
Freddie Prinze
Gene Rayburn
Burt Reynolds
Don Rickles
Joan Rivers
Carl Sagan
Mort Sahl
Doc Severinsen
The Smothers brothers
David Steinberg
McLean Stevenson
Barbra Streisand
Tiny Tim and Miss Vicki
Lily Tomlin
Gore Vidal
Betty Walker
Andy Williams
Flip Wilson
Jonathan Winters

And of the legendary *Tonight Show* hosts, Carson has certainly been the most influential. In fact, the entire spectrum of national television talk shows owes much to Carson. True, he has been attacked with some justice for knocking off in his time slot more serious talk-show hosts like Dick Cavett. But it seems unlikely that Cavett could have existed at all had not Carson blazed the trail. For *Tonight* in the Carson format is the prototypal talk show and has been largely responsible for the concept's general success.

Cavett and another intellectual, David Frost, still labor in the talk-format vineyard because America first accepted *Tonight* and the midnight talk show. On a less cerebral level, Merv Griffin also owes his career in large part to *Tonight.* Griffin failed as a Carson competitor but was nonetheless strong enough to return triumphantly in the talk format later through syndication—and in a dimension more exploitive of his own talents. The provocative and much-admired Tom Snyder, whose *Tomorrow* airs on NBC after *Tonight,* owes much to Carson. Without the *Tonight* lead-in, Snyder's ratings would be so diminished that it is doubtful he could muster a national audience.

In fact, Carson is the Great Communicator Mort Werner predicted he would become, and judging by the enormous size of Carson's audience relative to that of individual news shows, Carson has probably done as much for communication as Walter Cronkite and the other newscasters put together. For it is one thing to tell and interpret the news. It is another to put the news in humorous perspective, to give the public a handle on events in a form that helps make the hard-to-take acceptable—even a laughing matter—whether it be a political gaffe or an automobile Carson impishly and tellingly spoofs as unsafe.

It is no accident then that Carson—that deliverer of funny lines, that foil of clowns, that friend of the aged and listener to the famed and the great—is king of the celebrities, the most admired and best-paid man among his show-business peers. As the eighteen-year veteran of broadcasting's most important comedy forum—*The Tonight Show,* starring Johnny Carson—the Corning, Iowa, prestidigitator is undoubtedly the nation's number-one mythmaker as well as its biggest superstar.

Index